CW00802184

About the Author

J. D is an ex-vagrant, entrepreneur and reviewer who has recently become an author. This true story is about his homeless experiences in 2016 on the streets of London and the other irregular characters that surrounded him during that time. A time where himself and the country were at a crossroads.

Generation Tent

J. D

Generation Tent

Olympia Publishers
London

www.olympiapublishers.com
OLYMPIA PAPERBACK EDITION

Copyright © J. D 2023

The right of J. D to be identified as author of
this work has been asserted in accordance with sections 77 and 78 of
the Copyright, Designs and Patents Act 1988.

All Rights Reserved

No reproduction, copy or transmission of this publication
may be made without written permission.
No paragraph of this publication may be reproduced,
copied or transmitted save with the written permission of the publisher,
or in accordance with the provisions
of the Copyright Act 1956 (as amended).

Any person who commits any unauthorised act in relation to
this publication may be liable to criminal
prosecution and civil claims for damage.

A CIP catalogue record for this title is
available from the British Library.

ISBN: 978-1-80074-861-3

This is a work of creative nonfiction. The events are portrayed to the
best of the author's memory. While all the stories in this book are true,
some names and identifying details have been changed to protect the
privacy of the people involved.

First Published in 2023

Olympia Publishers
Tallis House
2 Tallis Street
London
EC4Y 0AB

Printed in Great Britain

Dedication

With Special thanks to: Flora Cordelia Raffles, Katie Arora, Oli, Nayarra, Ritchie, H, George, Jez, Alicia at Thistle Grove, Nell, Housman, Mother, Father, Sophie and Faith, Lottie, Olivia, Solus, Courtney, Alan Moore, and Amy Tez.

Chapter 1

I have decided to reminisce before I attempt some form of sleep. To discover how I got here in the first place – convulsing in the winter cold between two covering bushes.

Solus's grandmother has washed my sleeping bag and it has shrunk beyond practical use. Any movement in the essential head-cover feels as if my oesophagus will rip out of my throat. I wriggle my body, as if inside a cocoon while the cold water creeps up into the tent floor and consumes the roll mat. The weather has a particular savagery and it enables me to construct four considerations:

One: never in winter.

Two: feet and hair clean and dry.

Three: never sleep on the bare ground.

Four: four a.m. to five a.m. is the coldest of times.

I slither, looking for warm positions as I remember the day that I came up with the idea. An idea that started a series of events. A true story that I hope will help to make sense of a generation, lasted several months, felt like a lifetime, and is dedicated to the people who do it for a lifetime. A true story with many distinctions attached: elation, fear, incompetence, drugs, death, parties, destitution, dreams, and sex.

June 16th of 2016 and the psycho flat-mates had left their bedrooms quiet and empty. The constant warmth of June reflected off the white facades on Edith Grove – it would have been rude not to have a soiree. Rude enough for me to text my entire phone's intake, informing them of the evening plan.

The usual suspects were in attendance: Niccy, the stunning five-foot-ten model, she had invited a girl who she was 'seeing'. She flitted between boys and girls without warning but this girl was not her type: short, cropped hair and a broad build like a warrior dwarf from the Hobbit films. It was only when she purchased a substantial amount that their union made sense; she would rub it between her fingers, tilt back her head, and pour it down her nasal cavity as if attentively salting a steak.

Neza was there, the hot and curvy Slovenian who revealed her large breasts within ten minutes. She was a beautiful girl but eccentric, insisting on playing an Eastern European song over and over as she released a catatonic dance, shaking her entire body while flexing her legs.

'I'm half gypsy you know, this is a gypsy song!' she beamed. The warrior dwarf was into it, although she was with Niccy. Sans the girlfriend, she was soon caressing Neza's large breasts next to where I was clinging. Perhaps I should have been aroused at this stage? I was too busy climbing into some form of sanity.

Something was bad about the gear and this was confirmed by Niccy's grimace: 'I NEED TO BINGE ON GOSSIP GIRL OR I WILL FUCKING KILL MYSELF!'

Jerome was our usual boy but he was nowhere to be seen, so, the warrior dwarf ordered from an aggressive Albanian for ten pounds cheaper. That was the attraction of Jerome, you never got the shitty, clinging-to-the-carpet comedown; you were either high or dry. The downside to him was the belated arrival.

'How long are you going to be, Jerome?'

He would take his time answering, 'Erm, I dunno man, text

me your postcode.' We would wait out for him to avoid bad quality drugs. Many times, sitting impatiently for a phone call, tapping my toes with three to four hungry noses.

Niccy let out a childish squeal as piercing light peered from the door-sized windows. The piercing light that introduced a stark reality. A reality that this had continued to the next day. We were, indeed, consuming finite daylight. There were other people in the room but I did not know their names. Who was that girl gyrating on the cupboard in the corner? It was not Ellie the Freeloader, but she looked similar.

I wondered where Ritchie was, but then remembered that we had asked him to leave. He had pissed out of my small balcony and into my shoes before chasing his girlfriend with his coke-shrivelled penis. This penis, that had thrice been infected with venereal disease, was loosely hanging from his estate-agent trousers. Strangely, this was not why we asked him to leave. It was because he tried to throw a sofa out of an impossibly narrow window. When it did not fit, he proceeded to throw beer bottles onto Chelsea's pedestrians, narrowly missing an unassuming couple.

His girlfriend, Solus, well, she did not leave with him and proceeded to let Drew fondle her round fake breasts; Niccy was watching, pretending to be turned on. I tried to be annoyed with Drew but both he and Ritchie were my close male friends; I could do nothing. As far as I was concerned, with the regressing relations, I should be a mere spectator in a sport that should never be played.

Drew left with Solus in an Uber, audaciously dropping her off to Ritchie. He ceremoniously returned to the party with his high eyes blazing and excited. 'BUDDY, BOOBS IN MOUTH, I

HAD HER TITS... IN MY MOUTH!'

Niccy gave out a groan and I decided to acquiesce to her request. The girl came down hard ninety percent of the time and could get aggressive within a second. I once put Daddy's girl on a morning bus instead of in a taxi, all hell broke loose. The only thing that would alleviate her fluctuations was aiding with her fixation of "Gossip Girl". This was her escape, to a sleeker metropolitan world of rich men and snobby witticisms. The Golden Age of TV, with all its dramatic and sustained masterpieces wasn't for Niccy; she was fine in New York with Blake Lively and Chuck Bass.

I liked Niccy. I admired her dark, unrelenting beauty; the way she would curve her long elegant legs when lying down, the way she dressed and sipped cocktails. Being around her made you feel successful.

I resented Niccy. Daddy had rented an entire office floor in Pimlico for her art business and purchased a flat near Greenwich. What did she do with it? Fuck all, except discuss rich and abominable men and indulge the two C's: champagne and cocaine.

I was attempting to load "Gossip Girl", hands shaking and head spinning, and I sipped on a flat beer that had been left next to me while snorting the remnants of a line left on a fashion magazine. I realised that I had not finished an episode of "Vikings". As far as I was concerned, this was the golden age of television – gratuitous violence and history in one, though, liberal with fact. I watched some while Niccy was distracted. It concerned the ambitious Ragnar Lothbrok, the legendary Viking leader, who was the first of the Danes to enter the seven kingdoms of England. He had sent his son, another legendary Viking called Bjorn Ironside, into the wilderness for incompetent behaviour.

Bjorn Ironside changed within those three months: at first, he was a fidgety wreck, riddled with immaturities, but soon he grew familiar with the unrelenting cold. The trials and tribulations of being alone in the depths of Norway (which should have been Denmark) started to change him. It made him think faster and he became... how do I put it? More 'still' I suppose. Most importantly, most important of all, was his lack of decided fear. The climax of the piece: he kills a rabid bear in the cold snow as if he were killing his own demons. Blood strewn across his face, he shouts with vigour across the lands, a cathartic release of manhood that travels all the way to his father, Ragnar Lothbrok – the legendary king.

I thought of this in awe as I clung to the dusty carpet and it stayed in my mind for months to come. This, my lack of masculinity, my pathetic twenty-minute stints at the gym; a niggling anxiety that reminded me there was much to do and achieve for myself. I still could not drive, was not famous, and I was not married to Lily Donaldson. Though the quality of my life was rising, relatively speaking, in a way, I suppose? Some of my friends have an income but still live in their parents' spare room, still have to borrow money regularly from Mummy or Daddy, friends, even acquaintances. The list goes on with 'still have to's' for the majority of them, unless they were in finance like Drew. They were the chosen ones.

My marketing job that was fourteen hundred pounds take home at twenty-seven years of age. My rent in a flat share was eight hundred pounds, not including bills, which left me with six hundred. After bills, we are onto four hundred and fifty for the month, then there is a card repayment, travel, food, H Club, maybe a date with the girl I am seeing. Underwear, protein shakes, miscellaneous, you name it. It was a frugal lifestyle, though not impossible.

I thought of Niccy's flat, paid for. A mortgage is as far away for me as Andromeda. My mother had a bungalow, a large house, and a pad in the Mediterranean when she was a year younger than me and pregnant with... well... me. Imagine. You only had to look at the broadsheets to see that this generation was a write off. The Guardian stated that the previous generation (generation X) earned over ten thousand more a year in real terms, every year. The Daily Mail suggested that one in four of twenty to thirty-four-year-olds lived at home in 2016. It was not war or disease that was the enemy of this generation. The enemy of the millennial was inflation, exacerbated by the previous financial crisis. If wages were in line with house price inflation, the average salary would be above eighty thousand. This was clearly not the case, and the only people I knew that managed to purchase a house, which still seemed to be a tour de force, were the people who received inheritance.

There are more boring, technical aspects to blame: eight years of quantitative easing, thirty years of not building enough homes, the constant need for austerity. London itself was financially off the charts and there was an underlying sense of insecurity with my peers, wasted talent that did what many would do in their situation, I suppose. They moaned, drank, and drugged the night away. They did this to escape, and thus became a victim to excuses.

Conversely, if they had more cognitive dexterity, were more in line with the universe, then perhaps they would be more successful? Perhaps, just perhaps, if they never socialize, and when I say never I mean minimum human interaction; if they stayed at home in their flat-shares, by their bedrooms and worked on their deteriorating laptops until their fingers bled, success would arrive in abundance? Although it seems that I am jesting, there is depth to what I am saying. London is Darwinian in its structure. It is survival of the fittest but not everybody can be a robot; many need to feel. So why not move? This brings another moaning session. Considering London possesses a quarter of the GDP, the best bars, the hottest people, prospects and culture, why should they? Manchester is a romantic thought but it has not received funding since the Hacienda. I have been to the coach station – it looks like a scene from *The Purge*.

I was losing many friends to the wilderness of the provinces; Devon, Cirencester, Rutland, wherever the fuck that was. They seemed to disappear, never to be seen or heard from again, as if the surrounding trees and fields had swallowed them whole and into another statistic.

I thought of my psycho flat mates, one of whom woke me up at seven am last week, dragged me to the kitchen, and demanded to know who ate her pitta bread. They were all from Lyon in France, knew each other from there and besieged the sitting room for days on end.

I thought of the rise of the billionaire; I thought about how Ellie the Freeloader had to become a stripper when they would not pay her housing benefit. I thought of cocaine downers and the impending European vote.

I thought of the positive, fixating on happy thoughts and goals: my brain, plagued with escape and thirst for new adventure; I loved how I lived in Chelsea. There was a washing machine in the old building I used to live in and I still have the keys. If I could, somehow, not pay rent for months on end and… save. I could have my own place. My own home. Renting of course but imagine that? No running into the kitchen before they return. No fridge-shelf designation, no hiding in the bedroom. No pitta bread mysteries or pubic plugholes. Instead, there would be social status. Perhaps I could even make the on-and-off girl an honest lady. Theo Fennell rings and marquees. A mini dog and woolly jumpers; cups of herbal tea and Sunday roasts at the Builders Arms.

I had to do something. My rent was late and a downward spiral had commenced. I had the new online business but it was not enough to prop me up. Many people have the luxury of planning for years, but I did not. Time was of the essence; time, the most precious of human assets, seemed to throttle forward at a pace faster than life and there was no time for meticulous strategy. It was a visceral and pacey approach, an approach to avoid the stigma of being expelled from a flat-share.

I straightened my party-fatigued spine and said, 'yes' to myself; 'I AM JUST LIKE BJORN'!' I was going, with semi-careful planning, to leave my flat, obtain the deposit and live free for a while in the wild, like a self-made Viking hard man.

As I wiped my smoky eyes, I remembered an article in "Dazed and Confused" about an imaginative man who lived on top of a vast concrete block in Manhattan, armed only with a tarpaulin and a sleeping bag. He would work late and do his own thing in fashion photography. *How romantic,* I thought. It inspired the execution of my plan.

To be specific, I would purchase a tent. Not a complicated one: a two-man festival tent that violently emerged when you open the zip bag. Camouflage colour of course. I would carry it around like an oversized handbag and when it was time to sleep, release the tent in a designated area. Simple, though I expected not easy. I wondered if anybody else had thought of this in the history of London. With most of the homeless, it seemed to be uncalculated. Just sprawl yourself across the nearest ATM machine and hope for the best. I had an element of choice, surely. I mean, I could make up the rent if I really wanted to, but for some reason I did not.

I was sick of the feeling of owing.

This was a voluntary homelessness and there was nobility in that. Besides, I had many friends that would help me if I desired it. Wonderful and reliable friends – friends that would unconditionally help me when I needed it. I believed that if I got stuck in a situation and knocked on their door, they would welcome me, wide-smiling, as if I were some minor celebrity. 'John is here! Stay as long as you like!' They would throw pillows and sleeping bags at me and offer a cup of tea and a line. If the worst came to the worst, I had the parents to fall back on. No tarpaulins there, no begging and no flea-ridden beards. I would keep it civilised – it would be a very English type of homelessness.

This would be fun, I was sure of it, absolutely. The only thing I was worried about was liking it; 'Glory is fleeting, obscurity is forever.' So, I definitely needed to set a timeline. Two or three months should do it, yes, two or three months maximum.

As the wavering party started to dissipate, the duck-quality drugs wore away and I noticed that this was not an idea induced by narcotics. Technically, something had to be done. I was slowly spiralling into rent debt. I rang Rob the landlord, handed in my notice and told him to take the excess rent from the deposit, which he was more than fine with. I was fortunate to have a landlord that was direct; there were no agencies, no inspections and no county court injunctions. He was a relaxed, down to earth guy who had made his fortune at the height of Britpop.

A couple of days later, I had purchased a tent and

commenced drills in assembling and de-assembling. I needed to be able to de-assemble with pace in case I was discovered by somebody in whatever homeless orifice I found myself dwelling; I only had a week or two to arrange this.

Two days after, I performed these exercises with rigour while slowly sipping a beer and watching Netflix. Tamara was there and was supportive of my plight. Why wouldn't she be? At the end of the unpredictable rainbow would be a one-bed flat and she could move to vibrant London. She was a laid -back country girl with provincial sensibilities; she would calmly smile under her rosy cheeks and had the type of blonde-tuft hair that would sway with the wind. I loved her, I suppose, in a way, of sorts, didn't I?

I am not sure that I quite knew what it was. Did it mean to compulsively elope for better and for worse and be okay with it? Is it meant to be an unfeigned delight? Should I know the answer to these questions at my age? I feared it most of the time but there was a balance she created for me; home-like safety and care, a wholesome energy that garnered respect from blood relatives. Who cared if I was not sure? These reasons were enough to keep going… for now.

She was disappointed that I was not able to seal Florence and the Machine tickets in Hyde Park. She also counted the number of lines I snorted when Solus and Ritchie made an impromptu visit. 'Ten lines in less than an hour, John?' If it was true, it was excessive.

There we were, in my room, streaming online TV and relaxing in the flickering candlelight. A peaceful and safe setting that sheltered us from the crazy and combative world. It was then that I realised I had left the window open. As I went to close it, a cold chill softly blew onto my unwilling face and the relentless world closed in. I felt an emotion that I did not need at this time – vulnerability. Innate and fixed vulnerability.

I looked outside and saw the pink sky darkening and the eternity of London car noise; I saw the cold and stark reality of the outside world within ten seconds. It was then that I knew I was already hesitant, I was already looking to withdraw.

I decided on a masterplan that would include an array of concessions: I was going to give into pride and ask the parents for a new flat deposit, which I would pay back. Tammy had found suitable flats and the plan was to move in, worry about the financials later. My natural drive would make me find the extra money I needed to maintain a one-bed flat in the capital City.

I was on the phone to Mother. 'Okay, John, yes, you haven't borrowed money in a long time, so I can send you half, and your father can equal you the same amount… if he is not too busy that is.' This was great and easy so far. I asked my mother where she thought my father was, but she had no clue: 'Probably on holiday with the others'. I managed to get hold of him and he was reserved, but a new family would do that to you. I used the Mum card and he agreed if I pay it back; afraid that Mother would claim negligence.

I had a three-thousand-pound, interest-free loan with the blink of an eyelid, it was a one-off and I knew that I had to pay it back, well, at least with father. But to be fair, at my ripe age, it was time to generate my own wealth and independence.

Chapter 2

Of Brexit and Banks

Brexit

'Quitting the EU won't solve our problems.'
– Boris Johnson 2013

I woke to low but intense mumblings in the kitchen; the French flat mates had congregated there, spreading and eating French toast and I soon realised why. I always avoided the kitchen: the anxiety of knowing that somebody would be in there any minute, somebody that I did not want to see while I am trying to cook, trying to rest, trying to be alone. I promptly showered and got ready to evade. The vibration and mumblings became more intense which meant it was not business as usual.

I got dressed and, as usual, avoided anything at proximity to the kitchen. I ran out of the rumbling flat, down the 1920s stairwells until I was interrupted by a cacophonous shriek that sent shivers down my spine.

'VICTORY, SON! VICTORY!' It was the Irish lady who also managed the block of flats. A devout Brexiteer which you would not expect, but she was. I was confused as to how she knew I voted out, which I did; and I was confused as to how we won. You see, mine was a protest vote. Potentially like many others because 'the system was rigged' and that 'remain would win whatever happened' – why did I?

Because of one of their offices looked like the Tower of Babel. Because they funded and were affiliated with corporations, because they lauded austerity, because I hate the BBC… because I hate everything.

Now there seemed to be a caveat:

If the European Union, the UK government, and its band of pro EU media players such as the BBC had not managed to rig the election, there is genuity in the current system. This vote was genuine, therefore, we are still in a democracy. That, and its environmental laws, workers protection rights and I start to wonder – did I pick the wrong side? Especially when you look at some of the pro-Brexit stock including the Irish lady; I could imagine trying to revive a time that did not exist. I imagine myself sitting in a room with the Irish pseudo-landlord, Nigel Farage and a few neo-Nazis though this could not be the case. Brexit won the vote so there must be many evasive, silent, and middle-class telegraph voters. As well as tabloid junkies.

There was something noticeably clear; there was a voice, an unheard but progressively louder that had been released from the shadows. Inequalities throughout the country and the West had reached an unprecedented scale and somebody needed to be blamed for the suppression of wages, the suppression of spending, the suppression of just about everything. The scapegoat is Europe and its immigrants who had done nothing wrong.

Things were to change forever, I suppose, at some point although for me? I'm indifferent. Johnson is opportunistic and Corbyn is more interested in tory bashing. My goal will be the same as always, a goal unwavering and resolute in its scope. A goal to survive.

I ran away from the Irish lady, fisting the air in faux celebration as she smiled. I only ever see her when she is shouting about something: cigarette butts outside, excess party noise and now, nationwide votes. I ran onto the wide street and saw a ragged looking man who had a Union Jack taped to his back and front. He wore a Microsoft word printout with a word typed: 'independence'. Another voter found.

Banks

'There are moments that define a whole person's life. Moments in which everything and anything they may possibly become balance on a single decision.'

– Jonathan Maberry
'Rot and Ruin' 2011

Tammy showed me her research in the area and one stood out for the price: eleven-hundred-pounds for a one bedroom flat, all in. At first, I dismissed it as it was in Fulham, vacuous, and it was found on Gumtree: bound-to-be-bogus. Another in Earl's Court which was more in-line with the market and had bills to pay on top of rent cost.

I decided to view the Earls Court flat and probe the Fulham flat by calling up. They answered promptly: 'Yeah, man, the only thing is that we are having a viewing on Friday and I already have quite a few interested.'

I was panicked and thought I better move quickly. 'Hi, it's okay, I can come Thursday if you like? And I can pay the full deposit and rent?' I preferred to liaise directly with landlords such as Rob my soon-to-be ex landlord as there were less checks, agency fees and bureaucracy.

'I dunno, man; I should really prioritise the others.'

'Okay, well what about if I pay slightly more deposit to seal it?'

He seemed charmed. 'Haha okay, okay, come on then, man, bring I.D and we will take it from there.' Tammy seemed impressed with me.

I had the two flats to view and the plan was set in convention: to live 'normally' and have my own space in a flat devoid of flat mates. I would use this as motivation to get higher paid work. This would also include the push of the online fashion business. I said to Tammy that if we were still well in three months, she could elope with me, but whether I mean it, I mean deep down, I am not entirely sure. All I know is that it is an unspoken plan, a little like other unspoken plans between couples. Subliminal communication, like having to have children at some point, or having to fuck your loved one when you hadn't seen them for a week. This unspoken plan is the only reason she is patient.

Dark thoughts form in the psyche, thoughts to warn me against it: when she walked around naked with my ex-flat mate in the room. How she nearly ran off clubbing with Oli, and how she looked at the hunky model in the Juice café. Perhaps I am being paranoid, perhaps not. Perhaps it gives me the excuse I need…

I made my way to Fulham and up the multi-coloured side street that was idyllic compared to the hustle of the nearby North End Road. I waited outside and waited some more. I called the man profusely but it was to no avail. I was now at the side of the road in a panicked frenzy until finally he answered. I told him that I had been waiting for at least twenty minutes and he stated that he had to sort something, but his assistant would let me in, which she did. The flat was amazing: one bed but spacious and felt like a home; separate rooms – it could host great parties. It had wooden floors, a patio, well worth the sacrifice of leaving Zone 1. Tammy would be pleased; my friends would be pleased.

The strange looking assistant with dyed blonde hair was peculiar in her mannerisms. She stated that others were interested, so, it was on a first come first served basis. She did this while regularly twiddling with her tinted hair. She had prominent acne, acne that seemed to poke through her dense make-up, strange for her mid to late-twenties age. I told her that I could pay the deposit today provided I had a contract to look at, and that I paid into a bank account to cover myself. I thought that this would cover me whatever happened. I thought I was being intelligent.

She had a contract for me to look at and sign and stated that it would need to be signed, along with the deposit, in order to process the tenancy. This seemed normal. The next events are nothing but a blur, chronologically, I cannot see how and what, but I remember a feeling of excitement. Not the kind of excitement felt as a child when one obtains a new toy. It was a capsulated and reserved version of this, a satisfied relief, that things were now to change for the better.

I made a friend look at the contract; and a contract was signed, faxed and sent over via email for records. When they confirmed that they received it, they sent a signed copy in return. Only then was money exchanged. One month's deposit, one month's rent. Two thousand and two hundred pounds. Deal done.

I called to see if the money had been received and he said that he would double check. He said that it was likely fine but he was called into a meeting. So here I was, steps away from Tammy and the home-safe delight. House warmings and red wine, woolly jumpers and adulthood.

The elusive man's accent, ignoring political correctness, would be described as 'street'. With some, this would raise alarm but I liked to be open-minded. The foundation of this country is to make something of yourself. To progress and to enhance others no matter of their background, is it not? Besides, his name was Daniel. And while I waited for Daniel to get back to me, I realised I had another flat viewing in Earls Court. This would be in vain but I went to see it anyway, if for nothing else – curiosity.

While the Earls Court man was showing me around, still a good deal, thirteen hundred pounds a month but not including the hefty and inflated utilities. I remained smug as I had a deal which I freely told him about. 'Yes, it's a nice flat but I have just signed with someone else.'

He nodded. indifferently. 'Oh yeah, whereabouts?'

'Fulham,' I said. 'But I have been in this area for quite some time'.

Memory still a blur, I am not sure when he said to me: 'Good luck with that,' but he did. I informed him that I handed over two thousand and two hundred in a bank account without seeing an office or the person who owned the flat. And thus, with his tight-fitting suit and smug look he stated, 'Good luck with that.'

To say my heart sank would be an exaggeration; it was a familiar realisation that all was not well. That the confirmation of payment had taken too long, and that the blonde assistant was too weird-looking. I called the guy again, Daniel, the man I had not met but had willingly paid money to.

I like to think of myself as intelligent, relatively speaking, or compared to some? An impromptu IQ test revealed an IQ of over one hundred and thirty at some point in my life. Still, it only dawned on me when I called the street-style landlord back, 'To be frank, I still haven't seen it in the bank account, could you maybe double check or put it in again?' To say I felt shock and awe would be wrong, it was more of a numb fatigue, a confused dizziness, as if all the efforts to live in peace and security had come to a predictable and depressing end.

There were two mitigating circumstances to my stupidity: the first was that I had dealt directly with a landlord before. This was in my current dwelling and he was an honest and lovely guy, trustworthy, and it was a streamlined process. I assumed this would be the same; assumptions are the mother of all fuckups. The second was that I had warned Tammy that gumtree flats are scams, especially at that price and readily available. As far as I was concerned, she had indoctrinated me into her shitty pseudo-strategies, creating an over optimistic mindset which, in turn left me blind to the dangers of the world.

I rang the bank and tried to cancel the transfer that had already gone through, it was three p.m. and it had been a couple of hours since the money had transferred into 'Daniels's account.' The bank was vague; they said that they should be able to retrieve the payment if the money wasn't withdrawn. That it was my fault because I voluntarily put the money in. It was presumably my fault for thinking that the bank would be a blanket of safety as we are legally forced to create accounts. They subsequently make interest on our mounting debts and misfortunes. Any misfortune that they cannot make money on is literally of no interest.

I called Daniel back to the point of exhaustion, the man was not contactable even on an unknown number. Of course, if he did not answer before I gave the money, he certainly wasn't going to answer now.

I didn't walk back to Fulham, I ran. Running back to the road with the peaceful multi-coloured houses and within-a-distance-market where I thought I may settle. I ran frantically, dodging joggers and even cars and I called Ritchie on the way, purely because he was an estate agent.

'Oh, you forkin mug!' Ritchie exaggerated the syllables on the word 'fuckin' until it sounded like 'fork' – the commonplace utensil; educated at City of London, he did everything to extinguish it – from the grime-inspired clothing to his 'pedestrian' speech.

'What's the guy's name?' he said.

'Who?' I answered. 'The guy who rented you the forkin flat you doss prick.'

My daze engulfed me. 'Daniel Green, his name is Daniel Green!'

Ritchie flexed his 'I'm-an-estate-agent' search capabilities and discovered, unsurprisingly, that there was no Daniel Green on the deeds. 'You, forkin mug, you should have told me, I could have shown you who the house is owned by, you have been scammed!'

I ran faster into a sprint towards the multi-coloured street. A moment hard to remember other than the rush hour cars and the sky, a beautiful pink. So beautiful and serene it confused me. I arrived at the house and there was already a queue, this included a young couple from Crystal palace and another, non-descript, sobbing man. Whoever these scammers were, they had balls. It was the most tragic of scenes: groups of young, financially vulnerable innocents looking to enhance their lives. They had stumbled on a carefully planned opportunity albeit contrived, their world shattered in the short to medium term.

The angered couple were already talking to the owners who had opened the door, and it wasn't the strange looking blonde lady or Daniel Green. They were as shocked as us; they hadn't

Airbnb-rented out the flat to return home to a queue of irate theft victims. I staunchly hung at the back, more confused and numb than anything and I kept thinking out of all of this, at least I could go back and tell Tammy I told you so, I would tell her, 'I TOLD YOU, I TOLD YOU NOT TO USE FUCKING GUMTREE!'

Common ground and trust grew between the owners and the mob and we were invited into the flat. There was a caveat to the tragedy: the scammers agreed that they would drop the keys off at six p.m. As to what I assume would be to not get a bad rating on Airbnb. We were told that Airbnb had given them a profile without full docs, they did not help with the case or the retrieving of the monies which must have been over ten grand. Conversely with Airbnb, if you receive a three-star review on the flat you rent out, they put you on a watch list.

The couple's plan was to wait for them and then... ambush. The Wife wanted us to wait indoors and invite them in, but the husband said we should wait on the doorsteps. Two different strategies, but he got his own way. Soon enough, towards six p.m., a fast and modified car pulled up and then roared away as soon as it saw the populated doorsteps. It was then that we knew we should have listened to the wife. We managed to write down the number plate but it was in vain, it was all in vain. When they realised what had happened, the Airbnb wife shouted, 'Next time you listen to me!' The outburst was not going to help us now and there was an awkward silence in the flat which meant we were supposed to leave. They had done their bit, now we were to go it alone. We said our goodbyes and most people headed towards the police station.

I hung with the Crystal Palace couple, the male was sizzling with anger and probed me with regular squints of suspicion.

'So, when did you get scammed? Today?' he asked me. We

exchanged stories and although their realisation came promptly, the set up was similar.

We took a bus to the police station who, in turn, said they did not deal with fraud – we had to call a separate number. A lot of texts followed, a lot of reference numbers, a lot of evading responsibility. The police had heard of the case and said that there were at least twenty victims. Twenty victims. Forty thousand-plus pounds worth of innocent individuals looking for a place to be. They could not deal with the case directly, but they could give us confidential information? Probably to make it look complicated to the victims, evading responsibility once more.

My nonchalance was because I believed the bank, NatWest, would retrieve the money and, when that didn't happen, I briefly analysed the well-known structure and realised why:

The institutions that you have to be with in order to register for a job or pretty much anything, who in turn, take your money and are combined with investment banks, make money off your money that is now virtual – are there to protect your money.

With that being said, are they ever secure? They have stacked billions of laundered monies this decade, had to be bailed out in the last one and nobody goes to jail. As long as money is going in somewhere, it doesn't matter. My money goes out and put it into another account, so, they could not care less.

I agree, I was the one who put my money into the account and my stupidity is the cause. This was why I was not protected; they said that they would cancel my payment but they referenced every transfer. Mine was conveniently pulled out of a cash machine. A cash machine that lets them withdraw thousands of pounds at once, apparently the recipient bank, Barclays, are the only people with these machines. More evasion ensued whereby it was Barclay's responsibility to get my money back. To this day and to my knowledge, even with a self-serving ombudsman and the threat of legal action, the police have not linked with Barclays to track the scammers account. Barclays seemed more concerned about the rights of their account holders, which made me think I should switch banks to them.

Throughout the coming months I gave a perfunctory fight, deep in the knowledge that nothing would be resolved. The sheer pain of trying to resolve was more painful than losing the money. The two thousand and two hundred was nothing in the grand banking scheme of things, I was a wasn't a multi-million-pound launderer. To them, I am nothing but a struggling proletariat. Having said that, the amount wasn't insignificant enough for them to pay me back.

I lay on my back in bed that night, the sky mildly radiant from general summeriness and light pollution. It was to be one of the last nights in my own indoor dwelling. I fleetingly thought about the other scammed people, were they homeless? Were they suicidal? I thought of the universe and its increasing desire to thrust me into tent living, now, my undeniable destiny. I could not tell my parents of what had happened – the shame alone would follow me for an age. They would probably and begrudgingly lend me more if they believed the convoluted story but the guilt, the guilt would kill me – way before the rigours of outdoor living would. One thought prevailed more than tents and victims and summer skies: Daniel Green thought I was so deficient, he asked for the money twice.

Ritchie called as I slipped in and out of conscious thought.

'Oi, you dumb cornt, did you hear that Cameron resigned? Forkin mental these times! Anyway, Solus and me are getting high tonight, already ordered in and she has her tits out again… Solus! Solus! Oh my, forkin hell, there are a few people round here actually.'

I briskly hung up and he didn't call back. Through my pensive exhaustion, I thought a thought with the clear and determined definition: 'Not tonight, Ritchie, not tonight.'

Chapter 3

First Night

"English rain feels obligatory, like paperwork. It dampens
already damn days and slicks the stones."
– Maureen Johnson
– The Madness underneath 2012

Mother: Are you Okay?

Me: The flat is really good thanks. Thank you for the money, I will pay it back.

Mother: Are you all moved in?

Me: In a way, yes.

Mother: In a way John, why are you so vague?

Me: Sorry, I meant I am just moving the last remnants of my stuff.

Mother: Do you want me to come up and lend a hand?

Me: Oh no, thank you, I have it all under control, thanks for your help. Cannot wait for you to see it.

I cycled with purpose to Oakley Street, camouflaged tent strapped on me and a large vertical bag that I possessed from teenage camping. It started to rain, a constant but warm rain that summer in London is known for. The type of rain that was tolerable but nevertheless, people rehearsed panic by clinging under shop windows and sprinting with umbrellas. Of course it must rain on my first night but I was not daunted; if anything, I was excited at the concept that I was obtaining the adversity. I had the keys to the Oakley Street building which is where my mail was still sent to. My plan was to camp out in the communal garden on the pretext that nobody would give a shit, in fact, nobody would come out at night unless to deposit rubbish or to check on their bicycle.

Within this large and decrepit three-story, I had electric plugs and bathrooms as there were many bedsits. The garden had a washing machine in an outbuilding, a palm tree and a black and white cat I called Chaplin. I was grateful for the cat as my fear of vermin followed me to every dwelling. Many moons ago, in this very same building, a substantial rat leaped from beneath the sink and under the bed. At night I could hear it chewing on the curtain ropes and the trauma has lasted.

The tent, highly efficient, unveils with no assembly. I was glad I practiced because it was difficult to put the tent back in the bag with pace. This is what would be needed, well, if anything untoward would occur. I put my phone on silent and wriggled in my sleeping bag, as the warm rain continued to patter on the canopy, I noticed two things: the first was that I was already cold, and the second was that my lower back was pestered by the stony ground. Suddenly I heard footsteps, and then the footsteps paused as if they had discovered my dwelling. I could feel the energy leering over me and in the silence, I heard whisperings in Spanish. 'Quién es?'

There were two of them, but I remained quiet and poised. They quietly moved to the left of me to deposit rubbish and returned into the ageing complex.

I decided to retreat indoors into the small room with the electricity metres. Thank God I had packed lightly. Tammy had come up to help me with my belongings a few days before and said that she would return when I had settled. A gem move, especially when giving me the space to gather my thoughts.

But Tammy had an instinct for giving space to men. My mother had noticed this and cited it as a marriage-like strength. She had told her expat-from-Zimbabwe father what I was going to do and he told me that in the summer I could lay beneath the stars; I was a minor celebrity. I had almost bragged about the expedition, some thought I was bold, some thought I needed therapy.

Why not live with her? Tammy had a smart Norfolk house. Vast with several acres, an idyll by Theocritus could not do it justice. It was her parent's house. Even with the square footage, the chickens and the forestry, her parents were there all the time. It wasn't in the City and the provinces would be the end of me. Tammy did the most wonderful thing by taking my storage for me. It is still there to this day.

A friend? I previously discussed how they would greet me with open arms, but when the real exposure starts, the reality kicked in: in a world where few things are unconditional, 'friends' are predictable. Few things are less desirable than sleeping in a tent but I know of one: the niggling guilt you feel when outstaying your welcome. Friends are over-enthused for the first few days: hyper, excited, they can party; they can chat with you, a self-willed sleepover. When the honeymoon ends, the controlling begins. The questions: 'Did you use the entire loo roll? Who has seen my phone case?' Finally, the resentment; no matter how hard you tidy, how much you cook or try to maintain the entertainment, they will re-enter their abode and you will see it on their mildly grimaced face. Their suppressed eyes try to hide it, but you can see it because you feel the shadow. If you do not leave, you will suffer the enduring indignity of an excuse, 'my sister is coming up so you may have to leave for a while… my landlord has found out there is another person in the flat.' An Englishman's home is his castle.

Before I packed up, I remembered I had a small amount of white in my bag's top pocket. I remembered it was dud but would keep me alert while I changed around. I took a bump and, for some reason, the buzz was ecstatic. I did not remember it being this good, but it was. I twirled towards the electricity room and, wide–eyed, looked up at the limited stars. As I moved into the electricity room, my phone lit up though still silent; Coralie was calling me, Coralie the beautiful. I wouldn't say I was in love with her, rather an infatuation fuelled by mystery. Now that Tammy and I were estranged…

She wondered what I was doing but I could not take a session with her. She didn't understand the art of bumping – only twenty centimetres lines until you shake uncontrollably and the dramas made me too exhausted. 'Corawwie! I just haaad a bump, it was amazing, and I can see everything, THE STARS!' She noticed my slurring which prompted her curiosity:

Coralie: Where are you?

Me: I'm not around now but soon, how are you?

Coralie: I'm okay, just moving flat again, same old shit, sick of it to be honest.

Me: Did you vote?

Coralie: Yeah, I voted in.

Me: Gurning sounds while changing the subject. I'm living in a tent, Coralie! Come live with me, I have enough space for two!

She paused, as if to comprehend what I was saying through the slurring and to gather if I was serious.

Coralie: Erm... right, yeah well you never know, I best go to bed now.

We left the phone call, promising to meet soon and I tried to muster some morale. Perhaps this is how Bjorn felt in the wilderness when the cold and harsh conditions surrounded him. While the bears and perils made their way towards his humble abode.

I had little sleep that night, mainly through fear of people coming to check their electricals. I needed to modify and retry – namely a roll mat and a thick sleeping bag.

I woke in the morning; thirty minutes to an hour of medium-depth slumber and a crooked lower back. I left the electric room at six thirty a.m, overborn by the paranoia of impending interruption. The communal bathrooms were compromised by mould. As the showerhead scum travelled through the water and onto the skin, it left me smelling like fungi and dirtier than before. I forgot to pack a towel, so I improvised by drying myself with a much needed t-shirt and a radiator in the communal hallway.

I left the building and went to a camping shop on Tottenham Court Road to pick up a roll mat. Then I asked the man for a sleeping bag.

Man: What kind of sleeping bag are you looking for?

Me: The warmest you have; I'm going on a camping trip in winter.

Man: Where are you going?

Me: Erm... Iceland, I am going to Iceland.

(The man looked at me with fear and shock, then his expression changed. Almost as if he saw through me and had seen this situation before, perhaps recently, perhaps regularly).

Man: Wow, okay, I am not sure that we have any bags that are suitable for that. You may need to look at military grade? We do have this one for ninety pounds which has a firm insulation.

Me: Okay, and this is the warmest you have?

Man: Yes, but as I say. I am not sure with Iceland; I'm from the North of Sweden so I know how it gets. Even in the UK, at a certain time, it may not insulate.

Me: What kind of time is the coldest at night?

Man: I would say early morning is the coldest, around four thirty to five a.m. It goes through your bones...

(His eyes glared as if to warn me not to do it).

Me: But this is the warmest you have?

Man: Yes, definitely.

Me: I will take it.

Ninety pounds out of the funds but I was still above water; the shower situation could be resolved by showering at the gym, though the gym was a cyclable distance from Oakley Street.

Today would be a day of planning; the financials to be assessed: six hundred and eighty-six pounds and twenty-one pence in my account, most due to the spare money left from the parents. I had a 'needs work' credit rating that built negatively from my student days. No heavy debts but I would have to pay the parents back the money at some point. I had another three hundred from Robert's deposit that was coming in, the rest went against my debt. I would not be able to afford rent for quite some time. I would have to be committed to the situation. It was Thursday, my day off from the office which meant that payday was tomorrow.

I had managed to track down the photographer in New York who lived under a tarpaulin on top of a block of flats. Unnervingly, he withdrew from this, now a wedding photographer in a backwater state. Different people, different needs. He told me to take care, in a way that made it clear that it would be the last time I would talk to him.

I headed towards Chelsea and received an unwanted phone call from the gym.

'John, we had to move your belongings from the lockers as belongings cannot stay overnight. Please collect at your earliest convenience.'

My fatigue made me shrug the necessity of collecting but I called a few friends to enquire about storage. I should be working on my online business but I desperately needed sleep. Sleeping in the day was not part of this plan but it would soon become commonplace. It was now that the difference of the situation was stark: I did not have a base.

Psychologically and logistically, this will play on the mind of the homeless – you cannot take movements for granted. There is no, 'I am going to lay down for a bit,' or 'its cold outside,' or 'I need to get something from home,' – you are a part of London's harsh and populated streets and the elements that engulf them. You need to find a way to flow with them so that they are not against you: avoiding rush hour if you can, using the summer heat where possible. Utilise any public space that you do have access to. Be sure to minimalise – no fancy garments or excessive belongings. You never know when you may have to move on.

There were a few options when sleeping in the day. Firstly, one of the loos in the Oakley Street building (this was uncomfortable and would have to be done upright). I was a member of the private H Club in Covent Garden. This would prove to be critical for my workdays but hard to sneak a nap among the wannabe celebrity crowd. Lastly and the most likely: the cinema. I had an unlimited card for a chain that had a complex on the Fulham Road and Kings Roads. The Fulham Road cinema was larger and darker, with steep seating arrangements that allowed you to become part of the blackness without being noticed.

I received a ticket for Roald Dahl's "BFG" and the man looked at me strangely. As I entered screen one I realised why. It was full of screaming children and I, a full-grown man had entered with a plastic bag; tatty-looking and alone. I made sure I stayed at the back of the cinema and laid down as to not scare the parents and the children. I had left the large rucksack in the Oakley electricity room with the tent, the new roll mat and bag, so I used my plastic bag with a jumper in it as a pillow. I soon found out that the vibrations and noise of any action in the film went through me like an electric jolt, making it hard to sleep. Still, I managed to get a little and psychologically, it helped to get through the obscure first day.

That night I tried again, I opened the camouflage tent and lay on my new roll mat, opened the thicker sleeping bag and lay in the calm night. The palm tree swayed with the gradual wind and Chaplin the cat scanned his empire from the surrounding brick walls. I thought to myself that I could do this, like this, in these surroundings, beneath the moon-lit sky. The main roads noise was shielded by the building, the constant cars speeding down the Oakley Street were only a faint threat. The roll mat was adequate, I was comfortable and relatively warm. I thought of how strange things were, politically. How strange things were, personally.

I convinced myself that life was not in the definite; life began and remained in the grey. The black and white shades rubbed together like tectonic plates and amidst the friction, violent movement occurs.

I laid on my back with inner peace until I heard the rustlings of somebody. They seemed to tread lightly, paused, smoked a cigarette and left. I realised that however calm this place could be, there is a cold feeling of exposure. There would be human traffic every night with no closing hour. Then, suddenly there was another disturbance – my silent phone lit up and the dark night shifted a gear.

It was Solus, who was with Plum, a friend that I had introduced her to. Ritchie was nowhere to be seen and apparently the two of them were on a two-day party.

'Where are youuuuuu?' she squealed with her mousy intonation.

'I'm on Oakley Street, where are you?'

Before she hung up, she stated, 'We are coming in an uber, send postcode!'

From then, I knew there would be drama. It was strange as I was comfortable. I could have easily done this night without them, but curiosity had grappled me beyond any reason.

Chapter 4

Solus's House

*"Life may not be the party we asked for...but while we're here
we should dance."*
– Steve Gilliland 2015

I didn't dismantle the tent and as I let them in, they brushed past
me into the dark garden without a hello.

'Ah, is that your tent? How fucking cute!' stated Solus with
her erect used-to-be actor posture. Plum striding behind her with
a bottle of beer, cigarette already lit. Their confidence and don't-
give-a-fuck energy amused me, it flowed with the rogue
situation.

Plum started to look around. 'Babe, do you have a loo?' She
soon got distracted by Solus's music which was blaring out of her
phone: some kind of grime followed by Plums alternative
options... Shoreditch.

'Oh my word oh my word it's a washing machine! Look!'
Solus pointed to it and dragged Plum towards her, it was then that
I knew they were high on white. They giggled together and I
could not work out why, then again, I could never really
understand the intimate and private humour of the female mind.
They seemed to get excited at the most innate of objects: sugar-
free red bull, photos, a certain view... washing machines.

Solus pulled her four-foot-eleven frame on top of the

washing machine. She sat there and dipped a key into the clear wrapper containing the snort and nailed it in one. Plum was amused by this and started to kiss her while caressing the side of her shoulder.

I was not shocked by the kissing; Plum would always have a boyfriend but would aggressively seduce the bulk of my female friends – she had tried to seduce Tammy once by showing her the size of her fingers. Whether Plum's boyfriend knew this I couldn't tell, and whether Ritchie knew that Solus was Bi I did not know, though, he would have endorsed it.

They beckoned me over to the washing machine and mocked me. 'Is this where you do your washing?' Then, they proceeded to offer me a line which I unconvincingly declined.

'I did some yesterday, I shouldn't.'

Solus stared at me in silence and shouted with faux aggression, 'SHUT THE FUCK UP!'

Plum started to 'mansplain' her drug theory. 'Babe, babe. Coke isn't a drug; it's like a thing, a thing you do at parties, you know? You have to just chill with it.' To the onlooker, this would seem like a bizarre and vague theorem but this was Plum. Plum the fashion girl, beautifully voluptuous and tanned with a deep voice like a seventy-year-old aristocrat. She had a way of making partying with class A seem like an innocent past time.

We racked three large stripes on the washing machine and snorted them in unison. Plum stuck out her pierced tongue at me in an astute acknowledgement that the night had begun. She was riddled with silver-like 'fashion school' jewellery: a Louis Vuitton padlock around her neck. The only flashes of gold being on her tongue and her signet ring. It was then that Solus hiked herself back on the washing machine and stripped down to her thong.

At some point in the night this was inevitable. Her large, surgically enhanced breasts pointing towards us as she arched her back. I never thought it before, the numerous times she had enforced her nudity upon me, but for some reason, this time, I saw it as a cue. I grabbed her left breast and she didn't even flinch but Plum, Plum was furious.

'No babe, no that's disgusting! That's sexual abuse GET OFF! GET THE FUCK OFF HER!' I was mildly amused at her hysterics but quickly withdrew my hand. I knew better then, in the starkest of forms, to get between Plum and her conquests.

After another line, cigarette and some giggling, a tall blonde lady ran out of the complex and shrieked at us. 'WHAT DE FUCK ARE YOU DOING? WHAT DE FUCK!' The accent was hard to decipher. 'Keep the noise down you don't own place you know!' As she walked away, she mumbled, 'Fucking tents, fucking tramps!', which almost hurt my feelings. Solus decided that we would go to hers. They laughed at me as I dis-assembled the tent and packed it with the upmost diligence. I took the majority of my belongings to hers, a small terraced flat with her grandma near Sands End; a far cry from Plums: a mansion flat in Parsons Green where guests were never allowed unless the parents were familiar. Some people showed Solus an amount of snobbery, even Ritchie. The invisible class system, alive and well as she was true cockney who moved west. But we were welcome at hers; somewhere safe, somewhere warm. The flat was nice. The flat was not a tent. We got in and said hello to the grandma who was still watching television in the front room.

With Solus's house, it was about congregating in her small bedroom, sojourning and smoking out of the open window. We rushed up and they promptly stripped down to their undies, then, they strolled downstairs for a long duration and left me to my thoughts; were they having sex together? Maybe... quite possibly. I started to become pensive about something, maybe many things that were out of place for this night. So, I called Ritchie and told him that I was at Solus's.

'Mate, I am at Solus' by the way.'

He mockingly replied, 'Have you forked her? Oh my wooord!'

I stated fact: 'No, of course not. I just wanted you to know, and I may have touched her boob.' He appeared nonchalant, but I feel, deep down and past the bravado, he could have thought it a betrayal.

'What do I care? And tell that twat to call me.'

People loved the name 'Solus' in the trendy areas: Soho, Shoreditch, Kings Road.

'Wow, is that what she is really called?'

'Is Solus her real name?'

It was her real name and it was cool. Its origins? Perhaps not so: Her Mum and Dad named her Solus as she lay on the hospital bed, probably weeping from the pain of being bought into this world. They decided that they did not want or could not afford to have another, so, they named her Solus to remind them not to do it again. She would be the only one, the special one: Solus. The point was void five years later when her parents divorced, her name remained the only constant.

Plum's name was an equally inspired birth choice: when her mother gave birth to her first child, she was told that it would be difficult to have another. Then arrived Plum, a large baby that supposedly scratched the walls of the womb. They took it out early via incision; Plum came out unhealthily, nearly dead, and purple like Little Plum from the Beano comics.

I could hear the girls giggling in the depths of the house, I didn't see them for a few hours, but Plum sporadically emerged to get something out of her bag; her Calvin thong hugging her curved and tanned physique, the wavy blonde hair past her shoulders. She was a friend, but it was hard not to be attracted to her. She threw a wrap at me as she was exiting. A substantial amount remaining inside and she blew a kiss. 'For you, munchkin!'

They were blasting non-descript Rihanna downstairs and God only hopes the grandma was sleeping. I quietly put on my coming down tunes; more Avant Garde, more calm, female vocals: FKA Twigs 'Two Weeks' followed by Wolf Alice's 'Silk'. Then, always, Florence and the Machines 'Falling'. Always Florence, in a decade where culture is retrospective and otherwise vacuous, it can be argued that she is the remaining prophet. Some will say that she wails and exaggerates, but this is what is needed.

I lay on Solus's single bed and started to doze, but not before I re-clarified my plan: it had to be clean, disciplined. Up at a decent hour then to the gym which is where I would retry to store some of my belongings, the rest would be at my friends, Scatty Alice's. She had storage space on the idyllic Thistle Grove which is at close proximity to the gym on the Fulham Road. The sleeping place is equidistant to the gym as Alice's is, it's a small garden in a block of (mainly) council flats and I used to rent in one of them.

The garden was on steep man-made land and you had to go up steps to get to it. At this point you were exposed to the rear-facing apartment windows – a nightfall mission. As you travelled to the left corner, it was dense with shrubbery and there was a crevice between two of the thicker bushes. A crevice large enough for a tent. Once there, you could not be seen from the front because the garden was raised. In fact, it would be hard to be seen even if somebody were on the lawn because the shrubbery would cover some of the camouflaged tent. You could not be seen from either of the sides, to my right was thick shrubbery and to my left a tall brick wall onto a main road. The only place you could be seen was from behind; only a short wall separated oneself from a newly built tower of houses. Exposed, but with the darkness of night and the camouflage of the tent – it could work…

I didn't see the girls for the rest of the night. I started to doze but made sure that my perspective of the night was positive: free drugs and accommodation, my own Avant Garde tunes and two naked asses for the eye to see. I would name my project. In my high and tired state, I made it official. I would call this adventure after the great man himself: Ironside, I would call it Ironside.

Interlude

Benefits

*"I, Rooster John Byron, hereby place a curse upon the. Council,
may they wander the land for
ever, never sleep twice in the same bed, And may they be filled
with the melancholy Wine won't shift Jerusalem."*
– Jez Butterworth 2009

It was frowned upon in my circles to try and obtain benefits, though, I know that there are more than a few. For me? I found the option a poisoned chalice:

The government had practiced eighty billion pounds worth of cuts in the last five years: the longest and deepest period of cuts since the Second World War. It was an attempt to offset the issues caused by the financial crisis and the subsequent recessions. In short, it was to help the thing the government cared about: gross domestic product.

Local authority funding cut by sixty per cent, thousands of hospital beds and, of course, benefits. While I disagreed with the New Labour approach, where it seemed that you were better off on benefits than many jobs. The Tories used this and took advantage. With initial public support, it seemed like they would swipe any benefit or base support that even glanced in their direction. I did once try to obtain housing benefit under this new regime, which you could only get when on job-seekers allowance. You could tell that they will do anything to tried to stop you from obtaining any form of help. The organisers, outsold to private companies, are targeted to get people off benefits and you can tell this when on the chargeable call. It was an arduous process, a gauntlet to which only a few would make and if they did, the benefits received are purposely not enough to cover expenses; you would receive a pittance and you would feel like shit for doing so.

Cameron started a few initiatives with great foresight. One being a loan for people in benefits looking to start a new business. A sound idea, but you had to prove you could survive on the amount provided which I could not: I did not live at home, rent free. For me, a tax paying person, the benefits would have helped me to get back on my feet and obtain clarity while I re-arranged and became dependent. This would have happened very quickly but, as said, it did not work out. I was lucky to have other options but for the people that don't, if I think for just a second, these times must be brutal.

Many deaths seem to be recorded from the re-jigging, including people with disabilities and people deemed unfit for work. I think of the Ken Loach film released in this very same year of our lord, although socialist and contrite, shows the helplessness of the victim powerfully. It shows how cunning and manipulative, how outside-the-box you must be to survive. It was clear where the financial pressure and concentration would be, where the blame and cuts would be executed. It would be almost as always: not the banks, not the CEOs, but the dependent.

My close male friends, Ritchie and Drew would scoff at this. Both ardent tory supporters, they believe in working and general self-made-ness but they forget something. They forget that I knew Drew when he was made redundant. He only survived through friend's contacts that elevated him into the world of finance without any prior experience. Ritchie forgets that he was jobless, that he is lazy without his own initiative but a school friend gave him the Estate Agent job. Therein lies the angle of privilege: the majority of top journalism jobs are public school educated onto Oxbridge, even the wannabe socialist Guardian. This is echoed in finance jobs, property and, traditionally, Government. They are in and let their own in. Could I talk? Decent boarding school in the East of England but moved to a day Catholic school. I have learned to only mention the former.

I know that although everyone is smiling and drinking in bars, although everyone photographs their holidays with jubilation, the struggles are deep. I know that although Ritchie and Drew had wonderful jobs; suits from Hackett; disposable cash. I know. I just know that in this front line. Without the contacts, without the privilege, they would be the first to drown in the pool of poverty. I wish they could see that what was there for them without it; in this specific age, in this specific year, what was there waiting for them: nothing.

Many people will read this story and comment on how I could have done things better. They will comment that in general, the fault is mine and I agree. Some would say that I let it happen out of curiosity rather than it being thrust onto me.

I agree with a few exceptions. One of them being the brutality of the welfare system, where mistakes, bad luck (such as being scammed) and vulnerability were not justifiable. Where amounts given were purposely not liveable (I was quoted a combined housing benefit and allowance of lower than my rent itself). National Insurance? National excess prudence.

I would soon see with my own eyes, the exposed were to be

exposed. The number without four walls was rising and has not peaked. Since 2010, a rise of three-fold. Avid and abject discrimination for those who make it onto benefits (you are not allowed to rent in certain places if you are on benefits). The rich are allowed to launder money with buying London flats but benefit recipients receiving a legal fund are not allowed to rent. You should not discriminate with housing by colour, creed, if you are Irish or whatever your legal income. (I would allow being selective on dogs). A prejudice purely based on assumption that 'benefit people do not pay their rent on time' – an issue easily remedied by making the landlord take the rent from the council, though, to be fair, it doesn't cover the rent.

Chapter 5

High Summer

"Everything good, everything magical happens between the
months of June and August."
– 'The Summer I turned Pretty' by Jenny Han. 2009

July in London – a month to adventure. To enjoy the trapped heat between high-rises and to share the rising temperature of your blood with friends. They say that repetition is the epitome of strength and so I must be gaining it. My routine was the same: wake up at an ungodly hour from the two bushes or wherever I resided and into the gym, pump iron in peace for forty-five minutes and shower. Then to Scatty Alice's place on the Thistle Grove where I had my clothes. I would put on a fresh top and underwear but my trousers would stay the same. There was a lingering damp from my clothes which came from a culmination of things: living in a tent which collected residue and liquid, even in warm weather, and the dampness of the stable-style storage room at Scatty's. I would usually drop a protein shake at this point. My creatine and powder stashed up with my storage and I would add milk or water, purchased from the local shop. I agreed to pay Alice forty pounds a month for the storage room.

She said that it was crazy that I did not stay with her for a while, but, as I have discussed, I can see things before they happen. We settled on her letting me stay in the flat when she went to the country, it happened sporadically, and I was grateful. She maybe scatty, but she had a heart.

'John! I have lost my glasses? I can't bloody see! I have the opticians in two days I suppose I will replace them...' If I let scatty Alice continue to talk, she would talk all day, just at me, verbally leaking every bad medical condition that was harassing her brain. 'Of course I have this bad knee as well, still from when I was knocked off my bicycle by that bloody learner driver...' I found a way to mitigate it. I would consciously nod at the end of every point until finally there was a pause. I would look at the phone and the time and let her know I had a meeting – whether I did or not. A storage expense of forty pounds a month with twenty-four hours access was not bad at all.

I would go to the office if it were an office day; at the office they noticed nothing except my improving muscularity. I dressed like a tramp most days prior to Ironside, as we didn't have to wear the slick suits and ties like so many corporations and companies, but we did have to be good at our job... an intense job that gave me the essence of normality. Me, behind a desk, emailing with other office types around, emailing and calling. An occasional top boss entering to assess and check it all.

I called it the day job, but it was part time: four days a week that they cut down to three in July. Amazing timing – imagine if I was still in the flat? My take home sliced by a quarter. I was not renting, therefore money was better but things would take longer. My default and involuntary plan would definitely take longer.

The square mile is something to marvel. It's ancient and you can feel it; its oldness and the narrow streets that create its capillaries, an intricate network compressed into one square mile. The office backs onto an ageing church mentioned in a Charles Dickens book, "Great Expectations" perhaps, or "A Christmas

Carol…" I can't remember. When you walk past the graves you will soon hit Moorgate with the Great Fire of London statue. Turn the other way and keep walking, soon you will meet Liverpool Street and Shoreditch.

The bars in the square mile are great for quiet beers, that was before returning west to the chaos of my friends. One day, Niccy had returned from Hong Kong and had a model meeting in the City. She took me to a member's club a hundred yards from the office, a place I couldn't get into in my wildest dreams but she strolled in and was familiar with the door man. She looked sleek and told me of how she fucked a male model on a Hong Kong side street. We entered and Niccy paused, her face tweaked in disgust. 'John, you smell funny, kind of like B.O.' I woke up late and already, I had failed with timings to shower – I also didn't have time to change clothes. I hadn't for a while because suddenly I had slacked on my routine, and slacking on this routine meant the utmost danger, it meant only maligned consequences.

The office, its importance: I needed the income to flow while the fashion business elevated. Three days, it wasn't enough. Deep down I knew it was not the money – it was me and my expenditures, I couldn't seem to control them. After my pay and deposit, two thousand pounds in the bank account but it should have been more. The socialising seemed to be integrated into my life and it was hard to turn back, especially in the circumstance; drugs, then a drink, random snack and then walking to and from places, public transport, miscellaneous; perhaps the odd taxi or item of clothing.

There was minimal sleep in the tent, four hours a night. The dreaded four to five a.m. was cold and uneasy even in high summer, then you dealt with your own paranoia: the rustles near the bushes, the busyness of the road to my left and from six a.m, the knowledge that a gradual release of humans travelling to work was nearing.

When I had finished work, by six p.m. I would be exhausted. My calorie intake would be gluttonous to survive. Always a restaurant or take out after work, hearty sometimes elaborate meals as Pret and other cold-food chains would quickly become monotonous. If I could have disciplined my capacity to eat at this time, I would have saved a lot more. Sometimes I would venture to club H in Covent Garden if I were not too tired but it was far from my dwelling. Wherever I was, my laptop would be attached to my side. Lodged, as if it were a part of me. They say it was the hottest month ever recorded on earth, that climate change is here to stay. But here in London, the weather fluctuated between extreme heat and cloud. My food consumption took a substantial chunk of my finances, by the first week of July with travel, one wrap, eating and some old bills, I had already cleared three hundred pounds.

I could never explain the innate fear I experienced in the evening when it was time for bed. When I had to shower again in the gym (sometimes), promptly get to Scatty's and pick up my tent. Walk through the side road and past a Mews so that no friends would spot me on the Fulham Road. Sneak up on the lawn in the darkness and set up. You and the elements together in a tussle. Roll mat down and check behind you past the small brick wall for danger. Small rucksack to the left. Phone on in case there was a party, for which there were many, and I could stay in a building.

Once set up, I felt better but I knew that my time for sleep was limited. I found a way to take the edge off, give me more confidence and relax the muscles for the hard bedding ahead: one can of beer, maybe two, but no more unless I was partying. Other than this, I never understood alcohol in moderation. I have tried; goodness knows I have tried. The type of groups, huddled in bars on a Sunday afternoon. They are content with their lives and with their social circles. They sip the wine gently, the girls on rose, the men watching Rugby with a Guinness. One leg crossed by the knee, rubbing the cold ale up and down with their fingertips. Giggling and civilised. The men and women are platonic. No sexual tension, no fucking in sight. SW fucking six. I have tried to hang with the types, I have tried to listen to their mundane spluttering about their nine-to-five's:

'Yes, we have a new boss coming in next week, I should have got the role.'

'Yes, I move flat next week, I may bring the car down for my stuff.' Always an upward inflection at the end of a sentence, like an Australian. I would nod and wish for snort. Then they would say, 'Okay, this is the last one, I have work tomorrow' and I would think: 'that's it? Ever-so-slightly tipsy? Sterile conversation? We are not going to go until our brains expand and give us far-out ideas? Until we have an existential crisis?' I would then think that I could not remember the last time I was like them; I couldn't remember the last time I wasn't on edge. They would leave and I would hang with people that made ME want to stop. I would drink and snort through the depression, more violently than usual.

I take a large gulp of my night beer. Now I knew why tramps drank all night.

It wouldn't take much for somebody to find me in this tent. What would they do? Call the police? Set fire to the canopy? I told Tammy that in these times, in the evenings, when we would usually talk intimately... it would not be possible anymore. I needed to have full concentration; emotions and attachments would only deter from the mission ahead.

One night, while lying on my back in the canopy, the road eerily quiet. The constant low-key heat of the air gave way to a storm. The thunder was loud and crackling above me, the rain that started as warm patters of water on the canopy became threatening thuds of liquid; rapid, intense, and relentless. I was entertained, it was joyful. Me and the elements, everyone else safe in the well-insulated abodes. I would scream every time the thunder roared over the metropolis. I would scream as loud as I could with chronic laughter: "IRONSIDE! IRONSIDE!"

Thursdays were different; every Thursday the stars would align in perfect homeless harmony. I would shower in the gym but miss a training session. I would deposit my tent at Scatty Alice's and head to Café Nero for good Wi-Fi. Sometimes I would order coffee but usually, an orange juice with a croissant. Sometimes I would shave in their loos if caught short.

Finally, my own things – my own world. Where the idea came from in the first place: independence. Working frantically on the online fashion business while I looked for an intern that could work for free. The merchandise was stored at Tammy's and she agreed to send them when there were sales, I would pay her for every pair sold. There weren't many sales in the coming month, but that was to be expected. What there was? Growing traction.

I had even managed to corner Vivienne Westwood after one of her talks. Her marketing director from the U.S kept blocking me, then, she would show off to the hot fashion women in attendance. She would try to seduce them in her sultry voice: 'So, I am in charge of all the marketing for her, I am the head honcho.'

I dodged past her and spoke to Vivienne directly. 'Oh, John, that is a great idea,' she said with her robust Yorkshire tones. 'We may well be able to do a collaboration, you must speak to my team and set it up.' Her team meant the predatory marketing director, who saw me talking to Vivienne and soon interjected.

'Yeah, get in touch, John, by email next week and we will… have a look!' I had already emailed her the prior week. I wondered if Vivienne knew she had such a self-serving pillock in charge of her marketing and perhaps I should be given the job. There was no doubt that online businesses had levelled the playing field for people trying to earn. There was no nepotism, you didn't have to be a certain class, nothing esoteric – just a website and constant action and, with a serious amount of hard work… you could be recognized.

When I had finished my work, the cinema was two buildings down. I would catch a film and sometimes Solus would join me, she was jobless and sometimes she would be expelled from her home. To be honest, she didn't need to be as Ritchie had got her a job as a receptionist at his Estate Agents. She lasted two days. Perhaps it was the principle. Paid a pittance to slave away for a corporation that would marginally raise the pay. Monday to Saturday in property, no commission for receptionists. We would have loved her to take the job; she never had any cash and I would more than often have to pay for her drinks, drugs and transport. I tolerated it only because her company could take the edge off an anxiety inducing period, or so I thought at the time.

I seldom would sleep in the tent on Thursdays. I would attend Club H in Covent Garden or go to Soho or somewhere where people would be. Fortunately for me, tent living was sparser in this warm and notorious month. There were constant gatherings and sojourns where I would be able to go in and take advantage of people's slack-mindedness. 'With chaos comes opportunity'. I will tell you stories of a few:

Gathering 1: Dean Street

'No future for me.'
– Sex pistols

There is a noted member's club on the cobbled strip of Dean Street – I will not mention the name. A notorious club, a club lauded by celebrities since the mid-nineties. When you go in, they are the hierarchy. The celebrities to one side, everyone trying to be on the other. It's closed in, sweaty and huddled, but everyone joins forces in the smoking area filled with pink neon lights.

Among the plethora of member's clubs on Dean Street and with new ones emerging, this club was known amongst for creatives. I say creatives but now, instead, the pure creative was being overthrown by a digital media type with their spikey shoes, spikey hair and lack of aura.

Naomi was our friend that would get us in, she only had a plus three but we managed four: Ritchie, Drew, Lottie and myself. Amy Tez was already in, but Amy Tez knew everybody. We hardly saw her for the rest of the night, just compendiary flashes of tight jeans and long brown hair. Ritchie was glad to have a night off from Solus and Drew was rigorously pursuing Lottie. He had been trying to seduce her for some time as he thought she had the credentials for marriage: a Surrey blonde, ditzy exterior though highly intelligent and in finance in Pall Mall. He took her to Glastonbury last year, followed her everywhere... nothing happened.

Ritchie was dressed as an Estate agent and Drew was shirted, and it was clear we looked a little stiff. Lottie, well Lottie looked good but I had jeans with a deep hole in the groin. It looked like the ironic fashion rips of the time but it wasn't. I ripped them when briskly trying to climb on the lawn where I pitched my tent – I had limited options with clothes and restricted time to get ready because we couldn't miss Naomi's entrance. If we did, we risked being placed on the humiliating sofa. A place where some waited for hours on end.

Naomi greeted us with a genuine smile. She was draped in a black dress, black tights and Dr Marten boots. 'Looking trendy, Naomi,' said Drew. She turned to us and shouted over the music: 'Thanks! I'm imitating Churches!' Her eyes were wide and I knew that snort was already here. 'Chvrches with a fucking V!' Naomi was younger than us, still young enough to imitate musicians and to think that the world was there for the taking.

We started walking up the stairs when somebody shouted 'Oi! Naomi!'

We glared across and Lottie was soon to be vocal. 'Lol that's the Mighty Boosh guy, look!'

'Shut up, Lottie.' Naomi was soon draped on his lap, giggling and frolicking as they both came over. For some reason, rather than saying hello, he rubbed his hand up my abdomen. Was that sexual? I left the thought, wiped my tired eyes and decided I needed a line. I had forgotten to order and Drew was being tight with his stash because he was feeding it to Lottie. Ritchie didn't have any, he was playing it deep until somebody else purchased, then, he could snort it all in ten minutes. Naomi was skimming it from anywhere: friends, the marbled tops in the loos, naïve males.

The drugs in Soho were known to be weak but everyone in this club was at it, in fact, if you weren't doing coke, you were out of place. Even the bouncer and one of the Managers slyly sold it but I persuaded Ritchie to call one of his guys and bring him in town. We were lucky as he came in ten minutes. I snuck a bump on one of the dark side-streets, cobbled and full of shadows.

Back in the club and Ritchie started to sway, it was only a matter of time before he embarrassed us so I forced the wrap in his hand. Drew was laying it on Lottie who was nonchalant, sipping on a daiquiri, happy-go-lucky. She bought us all a few rounds for inviting her and I thought... maybe she is okay? Naomi wanted us to meet somebody in the billiards room and, as we squeezed through more stairs, I saw Alex James from Blur. To me this was the epitome of cool: Britpop, hair slicked to one side; my older cousin loved him. He was drunk and swaying and so I took my chance. 'Hey, I just wanted to say I'm a big fan.'

He paused, 'Thank you, you are an incredibly beautiful boy.'

I took on the conclusion that I was looking good today, two famous men doing something to acknowledge this but I noticed the lingering smell. Heat and damp had made the stench constant on my clothes. When my friends got to proximity, I moved discreetly.

In the Billiards room, Naomi beamed towards a shirted and older man who jumped on the table. He started to clap but jumped off towards us when he saw Naomi.

'Ello you, come here!' His name was Andy or Anton, and he was a DVD distributor. 'Look at this!' He pointed to a foot-long line he had made on the side of the billiards table. 'Nobody leaves this room until you or one of your friends snort this farkin thing!' Naomi dug in without looking at us; even Coralie would have been intimidated by its size.

Tammy started to call me and I tried to find a quiet spot. There weren't any. 'Where are you? WHERE ARE YOU?'

'I'm at the ********, the ********? In Soho?' I felt

remorse as I remembered she always wanted to come here. 'What? I can't hear you, babe; I'll call you back tomorrow, okay? I'll tell you all about it!'

As we hung up, I realised that I had not spoken to her in two days. I went to the smoking area to find some space and cleared the guilt with a cigarette. There was a Sugababes member, so high, drunk or both that she found it hard to move in a straight line. She started to look at me and I felt she would be the ideal candidate to use for a flat. I didn't feel like staying in Wandsworth with Drew, and Ritchie, well, Ritchie had been drinking wine. I could flirt with her; I bet she had an apartment in Central, two or more bedrooms, one of those showers with the round metal showerheads. I could even dry my clothes.

She was so inebriated that everyone was watching, I felt that they were looking at me; me the opportunist. My friends must have been in the billiards room so I decided to sit down and I heard two mumbling voices.

'Of course, South London, it used to be cool down there until the yuppies moved in the early eighties, yeah they used to tell us off for wearin' confederate flags so I would say to them how many black friends have you got? They would say none! None! Can you believe that? No black friends?'

It was Jonny Rotten and the drummer from the sex pistols, reminiscing over past times. They were with their publisher and I listened intently to their conversation. The outside area seemed to go quiet, as if to cue me to say something. The seventies I had been told: strikes, lack of electricity, the rubbish in Trafalgar square. I wondered how it compared to now. If their protesting lyrics were genuine, if they felt the struggle.

Arguably we have it worse, at least they had punk rock, and we have Chvrches with a V.

I stifled up to their publisher and laughed as they all spoke. They seemed to include me. With the strong snort pumping through the veins I soon plucked the courage.

'So, what was it like to be a youth in the seventies?'

Jonny Rotten kept his eyes down, took a sip of a drink, tilted his head and slowly asked, perhaps rhetorically, 'So, what's it like to be a FUCKIN MORON?' He was riled, and the drummer started to interject.

'What a ridiculous fuckin thing to say, you are just a middle-class yuppie!' I tried to defend myself, but the comment that came out of my mouth didn't just confuse them, it also confused me.

'My mum is from South London actually.' The drummer was taken aback, he paused for a second as did I.

'That's all middle class over there these days, all yuppies, what the bloody hell are you going on about?'

It climaxed to a point where the drummer wanted to fight, physically, in an area densely populated. Jonny Rotten pulling him back and quietly calmed him down as they promptly left the outside area. That left me and a flabbergasted publisher and the piercing eyes on my back. An awkward and reticent silence consumed the outside area and there was now no way I would sleep at the Sugababe's.

I apologised to the publisher four times, inauthentically. I was amused by it, I was high and, low-key threat of violence aside, I liked them.

I thought of the night so far... far from over. Celebrities from varying decades present: Blur from the nineties, Sugababes from the noughties, and the sex pistols from the seventies. I wondered what they thought about the parties of today – how they compared to their time. I wondered what they thought of fitness crazes, of alcohol down and coke use up. They have achieved what they have achieved, anything else a bonus surely. It was now my time; me and my friends. All of us, under the same queen. We would be older than usual, but it was still our time and we had to grasp it by the ageing horns.

I cautiously walked inside and looked for friends, I found Naomi in the main bar area, splintered from the group. She was talking to an artsy type with long unkempt hair, dirty looking, almost as if he were living in a tent. She was lapping up his chat.

'Yeah, you see the Young Fathers are the only real band this decade, proper raw.'

I asked Naomi where the others were, she didn't seem surprised by my absence and there was no surprise that Ritchie had been asked to take some air by the staff; he had been swaying by the bar, head flipping from side to side, and took it upon himself to start a fight with the entirety of a downstairs room.

Amy Tez joined with us and soon we were a mutual group. Drew had not left Lottie's side but Lottie, gurning violently, may well be a liability. Naomi joined with us as did Ritchie when he was allowed to re-enter. Amy said that her friend could get us into The Box. The Box was a place that needs no introduction but here is one: the last time I was there, a transvestite on stage stuck a dildo up their anus.

Amy's friend was a tall and flouncy type, draped in fashionista gear including studs streaked across his black jeans and long tassels hanging from his T-shirt. For me, I was game, game anywhere. It would be a mission to return to Chelsea and assemble the tent at that time, no sleep would be found from it. Just the damp and surrounding noise.

'Can you get us all in? All of us?' Naomi stated.

Amy responded, 'Yes, Naomi, yes he can.'

I befriended the fashionista just in case, being male – it was a necessity to take this precaution.

'Yeah, so I basically work for Vivienne Westwood, yeah, she's a doll.' When people say basically, they mean that they are not but I nodded dutifully, fake impressed. I didn't mention that I had met her, I couldn't be… bothered.

When he asked what I did I said: 'being a tramp,' with a laugh so loud it hid the depths of my gut.

We started the short walk to The Box and I realised the greatness of Soho's irreverence. Lost in the moment, going from club to exclusive club. Laughing and high together. I was surrounded by people in compromising situations. Naomi the consummate couch surfer, lived in Devon with her parents but came to London for weeks on end, moving from house to house, 'looking' for job roles. Amy Tez recently had financial and flat issues. Lottie, a financial pioneer. The streets were full of rhapsodic characters, some trying to sell duck quality drugs, some offering leaflets to the local clubs. Partying and frolicking intrinsically woven into the dark lanes and streets. As we were about to turn right among the dimly lit erotica shops, I remembered there was still a primary school on the left. Between brothels and bars there it was, active and unassuming. It was adjacent to Great Windmill Street and the great windmill strip club. I thought to myself if I, me, ever had the money and emotional dexterity to raise a child, they will attend that school – it will be the making of them.

We get to The Box and the queue was so-so. The door lady was on an inevitable power trip and was reluctant to allow the entire crowd. She yawned as Westwood man whispered and begged. The crowd were agitated but then, a break: door lady needed a cigarette but did not have a lighter and exclaimed loudly to her empire, 'Right, the next group to get me a lighter gets in!'

I had one and promptly gave it to her; she smiled and bowed in a kind of thanking display. She let the crew in and the fashion man seemed dishonoured by my initiative. We entered and the place had transformed: no smokey stages or elusive characters. The Box had transformed into a West End night club with a militant table culture: one or two men surrounded by beautiful women. The fashion guy told us to wait while his table got ready but we have all been in that situation. The thing was, at this point, I was a slave to whoever had accommodation. There was no way I could get back, assemble the tent and sleep. Luckily, Ritchie decided that he wanted to go home and he said I could sleep on his sofa.

I don't like to be with Ritchie alone, the last time he tried to trap me in my old kitchen. There was something sexual about it – like being trapped in a shower room in prison. Others have had the same experience; apparently Ritchie decided to get into his flat mate Si's bed and give him a spoon, kissing and caressing his neck. Si promptly threw him out. Oli had said the same thing but it's something we never talked about. He would always call in the morning and ask, 'What happened last night? I can't remember a thing,' and I could see that he was frantic, even vulnerable.

There was something underlying and I felt sorry for him, and so I would say, 'I can't remember.'

He would pause, leaving an awkward silence on the call to read the situation and eventually, he would say: 'Man, I shouldn't drink wine.'

He had drunk wine tonight – a lot of it – but his flat mate Si was at home and I don't think he would try to rape me on the sofa. We got back in a taxi that I insisted on paying for, I plugged in my headphones – Young Fathers followed by 'Charlie XCX - Lock you up' with the lyrics being relevant: '*It's a long way home but I'm making my way.*' I slumped myself on the large sofa and slept deeply. His flat laid on a complex that hugged the river Thames and Bishops Park, the air was good and I had the safety of the inside. I slept and made sure to concentrate on sleeping as I did not know when this would happen again.

Gathering 2:
Night with H

'Dark matter and dark energy are two things we measure in the universe that are making things happen, and we have no idea what the cause is.'
– Neil De Grasse Tyson 2016

H is Ritchie's younger sister but I knew her a long time before. Ritchie hated his sister because of the trouble she made at home. H, the unreliable but heart-is-right type, ever since she firmly gripped my hand at a club in Cavendish square and guided me through VIP. She was eighteen at the time. Now, twenty-three, she had been active on the local dating scene. Her main squeeze being a fifty-year-old drug dealer who pretended himself as a Consultant. His drugs were bad and he was a violent control freak but somehow, he had obtained a membership to an exclusive Dean Street club. A club different to the one mentioned in a previous chapter. With H, rather like when you spot a mouse in a house, if you see her with one man there isn't just one, there are at least three: in addition to the dealer, she was dating a millionaire on Sloane Street who wanted to marry her. Another was a man who was squatting in a mansion block on Portland Place – he also dealt drugs on the side. There was also Ritchie's flat mate, Si, who she fucked on and off whenever she pleased. The squatter in Portland place is where we would go today. The last time I saw H it was more than wild, the kind of wind-in-the-hair wild that never leaves you. The kind of night where you are unsure if you want it to finish abruptly, or if you never want it to end.

We were invited to the Dorchester and she had stolen three hundred pounds from Tara Reid, yes Tara Reid from American Pie's purse after a period of long and sustained tension. For H had history with her boyfriend. The time before that, she frantically ran into my flat when Tammy was staying, a bone was sticking out of her wrist. She had been grabbed hard by the police when they raided her boyfriend's drug den and although she managed to escape, they seemed to have broken something. The nights out I have had with her are hard to believe. The imagination and lavishness, compressed into twenty-four to forty-eight hours. Like a movie or dream but you are very much there; the thrill and adrenaline she creates. Her brother gets drunk and goes home. With H? It's an all-night affair. I loved her ability to find streams of cocaine and places to dwell, though, it was not all fun and games. it was never for the faint hearted. I could never introduce her to certain female friends for H, as amazing a character that she is, was a sociopath. They would soon be low-key pimped out and drugged for giggles – she had recently met a girl at a cooking course and took her home – within three hours the girl was hospitalised.

We turned up late at Fitzrovia, it was a vast and old complex with multiple floors and H was wearing a tight green dress – designer for sure. Her blonde cropped hair slicked back, and her statuesque figure walked ahead of me as she explained that the entire building was squatted. She seemed amused and excited by the prospect. We calmly entered as two men hugged H and took us up an array of wooden stairs. Then, we entered a room with a large dining table and underneath it? What must have been the largest Persian rug in London. A real fireplace was utilized in the corner; the flames flickered on the face of H's lover. He was at the end of the large table, neatly dressed in a cravat. H ran and hugged him violently and she seemed smitten with the man. I wondered what the millionaire on Sloane Street would think of this. Or Si? Or the fifty-year-old coke dealer.

The man was friendly and I reciprocated. H made sure to squeeze me tightly, to warn me not to get too introverted, to keep eye contact, to engage in jaunty conversation and at least look as though I'm not there for the snort.

She was nicer to me than others, never humiliated me in front of crowds, never stole from me or spiked my drinks. I was, I suppose, entranced by the danger of her. Like being on a tightrope, on the edge that could go either way – we could have a safe night, but we could also get arrested. We could meet nice people, but we could end up in hospital with stab wounds like her ex-girlfriend Jessie.

The man in the cravat took us to a smaller room upstairs, an intimate place with a small sofa which all four of us sat on. And I was thrilled, here, in the middle of Central London when we shouldn't be, in random rooms with the most beautiful and dangerous girl and of course I knew what was coming; he went into a drawer and pulled out a tray with his hand. A tray with a mound of white and a metal straw. 'Do you mind if you use your own straws? I'm a bit funny about that.' The other men and I made makeshift devices out of receipts. H ignored his instruction and nailed a line on the metal straw. I awaited my turn, trying hard not to look at the plate, acting surprised when they offered it.

'Oh! Thank you very much!'

H tried to get me involved in the situation, 'John, you should buy your stuff from here, it makes sense!'

The man raised his face from doing a line. 'Yeah, I'll get you a deal.'

I thanked him, but I never contacted him again... I liked my dealers to be mobile. 'It's a great house,' I answered and he smiled at me. He changed the subject back to drugs.

'No worries, mate, and if you ever need stuff, get it from us, we will give you a deal.'

'Amazing,' I said.

He continued. 'Yeah, it's amazing the lengths people go to bring stuff in, cut with nonsense.' I finally asked the question that I knew he wanted me to ask and hoped that H didn't think it intrusive.

'Where does it come from?'

The man smiled and winked to the other men who were amused with the question. As thought, they were baiting for it. He started to stroke H's hair while she lay on his lap. 'You see, people seem to go to great lengths getting drugs into the country, they ship it from South America, to Amsterdam, smuggle it up their arses, cut it with bullshit.' They laughed simultaneously and so I joined in, fake chuckles from the depths of the gut. He continued: 'there is no need when you can get to the source.'

This was my cue to ask for more detail, so I did. He promptly whispered, as if the vast squat was wired with listening devices: 'the Columbian consulate is across the road, we get it from there, CAN YOU BELIEVE THAT? They bring it through the building straight from Colombia!'

A good explanation for why it was so pure; my heart profusely pounded while I tried to keep my eyes from blurring. If it was true, they were telling too many people. H looked at me and I looked at her back; the buzz had started and we were grateful as we high fived. Two friends on the edge of society, between the line of danger and safety - what an unbreakable bond it makes.

Three years ago, I would have stuck to beer. I would sanctimoniously look while others snorted. It was not that I hadn't tried it before, I sporadically had and it did nothing for me. I would say to myself: 'Oh, there is an effect, yep, there it is.' I may have felt dizzy and not sober, but I did not know for sure.

Once, H paid an impromptu night visit, bottle of wine in the hand and a large smile across the face. I was honoured to have her there in my dimly lit bedroom. Nobody was around, and she was in the most reflective of moods. Usually, we would gossip about local human irritants but this time it was existential.

H: John, what animal are you in the Chinese new year's?

Me: No fucking idea.

H: Well, let's check?

Me: No, I don't like telling people my birthday.

H: Lol, you are so autistic, I'm a monkey.

Me: A what?

H: A monkey, in the Chinese years… and do you know what they do?

Me: Tell me.

H: They take things and just get rid of them, don't know what to do with stuff they acquire. So, if they found a box with toys let's say, they would just smash it to pieces for no particular reason. And that's my destiny I think… to acquire and destroy things.

Me: Like men?

She laughed while she elegantly smoked a designer cigarette. Then, she asked me to play something poignant on YouTube – something I thought was heavenly. I thought for a second, only one, and pressed Mozart's requiem as she handed me the plate. For some reason, this time, I didn't resist. I snorted it in one and it was a novelty – a novelty that stayed with me and stayed with my brain for years: when the coke is bad, when I shouldn't, when I have expended all monies but still go back, much of it is because of that moment. The unquestionable high, the choral tones of Lacrimosa, the heightened elegance of H. As if everything would be okay. Life would always be okay with moments like these.

H and lover number three were tactile. The other men were getting ready to exit and thus, so should I. H knew of my situation but she was nonchalant, she was homeless fifty per cent of the time and she viewed the night as a chronological adventure. She expected me to do the same, besides, I would say the same when her mother would expel her. It was too late to set up the tent and I realised that I had the office the next day. I didn't want to bother Ritchie when he had work and he may well ask where I had been.

I messaged Solus on the pretext that I would tell Ritchie the next day; meeting with her was fine but her house? Well, it breached many codes. I asked if I could 'hang' as I had some skim that H handed me from the squat. It was drugs-for-board in code and was highly effective with Solus. I stayed in her room on the floor and we listened to music while we snorted the rest of the skim. I loved it there when not in the tent, though, there was an illicit understanding. An understanding that I would always have to arrive with cocaine.

71

Gathering 3:
Shoreditch

I don't recall who was exactly there, but I definitely met Veronica and her minions on a rooftop bar where real-life shrubbery grew on fences.

Drew arrived accordingly and it was two boys, various girls. Shoreditch nights were great and we had our structure: Shoreditch High Street, onto the bar near Cargo with the beds and then into the Barley Mow for a Guinness. The Barley Mow was cramped and two stout men started a fight, the bouncer ousted them and we soon saw them scuffle outside. So, we took the girls to the West Indian bar towards some random housing complex, just past Old Street. We drank Red Stripe but the girls stuck with wine and there was a Jazz band playing in the corner; they looked strange in the dim lighting while playing in front of the purple walls. While smoking a cigarette, me and Drew met a girl who had a boyfriend but wanted us to come to her flat if we had snort. We declined, because the other girls wouldn't be up for it, she also stated that her boyfriend would be back in two hours.

From here, we hit a larger bar and some of the girls left us including Veronica, but Eve stayed and some others that I had never met. Drew was attempting but I was nonchalant, enjoying my beers, the view of Old Street through the large windows. The general vibration. We were told about this basement venue in Dalston. It was always the final stop so we negotiated with a taxi and arrived.

The event looked illegal until they asked for two pounds entry. Only one of the girls was holding cash and she paid for us. In return, Drew would pay for the round but soon enough, I recognized the bar girl. I used to do hospitality work with her, she was German or Swedish or maybe both. Quite pretty but super petite and looked high or even depressed. Not a coke high but weed or something glacial. She moved slowly, pouring the drinks and walking almost in slow motion.

She recognized me and smiled, then she beckoned me over and slowly started to pour beers for me and Drew. She didn't care that there were others waiting, way before us in the pecking order, likely waiting for several minutes in the sweat and the heat.

She handed the beers to us and shook her finger when we went to pay. As she did this, the base of the reggae was so boisterous it pierced through my drunken legs. The large crowd swayed in unison.

The summer night was warm and I was glad because I had left my coat somewhere in Chelsea.

We may have stayed at Eves that night, it would make sense as she lived in the vicinity. I do not remember.

Chapter 6

Tammy

"Calms appear, when Storms are past, Love will have his Hour at last: Nature is my kindly Care; Mars destroys, and I repair; Take me, take me, while you may, Venus comes not ev'ry Day."
                 – *John Dryden*

It was a warm weekend in late July and Scatty Alice left the keys to Thistle Grove – she was on her routine trip to the country. 'Darling, darling, you can have the keys this weekend, okay, but please water the plants… and no crazy friends! Oh, bugger! That reminded me, I forgot to take the washing out… I was going to sell my Nintendo on eBay but the wires…the wires!'

The flat had serious kerb appeal – instantly recognisable with the hanging flowers and a bench where the passers-by would smoke heartily on the narrow path. As you crept downstairs it had a studio feel; the bed could fold down into the long drawing area but the shower room was primitive: you relieved yourself in a loo that was directly in the shower bowl; I chose to shower in the gym which had its perils. Again, they had taken away the towels, so I would dry my naked body with the warm wind of the hand dryers.

Tammy finally came to London after a period of estrangement. We drank tea while watching movies in the coolness of the new basement. We went to the cinema and I would break for my gym showers – she was fine with showering in the basin. We went to H Club in Covent Garden and watched a movie there. There was a romantic dinner at Palm Court brasserie where I fed her onion soup, expensive, ate savings – had to be done.

I suggested ordering but she looked at me in disgust. – 'You better be joking, John.' I said that I was. She was worried about my strategy. 'Why not stay at Scatty's? Or a hostel?'

'Well, my theory is, that idea is just paying rent again and the point was to save and build from the back end.' It was easier said than done but if I could get used to my situation, I could do it and maybe even longer than the three to six months. It wouldn't be about making more – I could make more by default.

I could see that she hated this. She hated the back and forth . She hated returning to the country without me. We had a wondrous weekend, but a talk was inevitable.

It was wearing on her: the constant waiting, the lack of calls and affection. The elusiveness. I was struggling to maintain any relationship. I hadn't spoken to anyone other than party people, Scatty Alice, or people on the edge. Just like me. We made love in the makeshift bed that was put upstairs and we looked at the darkening sky through the roof window. On the last night we sat awkwardly on the bench as she made smoke rings with her roll up. We knew that a conversation was coming, and we knew it would be brutal.

Tammy and I decided to go on a break. From my side it would let me save and when I was ready to move somewhere we would see, just see. For her it was no more wondering or chasing. As she walked away, I felt sadness, I felt guilt but I felt relief. I felt relief because deep down in the psyche I knew that we would have to end someday, not so far away in the cryptic distance.

Because some day she would realise that she could do better. Better than me, me and my artistic temperament, better than my fluctuating fortunes.

Ever since she took the man's number on a train – a man in insurance, she readily wanted me to know that fact. That he was secure and had a purchased a large house in the country. I knew that the task was too big for me, the task was like walking up a downward escalator, masochism; the task, at this moment in time, was not my destiny.

As she got ready to drive, I remained positive. Her sun-kissed face showed a hint of melancholy but she was strong, way stronger than me. I did not want her to know that I was mentally preparing for the street again, that this time I didn't like the feeling – I didn't like it at all. We hugged and I waved her goodbye smiling, in pain but smiling. And I would call her when I could, I would definitely be in touch. Besides, she was helping me with the online business and we must keep it productive. This business we thought of together as a country fire crackled in her sister's cottage. She would create the remarkably simple, sustainable garments with her sewing and we would outsource the rest: socks, small totes, bracelets – and I would sell and market them.

When Scatty Alice got home, she called and groaned at me for leaving a mess: 'John, John, did you see the sitting room?' There were bits and bobs John and I need to go to the shop to get a vacuum but my friend said that they could get me discount and… With Scatty I felt that whatever the state, she would have found something out of place. Then, I waited for darkness to fall.

There is a star that appears before the others. London's pollution makes it hard to see stars but this one is resolute: a firm light that is larger and earlier than its counterparts. My father used to say that it is not a star, that it is Venus. That's why it comes out before the others, and why it doesn't twinkle, because it is a planet not a star. Planet or star, I could recognize it and, just for this strange night I waited for it to come. I waited and saw it, the firm and loyal white speck pinned on the dark blue night and I wondered if this was one of his elaborations. If it was only a star and he knew it. If the knowledge of the white planet above the darkened City was erudite… or meticulously contrived.

I started preparations. The tent out and the hard night ahead. You must hit the bushes not too early, but not too late. I washed clothes in preparation for the office day and laid them out neatly, folded and put them in the gym locker. Leaving things overnight was a risk in the gym and I had learned this the hard way; always pull clothes before forty-eight hours.

I could see there was a difference on the road when heading towards the bushes – roadworks seem to follow me in London and they had followed me once more as a big crane-like drill hovered over the trees by the main road. It was vast and yellow and dominated the side street with some of the skyline.

When in the tent, once it was erect and you were settled, those hours were never as dire as the preparation. I was slightly numbed by the alcohol ration, and I texted Ritchie or Solus for debased gossip. They did not answer. There was something different about this night. Different because I was beginning to sleep, deeply, and the clear air was fresh. A rare night where air and silence let me slumber in the camouflaged canopy. As I started to snooze… it began the evening drilling. Drilling from the crane-like structure. Strange, violent and likely illegal drilling. Drilling that went through me and made the very ground beneath me vibrate. Vibrations so loud that I would lift five inches off the ground on every beat, up and down at high repetition. It would stop and I would try to return to sleep once more. Almost as if it knew I was slipping into dream, it would restart and I would rise from the ground once more. I laughed hysterically, not caring if anyone could hear me from behind the rear wall. I laughed a laughter that was so violent I could not tell if I was hysterical; I could not tell if it was a happy laugh or because I had to.

Because I had to, to stop me crying about Tammy.

Interlude

Bocage Country

I was hard at work in the City, I wouldn't usually take an hour for lunch but this time I had to – a thirty-minute nap in an empty office, closing the door and locking it from the inside. Alarm on for dead on thirty, low level sleep; not a deep sleep in case anybody wanted to enter. I would need to be able to get up, speedily get onto the seat and pretend to work once unlocking the door. This time I was lucky as the alarm went off and I struggled to wake... but I managed. Sneaking out onto Cornhill and I continued to walk, just walking through Bishopsgate and past newly built high rises.

I went to Liverpool Street with the hope of flanking through to the narrow Jack-the-Ripper streets, straight towards Spitalfields and past an arcade that never seems to be open. Suddenly I saw these men, older men that were shaking money rattlers. Military medals everywhere, draped across their military chests. They were Normandy veterans, yes, Normandy in 1944. Not Iraq or the Falklands but Normandy – and this was 2016. My thoughts flittered between intimidation, admiration and jealousy. As I went to talk to one of the men, I spoke without a filter as if to foolishly test him. 'You look very young to have been in Normandy.'

And he took it well. 'Have you ever seen Sophia Loren?'

He asked and I replied, 'I'm not sure.'

The man was in a wheelchair and leaned forward, 'Well she is nearly ninety, so don't take appearances for what they are.' He was right. These old men were part of one of the most difficult campaigns in British military history. With my history knowledge so acute, it made me wonder why I studied English with only history modules attached.

I told the man in the wheelchair that I would be back. The cash machines by the escalators were closed so I went to find another. I noticed I could be late for work but I did not care and neither should they, though, I frantically returned and the man in the wheelchair had vanished. There were other veterans in the middle of the station and I ran towards them while a strange humidity reached my back. I thought that this may be the last time I see them, this rarest of occurrence. This gem.

They were talking amongst themselves about a cockney soldier who would get them anything during the war. They finished with: 'Yeah, he died in Normandy in the end.' What is a man supposed to be? In this century, perhaps it is harder to define the role. To provide would be one, yes, the ability to provide is certainly something.

I asked them where the man in the wheelchair may be and they stated that he had gone for the day. Whatever money I put in the pot would go towards the same cause. I hesitated, thinking that I should stay loyal to the wheelchair man and put it in his rattler, then I shoved the twenty in anyway. I asked the man, 'Were you in the Bocage countryside?'

'Yes, we were,' he said calmly and politely. Bocage Country and onto Caen; full of thick hedgerows and small fields with earth banks. Raining artillery and death; contrary to public opinion - it was as dangerous as Passchendaele. I said thank you to the men, three beams of hope among the monotonous drove of

City workmen.

When I finished work, I went straight to a hardware shop, purchased a small plank of wood and a small bit of ply. I forced myself to eat at Pret and into the warm night I went. Before I let the tent up, I scribbled on the self-made sign with a large sharpie: 'Bocage Country' and placed it deep in the foliage. A reminder for myself that there are greater than me, that adversity whether we like it or not, introduces a man to himself.

Chapter 7

The Crack Den

"Crack is ruining the drug culture."

– Hunter S Thompson

The heat had made me restless – sweaty humidity and lack of accommodation made me stay out and linger, deep into the uncertain night. It went well most of the time – I would slyly 'fall asleep' in people's bedrooms, on their sofas or floors while they mumbled in the background. They would be snorting and drinking, sometimes laughing, sometimes fornicating. Most of the time it was harmless. Most of the time people were unaware, but I saw things that will never leave.

I never saw crack until I saw the den – I thought people would know that crack goes beyond a limit. A secret code that things have gone too far in the world of narcotics. A joke drug for 1980s ghettos that left you looking like a zombie. For Whitney Houston and people with no teeth. I thought my friends would have the dexterity to realise that coke was as far as it goes. That what we were doing and sniffing was more than enough. Little did I know it was more commonplace and on the proverbial doorstep.

There was an old, semi-detached building close to the river with an array of cluttered and clustered artefacts. It was a hoarder's paradise I found out as I was introduced to an older guy with a husky cockney accent; he possessed a quiet and confident swagger and openly let me in. Through the drawing room we went which, although possessing more hoard, was surprisingly spacious. Most importantly it was warm. It had been three days straight in the tent and my tired eyes looked like eight balls. He sat by the fireplace with a blanket and produced a plate of coke before saying another word. The fire and fireplace were real and he gave it an occasional prod to stoke the amber flames.

Solus had always been crazy but this time she had surpassed herself. I knew she saw drugs as a priority but she could halt when she needed to. Unlike some of her contemporaries that radiated sensibility but, hidden away in the depths of their mysterious soul, lied something unrelenting. When I closed my eyes I could see their high face by the flickering flames and there was no stopping them. Tonny was one of these people I was to find out, but not on this precarious night. Then he reached for it, it looked like coke but it wasn't – tin foil and other contraptions were nearby and I saw Solus take a pipe out of her handbag. I turned my back while they did their... thing. I heard them inhaling in the eerie silence; as long as I could not see them, I was not a part of it.

Solus briskly grabbed my arm and it hurt. She was surprisingly strong for her under five-foot and thin frame; she looked at me intensely with wide and watery eyes that seemed to conceal a thousand horrors. She made me swear not to tell, not to tell anybody about this place.

I swore not to tell and I didn't, well, not that I can remember. Not even Ritchie.

The crack man showed me a book where his name was mentioned at a party next to a Rolling Stone. He was immensely proud and I encouraged him, knowing that it would get me a free line. Solus told him how tired I was and he said I could sleep on his bed. I was appreciative but the bed was full of varying debris: bits of magazines, some glass jars and needles, yes needles, probably for heroin. I wiped away the debris that was left on the bed and was careful of the sporadic needles, brushing them away with my small rucksack packed with the laptop. Then, I slept on top of the bed with the rucksack between me and the bedsheets.

I tried to doze but heard illicit frolicking from near the stairs, it sounded like the man and Solus; definitely Solus, I could recognise mouse-like squeals creeping up towards the stairwells. I did not want to see what they were doing down there but it didn't sound good for Ritchie. I thought to myself that I was probably mistaken, the man was nearly three times her age and I froze, waiting for it to end. They seemed to go into the other room for a crack-fix and I tried to doze on the bed. The bed, an island surrounded by broken chairs, debris and drug paraphernalia. Still, beggars cannot be choosers and I started to sleep, quite content with the situation and the knowledge that the hardcore drugs were at a distance of safety.

All of a sudden, there was a girl that I did not recognise. She came into the room so high that the lower half of the face was twitching. She seemed to dance on the spot with one of her legs to stop me from seeing that it was also twitching. She asked if I had ten pounds on me, which I didn't. 'Come on, John, you must have ten pounds.' Solus must have told her my name which meant that Solus asked her to ask me. It was as if they were saying that it was unreasonable that I wouldn't give ten pounds cash considering I was staying in the needle – ridden bed. I shouted into the darkness that I could transfer via bank, but by that time she had vaporised into the lingering dark – maybe downstairs, maybe wherever.

People had told me that Solus wasn't what I thought she was. She had secrets, secrets that were hidden and you could not see them on the surface. Perhaps they were right, but it was hard to disassociate from her. It was if we were in it together, the long and hot nights, the destitution. Whenever I called her, she was there – always up for it, up for a night with no conclusion. The chaos within her, for whatever reason, created an ease within me. My weakness is, I am at ease with the messy people...

Chapter 8

Scatty Alice's 2nd Weekend Away

"I turn the Ritz into a poor house."
– 'Low life' by Future
2016

Scatty was away for another weekend and gave me the golden keys to Thistle Grove. And so, I invited Solus over on the premise that we would tell Ritchie later. She bragged about a new guy who sold a gram for forty, aptly called 'The Forty Man.' And I spent 40 on a gram and chilled with a bottle of red... and another.

Without asking, she bought Tonny and Plum – two people that I introduced her to, and they confidently strolled down the basement type stairs where we had created an inviting setup. Tonny played some music that I could not understand or comprehend. She was twenty-three – a little younger I suppose. But not as young as Plum who danced along with her with the proudest of expressions, as if to say: 'Look – look this is my crazy friend.' Somebody changed the song to synthesized U.S rap: Future, and they all sang along:

'High high, getting high... I turn the Ritz into a poor house, it's like eviction number four now... coz I'm always reppin for that lowlife!'

I could see Solus's mind whirring, as if to say – it's time: it's time to get naked. She started to lift her top but had second thoughts. Perhaps she thought it was rude to get nude in Scatty's house? In the history of knowing her, I had never seen her retract from stripping, but the narrow space was perhaps intimidating. I told Solus that I had invited Ritchie and she recoiled at the idea

'NO! NO! DON'T GET HIM HERE!' We were shocked at the statement.

Plum asked, 'Why not? Aren't you going out with him?' Solus looked down to the floor – half upset, half theatrical. It seemed as though a tear was about to stream down her contrived face.

'Yes, we are. Although I am not sure Ritchie would see it that way.' She tried to persuade us. 'I do love him you know! We do love each other.' The girls hugged her and then hugged each other and Plum seemed to grasp onto every moment - you could feel she was in her element.

Tonny changed the subject to something relevant, something relevant to her. 'I'm looking for a flat, guys. My parents are getting tired of me at home.' Solus told Tonny that she could always stay with her, to which Tonny promptly chortled and changed the subject.

Tonny turned to Plum. 'Do you think you will ever get away from home?'

Plum looked as if she had been ambushed: 'I dunno, babe, I mean everyone is living at home right now, aren't they? Except for John,' she sniggered.

Solus interjected: 'Everyone is renting as well, so hard to buy.' As if in her mind, she was even in that race. As if in her mind, she was somebody altogether different. Sometimes, I pondered smugly as I convinced myself that my situation was a big fuck you to the system, a hack where I live and wander around freely through the busy streets… there is a sixty percent rise in renters this decade.

I started to worry about the noise. Scatty Alice had stated that the neighbours were draconian – that we must be quiet when going outside to smoke and my friends were constantly frolicking and giggling by the foliaged bench. I went outside to tell them to calm down but overheard them talking about me. And I halted.

Plum: Is he okay?

Solus: Yes, he's fine. He's just autistic, you know how he is.

Plum: Yes, but doing this shit when you have parents, is it okay mentally?

Tonny: Yes, he is quite like, autistic isn't he, he goes quiet a lot at gatherings, have you noticed that he never looks you in the eye.

Solus: Yeah, no. He doesn't look people in the eye.

Tonny: Maybe it's the other autism thing, like a mild one.

Plum: Asperger's?

Tonny and Solus: Asperger's!

I went out and they shuffled uncomfortably. I saw that Tonny had sprinkled some cocaine onto a cigarette and puffed violently in the outside area. Apparently, the knack was to inhale, deeply, and hold it in for as long as possible. They offered me and I was hesitant. 'Is this crack, babe?'

They laughed. 'Of course it isn't, it's coke on a cigarette. It chills you out!' I slowly tried it, holding it in and it seemed fine- a distinct but steady chilling effect. I noticed Tonny was looking at me, intently and constant, almost waiting to ask a question.

'I don't think John would… no he wouldn't like crack.' Tonny was still staring at me, a gawk that I couldn't quite assess as Solus looked down at the floor.

Plum interjected. 'No, never do that, babe. Coke is fine but that's it.' Solus and Tonny looked at each other and gave themselves a knowing grin. Plum was not impressed. 'No, guys! No, no don't do that shit! It's NOT GOOD!'

I managed to get them downstairs into the quiet and safety but Tonny wanted to skin up in the outside area. I had to get firm. Solus proceeded to order more snort from The Forty Man without asking and she stated in a childlike voice, 'I may have just ordered again.' We all looked at each other.

'Okay, well who is paying?'

Solus shrugged unapologetically. 'I don't have any money.'

So, Plum tested the water. 'Well, shall we cancel then?' And Solus said that she couldn't as he was five minutes away, and we didn't know what to do as the damage was done. He was coming whether we liked it or not. She didn't seem to understand that money was finite, and bills will not miraculously evaporate. We all held a silence and wondered when somebody would capitulate... but the silence unnerved me.

'I will pay halves if somebody else comes in?' Tonny had no money and Plum said she didn't either, although she lived at home rent-free, she was doing internships that paid ad-hoc at best. bearing it in mind, perhaps she didn't.

Nobody would help pay but Solus had an idea: I was to pay the full amount and get Solus's crazy Ukrainian friend, Angelique, to pay half or whole back to me. Solus felt this was resolved and rubbed her hands together with the nibbling sound she always did. Her self-declaring sign to show us that she was excited. Angelique got money in bulk from 'clients' and happened to be in the hotel two streets away. A hotel that charged twenty-four pounds for two rounds of beer.

The dealer came and I reluctantly withdrew the finite cash. We snorted more and had fun while I monitored the noise which varied in ferocity. They discussed varying politics from around the world. 'Isn't it terrible, the horrible shooting and choking of people in America?' said Plum.

Tonny nodded, 'Yes, there is a Black Lives Matter movement now.'

Solus, fresh from a line, gave us her theorem. 'There is so much bad in this world, there are too many people, one day... one day the universe will just lash the fuck out.' She said it while looking into the middle distance, pointing her petite finger into thin air.

Eventually, Plum tried to run away to her boyfriend – Assim, Wissam or Assam, something decidedly middle eastern but we did not let her. She was in the count like the rest of us, with the drugs that were of medium quality but due to the price, we knew we would see it again.

I looked around the room at the numerous unemployed people, their energy floundering and unsure and I thought, 'Is this who I am? And am I helping these people? More importantly, are they helping me?' All I knew is that I needed people around me, when I could, to shield me from the unnecessary thoughts. The unnecessary evils. Deep down though, almost with mean spirit, I thought I was different: at least I was in an office three days a week and I was trying to set up a business. Perhaps I should have been showing them the way – the amassed bundle of hopeless humanity and wasted talent; high as a kite and draped on a stranger's sofa. Plum asked me why I was so quiet but Tonny had the answer:

'You know John, he's fine – he likes to... observe." She scowled at me while saying it, her eyes with the upmost suspicion.

Angelique finally arrived by banging loudly on the door – she found the place easily and she walked in, statuesque and angry. 'You guys keeps me fucking waiting huh!' Tonny and Plum from Fulham were shocked at the raw emotion. Then, she changed gear, greeted us with a smile and Solus whispered in her ear. They came down and I was excited. Partly because Angelique would be paying me and partly because the warm night had much to bring. Angelique came down and exclaimed, 'Hi, guys don't worry I have loads of COKE!' She poured a load of powder on an empty metal tray without asking if it was appropriate.

Tonny suddenly became warm and polite, 'Oh well, thank you very much, do you mind?'

Then, Angelique swigged red wine from a bottle that she bought. 'Of course not at all, help yourself."

Plum rushed in next without saying anything. But for me? Angelique had bought over a substantial amount and I wouldn't be able to ask for money. We put music on the system, perhaps a little too loud for the neighbours but we did anyway – dancing and cavorting deep into the night. Angelique exclaimed that there was a party with a celebrity chef's son down the road and they all seemed excited at the prospect. By this time I had enough and had seen this celebrity's son on reality TV. I will not mention the name but I was not interested in hanging with him, moreover, he had fucked Coralie after a seventy-two-hour bender.

I calmly waited for them to leave, and I saw that Solus was getting prepared by putting on some lipstick and taking a spare pair of underwear from my laptop bag. She always insisted on keeping a pair there, I never really understood it. Why did she not keep her cloak-and-dagger underwear in her own bag? Perhaps she did not want to get caught with it, perhaps it meant something unbefitting for the women of her generation.

I folded the bed down in a hint to them and I heard Tonny

whisper, 'Will there be coke there?'

Then I heard Angelique whisper, 'Leave him a bit of coke.'

To which Tonny said, 'Yes, but not too much.'

Very kind of them... I suppose. They soon left and murmured while walking up the stairs, 'Bye, John,' or 'Bye, babes.' And that was it... for now.

As soon as I was alone, something in me hurried to the tray and snorted another. Then, I skimmed the rest and washed the tray thoroughly for Scatty's return. My phone beeped a few times and I saw that I had fashion sales, three sales in the night which was great news, in all the chaos, there was progress. I would inform Tammy in the morning then go to the gym and then the cinema – hopefully a wholesome day.

Suddenly, my phone was alight. It was Ritchie. I ignored the first but he kept calling and messaged: 'oi cunt! Where are you? Where is Solus? I'm nearly there!'

All of a sudden, I heard the door from upstairs banging and the neighbours would certainly hear this. It was Ritchie, drunk and swaying. He didn't even say hello when he entered the raised entrance, immediately scanning for Solus.

'Where is she?'

I told him that she left with Angelique to some party, but I withheld the part about the celebrity chef's son.

'She's fuckin crazy, John, she's... have you not seen her tooth? Her tooth is brown, she fucking pukes up all her meals! She shags around – she's a, she's a CRACK WHORE!'

He was adequately distraught, I could see it in his eyes, the connection he had with her, however convoluted it was, it was there. He stayed and drank some beer while calling Solus profusely. He would call one minute after the other and I made him steer clear of the wine. He left her messages demanding her whereabouts and to come back to Scatty's. She did not respond. Eventually, he left and I cannot remember the time but it was late. Very late – so late I forgot to take the door off the latch.

I was dozing and Ritchie had left quite some time ago. I was snug in a warm bed with a roof above me, then, something prompted me to wake fully. I heard somebody enter. I was worried it was Scatty Alice as I hadn't tidied and remnants of drug taking and empty bottles littered the room. It wasn't Alice, it was worse. It was Angelique and Solus and they walked in without saying hello. No eye contact, no welcome whatsoever. Angelique was drinking wine and swigged and swayed her way down the loud and gapped stairs.

Solus spoke as I started to wake up. 'John, John guess what? You should see Angeliques room at the hotel across the road.'

I couldn't help myself. Curiosity, yet again, consumed me and compromised my relative safety. As they giggled to themselves, they complained that there was a smell of must. It was a worry. I knew it was the mixture of my clothes and likely my sweat induced by copious amount of drug taking. When Solus smiled, I tried to look for the brown tooth that Ritchie had mentioned. And there it was, very subtle, but it was one of the front two teeth that peered out of her gums, almost as if it were dented, as if it was bruised.

We went to the hotel and Angelique had a large suite, I felt that I should call Ritchie now but I couldn't be bothered with the potential dramatics. It was a beautiful room, ideal for her clients – there was a large balcony and television and she had a mixture of drinks, but unfortunately, the coke had run out. This erked and panicked Solus who was now on the phone to the dealer. She used my phone as hers was out of battery, and I told her in no uncertain terms that I would not be paying. She left and took my phone with her so that she could locate the drug dealer. She was gone for ages, a significant amount of passing time, leaving me with Angelique who was panicking about us making a bad impression to the clients she fucked.

I was also told what happened at the party: Solus stripped down to her underwear in a matter of minutes, strutted around with her boobs out and shagged the strange celebrity chef's son. Apparently, they fucked behind a curtain that was in the same room as Angelique. Another thing to keep from Ritchie.

Angelique stated that another client was coming to visit soon and I felt that we would have to leave promptly. I looked out of the balcony for Solus who eventually arrived. She paused, half-way up the path and she was crying – but I was more concerned about the phone. 'Solus, Solus my phone, where is my phone?' She looked and paused – she glared at me with the upmost sorrow and said, 'You want your phone? HERE IT FUCKING IS!'

She threw the phone onto the dark street and returned towards the depths that she came from. She was gone for at least another ten minutes and then, unceremoniously, she returned.

I went outside to try and look for the phone on the street, there was nothing there. I even went to the reception and asked if it had been handed in by some narrow chance. When Solus returned, I asked her where it was. She said that she had thrown it into the black street and that I saw her throw it with all her muster. I could tell that something was contrived about it; I could never work out how she did it, but I could only think that it wasn't my phone that she threw in the first place. The way it was executed, as though it had been done a million times before.

I told her in no uncertain terms that I knew she stole my phone, and that she needed to give me the coke, or at least most of it, because the phone was probably what she used as currency. She stated that she would kill herself and faux attempted to jump off Angeliques balcony. I watched her – quite tired, maybe high. I watched her hopping around the outside area and realised that I had completely wasted a night of sleeping indoors. I didn't speak, just gazed at her part-swinging off the balcony, each time it was getting more and more dangerous. She was athletic as she completed half-suicidal somersaults around the metallic fencing, the risk becoming more and more apparent.

I left when Angelique came back in the room. I left with the words to Angelique, 'She's suicidal apparently.' And I went back to Scatty Alice's just across the road and made sure I locked the door. I didn't believe Solus's suicidal act for a second, for throughout London, she was known for theatricality. That was until I heard large kicking thuds on Scatty's door – the neighbours would surely be woken by this.

It was Angelique. 'JOHN! YOU STUPID FUCK! RING RITCHIE! RING RITCHIE!' She was panicked, not in her usual, trivial way. She was serious. 'Solus has gone to hospital she has tried to take some pills, overdose! The ambulance is outside.'

I told Angelique that I was coming and that she should follow her immediately. 'You selfish fucker!' she said. I didn't believe it totally, and I had no phone to call Ritchie, hence why Angelique had to nearly break the door. She left and thumped the door before leaving and I felt that there would be irrevocable damage from this noise.

It was hard to get asleep again as I heard faint sirens creeping from the upstairs area. I walked, half-naked in a daze to the front door and snuck a look to the right-hand lane. There it was, the ambulance that had managed to pull up on the narrow street. Fast lights flashing by the narrow grove. Deep down I knew that Solus was in that ambulance, but really, I felt it wasn't my problem. My fucking phone. I couldn't get over the fact that she had stolen my phone for drugs. It would take something this dramatic for me to even talk to her again and perhaps she knew this.

Who would do that to somebody's mobile? A device that lets you hide and escape throughout the arduous day. Essential for business, essential for emergencies just like these. My constant and loyal friend throughout these homeless times wasn't Solus, it was my phone. It was my phone that helped me through the coldest and most mundane of nights. My phone would never leave me unless it was for a compulsory battery charge. That, or being stolen of course.

I went back into the flat and tried to get some sleep. I would need to tidy before Scatty Alice's return tomorrow and another weekend under a roof was lost in drama. The next day, Scatty gave me a stern warning as the neighbours had indeed complained, and there were party remnants inadvertently left in the flat. Perhaps it was a few wine glasses and white residue on the coffee table? It was never denied or confirmed. One more of those and I would not be able to stay when she escaped on her sojourns. I was glad that I was paying her for the storage. It was great foresight. If I wasn't paying her, I would not have been exonerated for the perpetual frolicking and debauchery.

Chapter 9

The BBC

"I've been told by the BBC that if I make one more offensive remark, anywhere, at any time, I will be sacked, and even the Angel Gabriel would struggle to survive with that hanging over his head."
– Jeremy Clarkson 2014

I had signed up to an extra's agency quite a few years back, a remnant from my modelling days and I would still retrieve the occasional bits of work. When I was younger, I always thought I would be famous, though, I didn't know what it would be. All I knew is that I wanted the unrelenting fame at the end of it. It could be reality TV or modelling or whatever would fast-track me into the tabloids. Leaning out of a limousine, drunk with two models either side. I thought that I wouldn't have to work in a conventional sense – just day-time interviews, drinks and late-night partying. As I started to work and grow up – the reality hit. As I scrimped to buy food for the week and took public transport into an office with the grey and monotonous beings – it made me realise, it made me realise that it was never going to happen.

The BBC wanted me to be an extra for a celebrity – a star from a comedy show back in the 1990s. Off the top, I cannot remember the name of the show. And if I did, perhaps I should not mention its name. It was a lady, known for being hypersexual and flamboyant while the other members of the cast looked on sanctimoniously.

The pay was good for a day's work: three hundred pounds plus a taxi there and back to the vast complex that was the BBC headquarters. The lady who had organised it met me and showed me the canteen where I would help myself to breakfast. She was cold, almost jealous. You see, my role was to be a silent runner assistant in a building full of running assistants. My role was to get the celebrity out of the dressing room and lead her towards the stage of "Strictly Come Dancing". She was to say some token line in a flamboyant double entendre such as, 'I'm ready!' and I would have to act shocked. Therefore, the majority of the intellectually challenged and vacuous BBC support staff could have done this role, and they let me know it through a cold and slightly vindictive demeanour.

The main assistant let me into my own private changing room. It was nearly as big as Scatty Alice's, topped with fashion magazines, a sofa, large TV and a vast-sized loo-bathroom. Although I was homeless, it didn't take me long to get accustomed to it, as if I deserved it; as if finally, I deserved this glory. But I could tell that the assistant couldn't take it, that she was wreathing with my jump past her in the pecking order. She could have done the part herself – and probably quite easily. She was, I suppose, an assistant of some… form.

She left me to my own devices in the large room and I watched TV, excitedly waiting to be called for my role. To say I was fresh would be a lie as I had been out the night before: night drinks had turned into a bit of snow from The Forty Man – a few spirits later and I rented a small room that took another ninety pounds off my savings. I felt it was essential so I could be showered and ready for the journey ahead. The private taxi was picking me up from the flat with the washing machine, Oakley Street, so I stayed at close proximity and ready. I thought of crumpling up in the electricity room and braving the growing mould on the showers – but it was not a good idea.

They told me to come in black so I bought a black shirt, underwear and vest to alleviate any mould smell that permeated from my clothes. I couldn't smell me anymore but others maybe could. It must be like the tramps on the side-street, the smell of stale human consuming a thirty-metre radius, but they are blissfully unaware.

As I watched the screen in my BBC room, I realised I still had a load in my bag. These days it seemed like I was doing it daily, so what was the difference? And so, I went into the private bathroom and racked one. I nailed it through a folded receipt, thought I was clever as I wiped any residue, and subsequently thought it was a comprehensive fuck you to the BBC establishment. I sat back down and read some more, watched the weird and live BBC tripe that they had playing and wondered if they would give me a beer to take off the edge.

The lady came back and told me that I had to leave the fitting room. She revelled in telling me this, she could hardly conceal a wry grin and, at first, I thought they may have known that I snorted a line. She hurriedly placed me in a communal space but the buzz was coming – and there was nothing I could do. She placed me in that hallway on a small backless seat, a desperate but tallied attempt to thrust me back down to earth.

Then, I met the director. Again, I do not remember his name, and again, it is best that I didn't. He said that I would be on in thirty minutes. 'Great!' I said, wide eyed and realising that I would be high on BBC TV. And, because the damage was done, I thought I may as well do one more – so I snuck into the large bathroom and nailed a rounded bump on my wrist.

Eventually I was to go on camera, I paced myself and walked to the door where I was to get the celebrity and take her from her dressing room. A bit like the assistant who had helped me to my dressing room. And so, I would take my character study from her – without the passive-aggressive action of course.

I was introduced to the celebrity but realised my reactions were not what they were thirty minutes ago – they were slow and reactionary. Many times, coke makes you faster and hyped, but people don't realise it can go the other way. You suddenly can't comprehend unless it's at a weary and glacial pace. She said hello to me and it must have taken three seconds to reply, 'Hi!' I said. But I said it too loudly which made some of the film staff look in my direction. We started taking takes of me opening the door and letting the celebrity out. The assistant director, with his due diligence, was shouting while the main director, who was apparently well known, investigated a monitor. I was aware that I was rubbing my nose. I was aware that I was slow and the dense amount of apparatus was overwhelming me. I could tell that it was taking more takes than it was supposed to and when they were ready for another, I constantly seemed to miss a cue.

'John, John!'

I turned, snivelling, 'HUH?'

They laughed, all of them. The entire crew with their cameras and headphones. They then said, 'Okay, let's get in it again.'

To which I replied in a camp Carry-On voice, 'OOH PARDON?'

There were not as many laughs this time, the laughter being replaced by puzzled looks but eventually, we managed to move on to the celebrity talking. She loudly and flamboyantly came out of the door and said the lines with the utmost elocution. She did it powerfully and effectively and I could see why she was on a classic comedy series.

They tried a take and she said the line, 'I'm ready!'

I paused and forgot what to do, rubbing my nose with my hand. 'Another take, please.'

From then I tried to concentrate and it was easy, for on this bit I had to look dazed and confused at her line, while twisting around, looking at the camera. All I had to do was to be myself, me in my current compromised state, and look at the camera at the end. It was a wrap and I had managed the job. I couldn't work out if they were happy with what I did – but it was time to go. I was glad as I had arranged to meet Solus on the pub on the king's road and I had a digital interview for another part-time role. The mood I was in, I would complete the interview jovially in the pub with an iced cold lager and an add-on bump.

The BBC assistant booked a taxi and acrimoniously waved as I drove away; I was fidgety in there. The taxi man asking what I was filming, swearing that he wouldn't tell anybody. I had to write a contract swearing me to secrecy, and so, I lied: I said it was something to do with a big brother launch.

Back in Chelsea, I met Solus and the warm weather was good. We drank beers and discussed the night where she tried to overdose. I had pardoned her because she gave me a different phone two days later. God knows where it was from – but it was an iPhone, just something more primitive. She said that Angelique tried to call Ritchie that night to see if he would see her at the hospital. He didn't. He told me that she was attention seeking and it was too late in the night for impromptu hospital visits. I felt bad, but I didn't really want to know why she did it. The depth of it would surely be burdensome for both parties. She could blame me because I was angry about the phone, but it must have been more detailed and solemn. There were always other aspects with a reaction so extreme and the darkness of it already lingered.

I had the interview, a little high and pissed, and the large windows of the pub let in the breeze and violent car noise which they noticed. I did a nonchalant and under enthusiastic interview. Partly because of my state and partly because I was hesitant to commit to another job. My emails pinged while I was at the BBC office and I had another sale. It's hard to describe the buzz, every time I heard the distinctive decibel from the mobile - a small but relevant victory.

Even though they had argued, Solus went to see Ritchie for their routine sex and I went to the H Club to meet my friend Eliza, the actress, and her boyfriend. They were so grateful for the invite and ordered me a few elaborate cocktails. I would have asked to stay at theirs, but the boyfriend would occasionally give offbeat and suspicious glares, besides, they lived in the depths of South-East.

I thought, while we smoked and drank on the Covent Garden roof – the view across the City restricted but pleasant. I thought, firstly, that I preferred the decrepit pub across the road and secondly, that I really needed to obtain an intern. They could come here as my office in one of the smaller rooms. I would do it on my two days off during the week and work the same on the remaining. It would be glorious.

I packed myself up as they got ready to leave, they said their goodbyes with the obligatory, 'Are you sure?'

I was sure. I walked round the dark colonnades of the Covent Garden and wondered where I would sleep, it was far to West, there could only be the office… and so I did.

Chapter 10

Sleeping in the Office

"Oh, grant that I can stay the night
Or one more day inside this life."
– Florence and the machine
– 2016

The notorious City office, it was ancient and surrounded by ancientness. The heavy doors creaked as you entered and there was a strange energy when you walked up the stairs. It reminded you that the Dickensian graveyard was attached to its rear, and the basement must have been at real proximity to the ancient bodies. Rumour had it that Boudicca was burnt at the stake one hundred yards from there. The Fire of London consumed the area from Pudding Lane – the list is endless. I crept up the narrow stairs in the dead of night. A silent night. So much different from Chelsea as the square mile was sparse in its population. The office was cold and it was as if something was watching me.

I could not make a habit of this for varying reasons. Firstly, the employees were sure to find my dwelling and secondly – it was as scary as fuck. I made sure to sleep in the corner office on the second floor if I had to, this was because the room was large and the heater's convection filled it. The window view let me see the Leadenhall skyscraper and the building works on Bishopsgate. For a split moment, I was taken back to memories of my childhood bedroom, playing with airplanes on my single bed but I was soon interrupted. As I turned on one of the office lamps, I heard one of the lifts going back and forth at an unnatural pace. People will read this and say it is just my imagination, that I was stuck in my in own world and my prepossessed knowledge of the area, but for me, it was unnatural and intimidating. The lift doors, sliding back and forth violently and fast to where there was no logic. I put on Florence's new song to drown the noise – on my headphones of course. A song she produced for a video game and it is called: 'Too much is never enough.' Fresh and relevant poetry to my oversensitive ear: '*A year like this passes so strangely, somewhere between sorrow and bliss.*'

The crescendo was sublime, I listened to the final third three or four times before using my rucksack as a pillow as I lay on the floor. Not so long ago, I had gone to Nayarra's to watch a horror film about the Enfield haunting. Based on a true story, a little like this one. A huge mistake. The image of the demon nun was lodged into my warring psyche. I envisaged it walking around the dark halls of the multi-halled office space, my mind flitted to it while checking if I had locked the office door from the inside, it was then I realised I needed to have a piss.

Reluctantly, I got up and turned on every light in the dark halls; there was a loo on the second floor and I routinely used it. Then, I thought I heard creaking behind me, and I froze, the horror film lodged in my imagination. I could envisage Nayarra laughing at me as the image of the nun haunted me again. It had reminded me that Nayarra had invited me to her housewarming party, or was it her birthday? She said that there was a special guest that she was going to set me up with, a celebrity guest, blonde and beautiful apparently, and I would look forward to it.

As soon as I felt that I could not hear anything, I ran out of the loo and through the door into the corner office. Firmly locking it shut behind me. I tried again to sleep but, of course, the phone had to light up in the silence and dark. Why did I not switch it off? I answered my own question in my mind: in case there was an emergency or something so tempting and depraved I could not resist.

It was a strange one. Martha, a voluptuous glamour model who Ritchie was obsessed with. A deep consistent love. If you mentioned her to Solus, she scowled in fear and acknowledgment that she could not compete.

I did not know why Martha had called me, I was bizarre as a choice considering I was Ritchie's friend, and she knew he was profusely in love with her.. She asked me as the dim glow of the Leadenhall building came through the window, and the light dimmed consistently from the office lamp that kept me safe from centuries of ghouls. She asked me what I was doing and that she wanted to party – with copius amounts of narcotics. On that night I was tired from it all and I was starting to feel ill and drained. I certainly didn't want her to know my situation, besides, she would have to come here and party, she would probably snort all over the table and the workers would enter in the morning while we were still at it. Although I had my rules, we would still probably still have to fuck and she would tell Ritchie about my unwashed body and how she had to sleep on the hard floor.

I responded, 'I dunno, Martha… if you told me earlier – '

She interrupted me, 'Listen, John, this is the only chance you will have, it will be tonight only that I will party, tonight… or never.'

I thought it may be a test, it sounded too good to be true. I pretended that I would try some numbers to get a delivery and call her back. I didn't call her back and she did not either. Perhaps

105

she was with Ritchie and it was a test, but perhaps it wasn't. All I knew was that she never called me again, and I never mentioned it to Ritchie.

The hard floor and unseen entities made it difficult to sleep, as did the itching and the knowledge that I would still need to be up at six a.m. so to avoid anyone. I left in the morning after opening the window and wiping with antiseptic wipes that were left in every room. Double checked for anything left behind and snuck out and down quietly, turning left into the narrow streets. Three things struck me on that early morning: how I felt quite ill, nauseous even. And that there was a homeless transvestite on the narrow path blocking my way to the coffee shop. She had surrounded herself with a cardboard box and was muttering out loud.

The third was at the coffee shop – I ordered a coffee and the man looked at me, he looked at me with concerned and empathetic eyes. I had the money but I was struggling to get the loose change from my pocket. I must have looked like a tramp that was struggling to get the money needed for the coffee. I looked like it, I stepped back and thought to myself: 'I am like it.'

The man said to me, 'Don't worry, it's okay, you can have the coffee for free.' I never forgot it, not so much the man because he remained a silhouette, it was the unconditional act that moves and remains. A truth that will forever be constant.

I walked towards Monument and turned around, back towards the homeless transvestite and the cardboard box. She didn't have a money jar, she wasn't even begging but I gave her the rest of my coffee, I had only taken one sip and I left her to her thoughts.

Interlude

Lady in the Cardboard Box

She was dressed as a woman: a pink dress with bright red lipstick shoddily placed on the lips and smeared across her face. She smoked roll ups and talked to herself. She would flit between two places: the narrow path near the office or outside the sandwich restaurant and surrounded herself with a cardboard box. It was as if she was making a base for herself, you see, psychologically, the tough part of homelessness is the lack of a base. Effectively, it meant a lack of security. A base is a key element that keeps you safe.

Element… an apt word. Four walls and a roof, or a cave, a hut or whatever humanity has used in the past protect you from the elements. There is an evolutionary warp that happens when you lose it: it's not natural. It's not supposed to be. Probably from the days of hunting and gathering and, although, they were probably nomads in prehistory, humanity has evolved to have a base. A static one. One where you base yourself, do your thing and come back. Wash, elope, sleep while the rain and wind batter it into the night – you are safe from the elements.

She, in her upmost desperation, tried to emulate. The four walls of the cardboard box, always with her while she laid on the pavement. Long cigarette ash burning down in her hand and likely inebriated – people seemed to walk around the cardboard to avoid proximity. The box was intimidating, and I could see she stayed by the restaurant for some form of attention. I wondered how she got there in the end – to her current destination, in a dress, talking to herself enclosed by flimsy wood. I thought I would talk to her, well, one day at least, but her energy of despair was overwhelming. People created a diameter around her so they did not get sucked into dark matter.

People in the office, with their pharisaic views, would comment when they had seen her. Something along the lines of, 'She's crazy,' or, 'Is it a man or a woman?' I would not stick up for her, but I would not join in with their attempts at humour. They were a herd where off-the-key behaviour was considered weak and threatening to their infrastructure; the world, the corporations – the man, the royal exchange across the road and the central banks want them this way.

I was glad that it was summer for her but wondered if she had any friends. I bet she had fashion ones, somewhere, maybe Soho or Dalston. I bet they extradited her as soon as her troubles were real.

Chapter 11

Earls Court Bedsit

"...but today the area has gone up considerably in price and there are not too many run-down properties of grim bedsits. But on the main drag – it still does feel for the most part a bit of a place to go through rather than to live."
– Earls Court on London postcode walks
– 2013

I don't think many could take tiredness like this. Tiredness to the point where my immune system petered in and out of existence. I was walking and snivelling, walking and sweating, hunched with a rucksack and my laptop bag. The weather wasn't August; it was overcast and depressing and the noise on the Earls court road loaded my anxiety until it hit anger; an overly loud police car, an ambulance that blasted the sirens as soon as it was alongside. A fast Audi and vexatious twits shouting for no reason to my left.

I was almost sleeping while walking, thinking about catching a movie to sleep, but the constant option of the cinema had its perils. I took it upon myself to go to a bedsit. To have a bed where I didn't have to pay in cocaine. The dinge of Earls Court had a plethora and this was seventeen pounds for the night. It was a shared room, six people huddled in to a dorm-like existence but... whatever... I just needed to lay down, quietly and surely, if only for a few hours. A few hours on a purpose-design bed was more valuable than a night on a deck.

At the front desk, I had forgotten to transfer money onto my account and my phone had died. I wanted to scream as the small transaction declined. I ran to the Café and had enough to purchase a tea – non caffeine as I didn't feel my heart take another stimulant and, as I hugged the warm tea, I could see that my hands were shaking. The Barista saw it too but looking at the crackheads on the nearby side-street, he was probably familiar with warped bodily actions.

My phone charged and I exited swiftly, back to the bedsit near Collingham Gardens that overlooked a garden square and three-star hotels. I had already asked a couple of hotels on the other road, one hundred pounds a night and I was trying to save. I was dwindling – down towards one thousand because of travel, nights out and miscellaneous turns of events that seem to riddle my existence. I returned with a successful transaction and the man gave me keys, keys with an oversized electric tag.

He told me where to go: 'Down then up then right.' I did so and went past a dank and dark basement, then some shower rooms and weirdos on the stairwells. I then hit my room; I took a top bunk and there was nobody in there but the stench, the stench was insane – pure stale, male body odour – permeating and persistent. I could see that the cleaners had been here. The surfaces were clean and the carpet was vacuumed but it would take an age to get rid of that smell. It was a smell so potent that the culprit could still well be here. I managed to crawl out of the top bunk and open the window. Ajar. It was as far as their security locks would let them open. And I crawled back up to the top bunk and tried to forget the stench, with my flailing condition, I tried to forget everything. It almost worked; I could almost forget the smell that seemed to be dissipating in my mind. I even dismissed my fluctuating pulse, a pulse that would move from glacial to as rapid as the human traffic on the Earls Court Road. That was until I heard faint footsteps. Footsteps that got nearer and louder until they entered the small room. I pretended to be asleep but had my eyes open enough to see what was going on: a rotund man, hairy and sweaty and clothed with jeans and a T shirt. He went to the bunk below me and paused, and he was looking at me in stillness, tenaciously staring at me in the bunk, not giving a shit about the consequences. I wanted to turn my head so badly but I did not want him to know I was awake, and quite frankly, as well as the stench of human, there was the smell of danger.

He finally moved but it was towards the window, then, he shut the window that I had opened with so much energy. The stench was now back to the original strength and he may well have been the one causing it. He left at least for a while. I would have loved to have re-opened that window but I was scared to do so, as if we were prison bunkies and he would attempt to strangle me.

I tried to sleep again, struggling through the lack of air and he returned. This time he was only in a towel, rubbing his fat hairy body but there was no ointment in his hand. I made sure I was pretending to sleep but he came again towards me and stopped abruptly. He was glaring, static and semi-naked. This time I was fearful; I was fearful of being raped, I was fearful of the stench, I was fearful that all six beds would be occupied by a freak like this. I tried not to move but I could see that he hadn't either. He was just watching me, almost naked, adding to the stench while the window was closed… I couldn't take it anymore; I couldn't see his hands and for all I knew he was touching himself in the large hairy crevices. And so, I made myself wake up. I was already awake, but I acted one with a fake yawn and suitable movement to make it convincing. I made sure that I was assertive, no eye contact, just a nod and an acknowledgement that he was there. He backed off a little, looking down while I promptly packed up my stuff and climbed down the small bed stairs. I walked out of there to the nearest communal loo where I strategically puked, wiped my face and exited. Ritchie and Drew were at work so that was not an option. I thought of sleeping in the small storage room at Scatty's or Oakley Street, but I needed a conventional mattress. I had just had a taste of one and now? There needed to be a conclusion.

There was only one option... it was Solus. I texted her, 'hey I have naughty's' – the usual entrance fee. I took a gamble with the last part of my energy and messaged The Forty Man. Solus hadn't texted me back yet but I was banking on it. I could arrive with the drugs ready and get on that single bed of hers that had saved me in many dire situations. He came quickly and I paid him the cash, and although expensive, it was still cheaper than a hotel. I waited on a street corner until Solus texted me back, which she did, she was on the way home from somewhere, somewhere elusive.

Probably another guy, a guy other than Ritchie or she would have disclosed, and I was to meet her in thirty minutes – thirty long minutes and I started to shake again. I found a small side road and dipped my fingers in the bag. I thought this would help me to keep going until I hit my destination and to support me as I pondered my recent encounter with the hairy raper. I left it for thirty-five minutes before I got a black cab to Fulham. There was no way I could cycle there or walk – I would simply collapse, full flow, on the busy concrete.

I got to Solus's and forced a smile; she looked excited but I

112

knew it is not for me. She wasn't even looking at me, rather at my laptop bag, glaring and guessing where the goodies were hidden. I briskly said hello to her Grandma who was sitting in her usual chair, watching her familiar shows.

When up the stairs, I falsely nodded to Solus's conversation and threw the bag at her. I didn't tell her how ill I was, how at times my vision could be impaired to a yard; she was someone who was likely to use my weaknesses against me.

I had readily been trying to see her less after the hotel and ambulance. Things were getting too deranged, crazy, but the truth was, it was one of the only places that I had and I should be grateful. She took the bag and proceeded with her nibbling noise. 'Yum! Yum! Yum!' She started pouring coke on to a magazine and rolled up a piece of paper. Then, she asked if I wanted one to which I steadily refused... The previous bump was readily flowing through my blood to the point where my heart popped through my chest...

'Knock yourself out, all yours Solus, I am just going to have a nap.'

She shrugged and snorted in silence while I curled up on her single bed, not even moving the various magazines and bags placed on there – not even removing my sweat-laden shoes.

Chapter 12

Intern

"Buy less. Choose well. Make it last."
– Vivienne Westwood, fashion designer
– 2014

Sustainability was a buzz word in 2016. As the planet burned and populations continued to grow – our little garments: socks and small bags and recycled-piece earrings were getting noticed by large organisations. PETA, the animal charity approached us, and had asked us to collaborate on a range of larger bags that would be designed by a vegan celebrity. It was an ex-Wife of an Oasis front man, and her daughter would also model for us. She lived in Primrose Hill and the range would aptly be called 'The Primrose Hill Set.' For that is what she was, back in the noughties with Kate Moss and Sadie Frost and all the others but I wasn't intimated. I felt that this was now our time, not hers. Even though this all may seem glamourous and fortunate to which me and Tammy were eternally grateful, our margins meant that we weren't making millions. And really, looking back, Tammy should have had a slightly bigger share. Although it was my idea and there wouldn't be a sale without me - she was creating some of the product. We were still tiny, but the website was executed so well, it made us look bigger than we were.

And so, I had to go to the celebrity's house in Primrose Hill and I was late due to sleeping over at a party. Understandably, she was not happy about this. She stood upright and angry, and pert nipples that were at the end of very large breasts were poking through her top which reminded me of Solus. I bet that's how they used to wear tops up here, frolicking with each other and wife swapping; the notorious Primrose Hill way. She was in a foul mood and looked at the prototypes that we had made and threw them on her white sofa. 'I don't like them, nope!' She would be the face of the product, but we would do all the work. PETA, however, was a marketing powerhouse and it would be foolish to say no. We modified the range and did a photo shoot and lo and behold the press came: Cosmopolitan, the Telegraph and her daughter who modelled was in teen vogue. Hello magazine, the list went on. And the sales got better. This, considering that it was August when people tended to be out and about or on holiday, so they had less time for internet sales. Well, at least that's what they say.

We would get a sale, regularly now, weekly, and I would text Tammy and say, 'Woohoo!' and she would say the same but that would be the end of the basal exchange. Communication kept to a compulsory minimum.

They were expensive stuff. Handmade and in the UK and I found the supplier myself if Tammy couldn't make them. I was buying them for five pounds each and selling them for thirty pounds. Faceless and classless digital progression. Minus Tammy's share I had managed to stack three hundred and twenty pounds, not millions but a start and could go towards my deposit. Back up towards sixteen hundred pounds.

There was other good news – I had finally found an intern: a girl named Noda from Luxembourg had emailed me and was interested about the sustainable aspect of the accessories.

'I am a fan of Vivienne Westwood and Stella McCartney,' she put on her cover letter. She was coming to live in London anyway and I presumed that her parents were rich. Not just because they were from Luxembourg, but because they had already acquired a flat in Central London for her.

My plan was to do the interning in the daytime at the H Club, it looked sophisticated, and I could say that my office is being renovated or something along those lines. She could help me to obtain wholesaler information and we could help to create a company that had an avant-garde feel. She could also help push this new range with the celebrity and PETA who expected regular donations from the sales.

I didn't want her knowing I had another job, I wanted it to be as if I was engrossed in the project and that we were going, without any doubt, to rapidly expand. More time in the wonders of Covent Garden and if I allowed myself I could get fucking excited...

I would say to her that the internship only needed to be part-time, so at the moment, she could feel free to do other work. This might change in the future depending on how well we did, together, as a team. I could also say that I had meetings on some of the days hence the part time arrangement, and occasionally she could come to these meetings. A business carrot on the end of an endless business stick.

The first day she was impressed, I set up her email and she started to approach the much-needed press contacts. We used a room that was at the back of the club, quiet with large sofas and plenty of plugs for laptops and phones. Only the occasional company; the occasional minor celebrity that would be pitching an idea to somebody that was barely relevant to their needs. The pitch would always be to restart their careers, somehow and someway.

My intern would order a coffee that would be on my tab, and she told me how she had settled into London quite well. In fact, she used to be a regular here in London, amongst the West End nightclubs and the partying scenes. A rich girl seeing the sights of the great hub of Europe. She moved back for a University course and now, back here again, to the large and aggressive metropolis.

We worked out a list of German and French speaking Fashion compilations – being from Luxembourg, she could speak both. We worked at proximity, and we were both comfortable with that. It was not my intention to seduce the intern, especially on the first day, but we were remarkably close. Literally close. Our laptops almost touching as I noticed her long vegan legs in tight fitting jeans and a tattoo of a heart peering from her ankle.

She saw me looking. 'Did you want to see my tattoo? Wait, look.' I stood up to get a better view and she placed her legs in a yogic-style split until they were wide apart, the leg with the tattoo bent to an angle. I pretended to fixate on the tattoo, I tried to, and then I sat back down.

She was good at the emails and I always left her some homework to do. Usually emails to send and some leaflet designs for our next meeting. She had the eagerness of youth: piss and vinegar. 'When will we meet next? When do you want it done by?' I always tried to set a date. I told her that I would meet her in three days' time with a vague promise that the internship would get more intense. She left and the session had given me energy, it was only four hours, it felt like a day.

I decided not to go anywhere else for the day, just stay on my laptop and achieve minor work while I waited for Eliza who was working in Covent Garden that day… she had an argument with her boyfriend since the last time we spoke. It took me back to the first day we laid eyes on each other. On the shop floor we both worked in, selling trendy canvas shoes. I remember going for drinks that very same day and she told me she wanted to fuck me.

On that very day, we smooched and waved goodbye as her boyfriend picked her up. Nothing happened after that. Shortly after I got with Tammy and, well, Eliza had a boyfriend. Whenever we worked together it was a bad idea. Once, we closed early and took off for drinks with a post-it note stuck on the window. Onto an underground Belgian restaurant and dreamed and dream together; a dream of art and only working for ourselves.

At first glance, it looked like I had got further than her in this: I had a business, I had an intern, but I was a homeless man. She worked for a retail chain, sweating and grafting on the shop floor, always straining with the small amount of money they rewarded her. She was flat sharing, two boyfriends since the last one she cheated on with me. But there was always the niggle that I did not know where I would sleep from one day to the next. Who was winning? It is close... so very close.

She loved the H Club and I had a feeling it was to get away from her boyfriend who I believed she was, again, unhappy with. We would smoke profusely on the H Club balcony with our alcoholic drinks. She found me sleeping in a tent so exciting, so daring and I would soak up the admiration as she would hunt for people to talk to. The people she sought were always the same: entertainment people that could enhance her career.

While I thought about where I would sleep that night, I enjoyed watching her in her element. Smoking and working the room with unfeigned delight. She would put her long auburn hair in a ponytail in a sign that she was about to work the area. Her boyfriend came to pick her up at ten-thirty and she asked if I wanted to stay. Again, I said no – they lived so far away, it would ruin my plans for tomorrow or for any day, such was the distance of their abode.

I was not in the office tomorrow but it was late and I needed to get used to tent living again. I wanted to break away from Solus and her ways, her subliminal ways of making me pay every time I slept there. I was reserved about bedsits, especially after my last evocative experience and sleeping in bedsits or Airbnb's would be a slippery slope for my finances. If I could get back into the routine of the tent, I could get into the routine for my business and intern. Besides, my monetary situation, although bumped up by the business had not been disciplined. Still due to suppers out, cocaine, travel, drinks, and socialising to feel a part of the excluding world. I needed three or four grand and, already two or three months in, I had less than half of that. At this point I could not remember when it started. At this point, it seemed I had been doing this for the entirety of my twenties.

The rain started to patter as I took an alternate route, a blurred and misty view towards the market and onto to the tube – I needed thick skin tonight. It would be a tour de force returning to the Fulham Road, pulling the tent and setting it up in the progressing rain. I still wasn't a hundred percent, and the occasional episode of shakes consumed my body. Then, I received a phone call from Liv, Liv was a friend of Lottie's and ran an ambitious Magazine based on luxury lifestyles. It was certainly luxury how it was managed: up at 10:30 or 11:00 each day after partying, a few hours work and then to a late lunch. Before I got with Tammy, I used to see her for brief and intimate relations; Lottie must have told her that I broke up with Tammy.

And that's why Liv asked what I was doing, she stated that she was lonely – she had also acquired some drugs.

She was aware of my situation but would never invite me if she wasn't lonely. She had probably approached a plethora of acquaintances before me and usually the offer would be enticing but I just wanted to... sleep. I said if I came, would I be able to sleep? To which she sighed and agreed, 'Yes, John.' And I made my way to Holland Park.

It was raining harder now and the sky was a decisive jet-black. This was strange, considering it was still the bright month of August, considering the nights seemed to be clearer in summer even in London. I made my way to the exclusive but monotonous white square with a sterile communal garden between the crescent. This place was built for and by posh cunts.

I briskly entered the high walled building and she greeted me with a glass of fizzy wine. Cheery and hyper. I could smell the damp on my clothes as I walked into the well-tidied living room, so, I tried to mitigate this by hanging my coat and leaving my musty bags in the hall. I quickly used her loo and sprayed myself with whatever perfume she had stored.

Liv was wearing a figure-hugging dress that was painfully tight, accentuating the womanly curves that got her a profusion of male attention. There was no doubt that she was beautiful. Her long wavy hair was radiantly blonde, all the way to the root and her blue eyes pierced through her porcelain tones. The type of Nordic beauty you might see on Vikings, with a shield and sword and blood wiped across her face. I smiled and forced eye-contact, trying not to let her see that my bulging eyes and thoughts were transfixed on the expensive Chaise longue. I listened to her conversation, 'I had to take doggy out for a walk and then got accosted!' I falsely laughed at her dramas and took a sip of the prosecco that she had given me. Then, I slowly made my way to the Chaise and sat there contently. It was beautiful, the room was so clean, the chair so… comfortable. I saw Liv help herself to a line to the left of me as my eyes started to close – I knew then that I was exhausted. My haggard body was ready to shut down at this very spot. She asked me if I wanted one and I declined which made her pause. I could feel the inquisitive stare pierce my head.

I told Liv that I would lay, just lay for ten minutes in sacred silence and dryness. I played the homeless card to which she shrugged, as if to say, 'Fair enough.' And so, I briskly laid on the chaise and it took a lowly minute for me to fall into slumber. Rest and warmth had found me at last – at least for a small moment. While I was there, in my own lucid dreams, I felt a hand touch my abdomen. What started as a touch evolved into a deep rub, a sexual form of rubbing that went towards my groin, to the extent that I woke to Liv, inquisitively peering over my tired head. I made the foolish move of knocking her hand and turning on the chaise. A knock so prompt and violent that I even offended myself. To this, she stormed two metres away to do another line and then hit me with it: 'WELL, IF YOU AREN'T GOING TO ENTERTAIN ME TONIGHT, YOU CAN LEAVE!'

I thought to myself, 'Really? Now? In the relentless rain?'

She continued while angrily hitting another line in succession. chopping on the plate with unnecessary vigour. 'In fact, it's probably best that you go, I could have brought other people over. Now I have to call around.'

I thought to myself, 'Call who? And why?' I wasn't going to beg; I was so shocked at her venom that I found the energy to get up and exit, hoping that she would be remorseful… but she was not.

I realised after this incident, and the incident in the hostel, that vulnerability has sexual appeal. As if people can sense the helpless energy on you and some embedded, carnal trait is released. For some reason it was sexual, a warped instinct to aid in procreation, and this was not the last time it happened.

She was already on the phone to somebody else. I didn't say goodbye, just hastily ordered a taxi back to the Fulham Road. Sleeping in the tent would have been okay if it was two hours ago. Now I was snivelling, now I was half asleep and had to progress in the dead of night. Now I would have to accept my fate. My fate that there wouldn't be sleep tonight – the camouflaged canopy would be a mere cover until the morning. I returned and went through the routine, through the motions in a stoic manner. Pretending that my body was down on the path and I was looking over from a lofty height. Me, slugging with my portable tent and bags, hunched over in the rain. I reluctantly set up in the battered bocage area, the self-made sign was soaked and sorry looking. I lay there quite ill and sniffling and, although the vision was blurred through the rain, I thought to myself a thought with upmost definition: Liv is not a friend – she is not a gem.

Interlude

Covent Garden and the Strand

I would wander around, mainly on my lonesome. Sometimes I would go to see Eliza, other times I would hit the plethora of corner pubs in silence and solitude. The numerous bars in H Club are great but there was something about the Cross Keys with its dim lighting and low walls. You could hardly sit on the seats – it's as if they were about to break with every swing back. The knees right up to the tables and the strange thuggish folks in the corners whispering with their pints of French beer.

Sometimes, I would have a pint and wander towards the Strand. It was crowded full of people just like me – homeless. Many of them queued for what seemed to be a soup kitchen. When you headed back up towards Covent Garden there were many more, but they were more organized. Around there, I walked through what seemed to be a community.

I was drunk enough to approach and I spoke to a man who had a large bag stacked neatly next to a camping stove. Then, a lady: fifty-something and sitting upright. Her clothes clean and her immaculate sleeping bag around her legs. Her portable lantern glimmered on her face. Her main bag was neatly placed and beside it were a pile of books. She was reading one while sitting there upright.

'Hello, how are you?' I said, and she greeted me with an open smile. Upright and regal. I then wasn't sure what to say. I am not one for real chat and I soon started to look down to the floor. 'Do you mind me asking how you got here?' Forward, and to the point but she told me:

'Well, I have made a few mistakes but now I hope to get back on my feet.'

She smiled and engaged but didn't put her book down. I bet it was one slip up, a sudden loss of cash or house fire. All I know is, this shit is coming for the middle classes.

I wondered if she had children or any family. She was too neat to be a drug addict – but that was not certain.

I would be sure to give one or two of them a pound if they had a cup, usually the most vulnerable: the young and female. The ideal night around this place would be to take a date to Palm Court brasserie by the market square. This would be followed by the H Club for a few drinks and smooches. Then, to the underground wine cellar that hugged the park next to Embankment station. A few glasses of expensive red and to the river to watch the ripples glistening next to the Cleopatras needle.

Chapter 13

Viking Reminder

"If you are fated, it doesn't matter if you choose or not. You simply have the illusion of being free to choose."
– *Ivar the Boneless in Vikings, 2016*

I was in the office for the day and I would see the intern tomorrow. For the next few days I felt occupied at least but, for some reason, the work in the office was more intense. People were coming up and asking questions, I had to get varying spreadsheets ready for 'end of play' and the heat in the office was making me sweat out all the excess coke and toxins that were haunting my body. The groups in the office had some graphic banter on this day, they were talking about graphic sex: rimming and golden showers and laughing so loudly to the extent that I had to hide in the loo and sit on the seat. I sat there and had a sleep and tried to get rid of the minor shakes that would still thrust themselves upon me.

I drank numerous coffees and tried to make sure that nobody could see me looking at the ground, deep in thought. More than usual, I seemed to be allergic to anything that resembled corporatism.

'John have you ever worn a suit?' they asked me while grinning to each other. Earlier on, the boss had stated that my jeans were not protocol, but my other pair were ripped to oblivion and I hadn't found time to wash the work ones. Finally, the day ended and I left the office. Many stayed on later than closing and when I said goodbye to them, they didn't acknowledge. This stayed with me until I walked to the tube – an underlying sense of guilt for not going the extra mile. For not trying to grow within the institution that could easily shrink you. Outside, towards the tube was intense enough: two City boys bump into me as I'm looking to the floor, smoking a cigarette – I would call myself a social smoker, but this had evolved to buying packs and puffing when on the move. I stopped on the street and somebody banged into my behind, cursing under their breath. I continued walking where a loud car beeped and a police car with sirens shot past. The shakes returned and I was unsure if it was body illness or anxiety, all I did know was that I WANTED TO FUCKING SCREAM.

On the tube I looked down on the floor, headphones in as it became more and more packed with bodies, people moving around, scuffling their shoes loudly, expanding the selfish wingspan by reading the papers and it was at this point that I decided I needed a release. I got off at Gloucester Road and walked towards the Swedish bar that was next to Scatty Alice's – they gave out free popcorn which I indulged in and ordered not one but two beers. It was still light, but it was getting darker, reminding me that August was nearly over – and soon so would summer.

I drank my two bottled beers briskly; it must have taken ten or so minutes and I looked over to the other corner of the small and dark bar. I saw a girl, a beautiful girl, petite but beautiful with long blonde hair – she was sipping on a cocktail and all alone. For some reason I knew that this girl was approachable, almost wanting to be approached – and so I did. I wasn't sober, the two beers that were drunk in quick progression had made me buzzed and cocksure. And so, I approached quickly and firmly which is the only way. When talking, you occasionally look the other way to show that you are not too interested, but that you are still confident. Some men find this difficult to do, but I do it naturally.

I asked her what she was doing here and if she lived locally. She told me that her name was Alicia and she was a genuine Swede in a Swedish bar. She smiled at my chat and asked me to come outside for a cigarette. For me? I was doing nothing wrong. Tammy and I were estranged, and the soft touch of a lady may have helped me get through the anxiety and the unknown territory of homelessness in late summer.

Outside we smoked, one of hers, and she asked me what I did. I told her that I was in fashion to which she was pleasantly surprised. My lacklustre dress probably suggested otherwise. 'Oh wow! That's great, I am a creative too!' she said while smoking on a cigarette.

'Oh really? What do you do?'

She smiled at me. 'I'm an actress.'

I kept up the enthusiasm, 'Amazing, anything that we would have heard of?'

She rolled her eyes coyly but excited.

Alicia: Well, I am going to be on the next season of "Vikings", the TV show.

Me: Oh my, no way, are you kidding?

Alicia: No, I am not. Why, have you heard of it?

Me: (I gulped with genuine intrigue) Yes, yes, I have I am a big fan, do you mind me asking who you will be in the show?

Alicia: Well, I can't say much about it, but I will be playing the Wife of Ivar?

Me: Ivar the Boneless?

Alicia: Ha-ha, yes that's correct. I cannot say much of course, but he really does start to kick ass.

Me: I am a big Bjorn Ironside fan.

Alicia: Byurn, it's pronounced Byurn.

Me: Oh, sorry. Byurn, yes, I think he is great.

Alicia: Yes, he is, and he is such a nice guy in real life.

I was annoyed that she bought the conversation back to reality and I was reluctant to tell her that I lived in a tent, kind of because of Bjorn, kind of, in a way. I chose to test the waters:

Me: That sounds amazing.

Alicia: Yes, it has been such a great experience.

Me: I love it when he goes out into the wilderness, on his own, it nearly inspired me to do that, you know just live in a tent in London and find myself? (I giggle while taking a puff of a cigarette.)

She looked at me with a specific look, as if to say she was previously interested but now she was not too sure.

Alicia: Shall we go in for another drink?

Me: Yes, of course, on me.'

We went back into the bar and I got her an expensive cocktail, I decided I would analyse the financials later. In the meantime, Nayarra had called me to state that we should meet, something I agreed to, and something that may prove essential, though, this was for later in the long night.

Me and the actress spoke for longer with our drinks and I was flabbergasted at the situation. It must have been an omen: 'The Vikings'. Perhaps I was on the right path after all – the

Romans would have said so at least. Fate they would say, fate cannot be altered by any means.

She stated that she needed to go home, this was not good for me. I asked her which way she was heading which was deep into Fulham, the same direction as Nayarra. We finished our drinks and I insisted on getting us an Uber. I asked what her address was and she readily told me. Not in a way that she expected me to follow, more a declaration that I had won her trust.

Nayarra. I knew that Nayarra would have to be the priority, and so, I would get out of the car and meet Nayarra when the time came... or when I needed to. While in the taxi, she giggled at my chat once more. I realised she liked the idea of a Chelsea boy – the idea of neat shirts, fake charm and rigid order but this was not me, well, not right now anyway. For now I was a paradox, or maybe a parody. It was something I would need to think on when I was alone in my thoughts.

We went past my destination and I half-heartedly stated this. 'Oh, I think my stop is somewhere around... here...'

She left it open ended. 'Are you getting off here, are you?'

By this time, Nayarra was calling me on the constant, it was profuse, and I knew I had a decision to make: risk going to the end of the taxi ride with this girl and get rejected? Then I would be late for Nayarra, potentially losing my guaranteed bed.

In error, I told Nayarra exactly where I was. This made her more aggressive, wanting me to be by her side with the upmost immediacy but I continued with this girl:

'It's fine, I want to make sure you are okay, I will travel with you for a bit.'

To this she laughed, rather than say, 'No, you should get out!' She... laughed with me and agreed with my improvised strategy.

It was not a good sign, it was a great sign but Nayarra,

Nayarra had been unconditionally good to me, a rare gem, and an important one.

Another five minutes of the journey and I decided to withdraw while taking her number. She said, 'Okay,' and I hastily typed it in my mud-stained phone. I returned towards the Broadway by foot and met Nayarra. She was with her female friend and her property developing boyfriend: five foot six and friendly, gentle and all-round nice. I greeted them with a smile but with a deep and underlying frustration that I could have been with a Viking.

We went back to Nayarra's and, sure enough, we partied in her basement – we partied and danced to Brazilian music and Nayarra shouted, 'John, get Solus over, let's make it entertaining.'

I thought to myself, 'Are you sure? Is it a deal breaker?' My mind was fleeting in semi-anger and regret about the Viking.

I was trying to avoid Solus but I wanted to keep Nayarra entertained, subsequently guaranteeing my bed… Having said this, Nayarra was different from the others. When she said she would do something, she would do it. Whenever she asked me round, I never felt as though she would retract the offer or that there were conditions. I was never a sexual threat to any of her lovers because I wasn't. She only fucked hench, steroid using broad beans that thought they were some kind of model. Men who pumped in the early morning before their shift in Zara.

I messaged Solus and was glad she didn't pick up, undoubtedly, she was with Ritchie once more. We had a great time dancing and drinking and eventually we went to bed. Me, in the large basement bedroom, empty and spacious as her flat mate was in the provinces. In the morning, Nayarra reminded me that her party was coming up, and that she was going set me up with the celebrity. After last night, she owed me a fucking celebrity.

I messaged the Viking lady in the morning and she didn't respond, in fact, to my disappointment, I never heard from her again. I received the omen, but the rest was likely inevitable.

My destiny that could be clear and unclear, and as I have now concluded with some conciliate relief: fate cannot be altered by any means.

Chapter 14

Coco

'Siren: a woman who is considered to be alluring or fascinating but also dangerous in some way.'

The opposite sex, with their soft-caring and whispy voices. The dainty touch they give while their long hair grazes your back. Their sweet smell and their tender kisses.

Not sex from the opposite sex. A form of affection – a form of assurance from a fairy-like beauty to stifle residual feelings I have for Tammy. To feel like somebody may find me attractive for how I am, in my current state. Living in perils of the bocage like so many in my age.

There was always hope with them. The beautiful girls, the beautiful crazy girls – Coralie was one, Coco another.

Coco had returned from whichever European ski resort she was shacked up in to spend summer in Putney's claws. I had met her with Niccy in my early twenties and they were the best of friends. Always chasing and taking advantage of the rich men the town had to offer; scheming for long nights of glamour with someone else's fat purse. The last time I saw them together it was, of course, with a middle-aged man – a property tycoon from Pakistan that Niccy had picked up from Annabel's. They had met me and Ritchie in the H Club and huddled in one of its small balconies, talking privately without us. Then, they decided to see this man, the property man with a serviced apartment near Harley Street. There was no need to meet him as we had the drugs and we were in a member's club. But this was not enough for them – what they needed was millions. Someone with millions. Someone with an abundance of everything so that there was a sense of security – a sense that they were as untouchable as their beauty made them out to be.

They invited us and we tagged along, knowing fine well there would be resentment and ill feeling towards us. Us the other males. Sure enough, it happened when Ritchie was asked to leave. He had been arguing with the man about his own properties, calling the Pakistani property tycoon a liar. The way Ritchie did it was weird, with his mid-level Fulham Estate agent diatribes on anything that may present glamour without order. The man asked him to leave – as did the girls. They said I could stay, Niccy especially said I could. Man-code should have prohibited me from staying but I was transfixed on Coco. I helped Ritchie into a taxi and pretended that Niccy begged me to keep her company.

Ritchie seemed to take it well and understood that, when you took yourself out of the situation, it wouldn't be fair to make me leave when there were not one but two – what he would call MACs. MACs an abbreviation for 'models and celebrities.' The highest honour you could bestow upon a beautiful woman.

And so, there I was, in the serviced apartment with Niccy, Coco and two rotund and ageing guys, one being the tycoon.. It was hard to hold any resentment towards him for telling Ritchie to fuck off. If he didn't, somebody would eventually. He beckoned me over to apologise for asking my friend to leave the premises. He explained that he didn't like to be called a liar and it was fair enough. For Ritchie, it was self-entitlement gone wrong. There was a lack of need to drill our host on his credentials. He then asked about the girls. 'The girls – how long have you known them?'

I told him, 'For quite some time.'

I knew that he wondered if they were sexual, even up for shagging quickly and unconditionally. That's why he asked me, and that's why my answers were astute.

Then, the night degenerated. The men played strip poker with the girls but, somehow, they were the only ones who ended up naked. Wrinkled men in their stained underwear, hoping that this would turn into an orgy. I left promptly after that; Niccy told me that the tycoon booked them a holiday to Capri, but she forgot to go.

Aesthetically, Coco was pinpoint: long, blonde ethereal hair, almost down to her waste. Tall, gangly but voluptuous with a bit-of-hard tattoo on the right arm. Her skin was tanned and her smile was infectious. Niccy was just as beautiful, but sometimes it's a carnal energy we never understand.

Coco had fucked Ritchie when she was seventeen, played piano to perfection in his old family basement and then eloped with him in the dark. Whenever I mentioned her name he would smugly mention this to me, trying to stoke a reaction. It was a cognitive stumbling block but I still wanted her, just for me, on my own and without the statistical noise. And so, I travelled to a high end and snotty bar to meet Niccy and Coco, somewhere near Westbourne Grove, and in the peripherals of Notting Hill. Coco, smartly dressed, had her Pomeranian and they drank wine and laughed with an older man smoking a pipe. He was definitely into the girls, either of them, and was not fond of my presence. He tried to shrug me as a major threat by ignoring and another man inside the pub was staring at Coco with curiosity and attraction.

She didn't notice, in fact, nobody noticed but me. He had a child who kept coming to our table, and when she returned to her father, he would make her go back to our table as a form of luring bait. The child would ask questions until Coco stated with a smile, 'Hi, darling, I am with my friends now so do you mind going to your father while we dine here?' The child left and we soon dispersed with Coco, walking back towards her flat with her designer dog. The pipe-smoking man offered to walk with her but Coco declined. I wasn't sure if I would ever see Coco again, but I was glad to get out of Westbourne Grove with its sterile Euro-poshness and non-commercial shops.

Before Coco walked out to the sunset, she turned around and acrimoniously stated: 'Thanks for offering to take me back, John.' She performed a nervous skip with the dog and turned her back towards me as I walked back to the tube station with Niccy. Niccy was completely unaware of the chemistry that was exchanged. Us. A definite and clear reciprocation. Niccy just smiled as we parted ways and she went on her way to her beautiful flat in the depths of southeast London. I never told her of my situation. As far as she knew, I could be staying at the Ritz.

A day later I messaged Coco on Facebook, just my phone number and a kiss, nothing else. I saw that she read the message, but she did not reply.

On a weekend towards the end of August, Scatty Alice let me stay at hers for the final time that summer. I flitted between hers and the cinema, the cinema and its adjoined Starbucks was a second home to me, just like the friendly Café Nero that was two minutes away. I was in the safety of the cinema, watching Margot Robbie in the Suicide squad with a large popcorn and coca cola, content in the dark with the ice and fizz.

I always left my phone on in the movies but on silent, just

like with the tent… just in case. Just in case there was a party, or there was gossip so intense it justified altering my plans.

I had always felt at home in the cinema. Ever since mother took us in our local town in the country on a summer not unlike this one. I would escape there in my university days – just leave and embrace the darkness and the theatre layout. Leave the busyness of this world and its people by sitting for two hours in the black. Now, I needed it. I needed it spiritually and I needed it physically. The building was essential on certain days: when it rained; when I could not keep my eyes open; when there was nowhere else to go. I sat there, flaccid, with the upmost relaxation. Safe in the knowledge that I could walk across the road to a bed, heating and tea.

Soon enough my phone lit up and I did not recognise the number. I quickly shuffled through the dark cinema lanes as to not disturb the sparse crowd and answered the phone in the corridor. It was Coco.

Coco: Hey.

Me: Hey.

Coco: what are you doing?

Me: I'm in the cinema, on the Fulham Road.

Coco: Oh well…

Me: Well, what are you doing?

Coco: I'm in Putney, bored, I wondered if you wanted to go for a drink? My brother has the dog.'

I didn't hesitate; I hated leaving films but this could be my only chance to see her alone, without the interruption of Niccy. I ran and changed into a shirt and made my way out of Chelsea towards Putney. I was supposed to be saving money but I did not want to be late, so again, I took a taxi.

I arrived and she told me to wait in a specific bar, just past the bridge. A bar with large clear windows and two floors. Suitably packed for a weekend night with week workers and masters of seduction. I asked her what drink she wanted and she said a Mojito would be fine. Of course she liked Mojitos, an easy going drink though relatively slick. A drink that works for any occasion.

She arrived, tall and snow-piste tanned with scraggled hair falling below her shoulders. She was wearing a summer dress that accentuated her toned frame and showed the tattoos sporadically inked on her body.

We were sitting and drinking on the top floor and, though there was the element of nerves, her aura comforted. She was different from the crazy days of old. Ritchie said she had slept with over a hundred men. Niccy had coyly mentioned how she found it hard to not cheat on her boyfriend – but I did not care. I knew that she had recently broken up with her latest amid the ski slopes of France – a tattooed snowboarder type with a campervan from what I could see on the tell-all social forums.

She spoke calmly and told me of her time skiing, how she loved being on the snow and riding motorbikes in her spare time. The situation was strange because she never used to like me, maybe because of my association with H. You see, H and Coco used to be inseparable partners in crime. Coco had her parents pay for H to go skiing with them, but anyone who knows H will know one thing – she will turn up when she wants to, usually unexpected, but on her own disconsonant terms.

Coco couldn't get hold of H a day before the trip, but H finally messaged to say she had cervical cancer and could not attend due to the strains of chemo. Coco decided to pay H a visit and H swung the door open, flashing a missing tooth without saying hello. The tooth was apparently a side-effect of chemo.

Coco was devastated, thinking that her best friend was a premature victim of inevitable mortality. Although she was shocked, Coco had her suspicions and called Ritchie who told her that there was nothing true about it. Ritchie relished in telling Coco that H had been on a seventy-two-hour bender and knocked her tooth out when a girl punched her in the face.

Though I was not estranged with H (I neither confirmed nor denied), it made Coco comfortable next to me – because she thought I was. She carefully brushed her hair back and asked how London had been in her absence. It produced an involuntary *guffaw* as I thought of it, as I privately recollected the precise dramas of the previous months. There was no need for her to know details. I had Scatty Alice's flat for the weekend and Coco had decided to fly somewhere again next week. With these timelines, exposure was unlikely and unnecessary.

I had glanced in one of the bar mirrors and saw a sight of declining muscularity; I hadn't been to the gym as much as I liked, so, to compensate, I curled my arms up in my shirt to form a bicep. Hoping the mass would be satisfactory for this most sporty of females.

Coco looked around at the loud bar and there was a momentary change in her energy: she started to move, nervously, fidgeting with her long athletic legs as if suppressing a twitch. I asked her if she was okay and she whispered in my ear, 'This City brings out the darkness in me.'

I'm not sure I will ever know why, but I know that she had always escaped the grasp of London's intensity – snowboarding in the alps, surf areas; vast expanses. It was something about her childhood but I can't remember the stories. For me there was no choice to leave, flat or no flat, London was attached to me. It was like a metropolitan boil – if cut off, I would soon bleed out on its concrete.

She asked for the bag I had bought and discreetly walked to the loo, but I wondered if the powder would make her feel worse.

This wasn't the quick-drink-because-I'm-bored scenario. I could tell already that we would be out for some time. Her and me by the glistening riverside. Her hoping for the future, me only hoping for her.

She descended to claim two more drinks that she insisted on paying for. I was fine with the alcohol, the occasional line and her unrelenting beauty but I became fidgety on my own. Perhaps, deep down, I thought that she would see my vulnerability in the temporary solitude. Perhaps then, it would take many more years for her to like me how I liked her.

So, I talked to two girls to the right. We went to the balcony to smoke as I watched them walk and wiggle in their bodycon dresses. I was here for Coco, but it was as if I was supposed to do something while she was momentarily away. They wanted to play a joke on Coco when she returned by pretending that they were both ex-lovers of mine. They said it would make her more interested – and so, I went along with it. Coco returned to see me talking to the girls and they started with the sketch.

'What are you doing with our guy?' Convincing enough voices.

But Coco said to me in a soft and calm whisper, 'I want to get out of here.' A voice that made me melt and shudder in within the hustle of the balcony. A voice that could cause an involuntary frenzy. This voice could make me jump in the nearby waterway if she so wished it.

I smiled back at the girls as we walked away and Coco left the drinks on the glass table.

We hailed for a black cab back towards Thistle grove to

attend the Swedish bar, another man was waiting for the cab but we got their first. 'Excuse me, this is my cab!' he said to us.

Coco smiled at him and said, 'It's okay, we can share.' He looked at her and her hair and did not need convincing.

I let Coco and the man sit in the normal seats, part being polite, part testing her as I sat in a fold-me-down. I was shocked at how flirtatious it was. It wasn't 'I'll make the guy I am on a pseudo date with jealous' flirting. There was something compulsive about it – she even touched his leg, in a casual and nonchalant way but enough to send a message. Perhaps it was because of the girls I spoke to?

The man enjoyed it until he realised I was there. He did not fear my reaction, but he looked at how pensive I was being with my head down and increasingly depleted. I knew that my lack of protest would create question marks in his mind. 'She must do this all the time… maybe she is crazy? He looks depressed with her!' With this, he started to reign in interest and luckily, his stop was sooner than ours.

For the rest of the journey I was quiet while Coco had an air of unapology. Unaware that her actions may have been untoward, unaware that she had revealed herself. I let the thought fade into the background as I tried to look ahead. There was the distinct feeling that she was only with me because she was bored, which to be fair, is what she had confessed when I was still at the cinema.

To an extent, I was proven wrong as we went to the Swedish bar, the same one where I had seen Viking Lady not so long ago. Coco sipped on a cocktail and kissed me. I had kissed Coco. Beneath the darkening sun on the Fulham Road, I had achieved what I thought may never happen. I did wonder what Niccy would think of me, sneaking around with her best friend without her knowing, I also wondered where Niccy was. As far as I knew she was not abroad but she was not with us. Coco would have surely asked her to cure the boredom first.

Coco did another bump and said she felt like going out, properly out, Kings Road out, to Raffles out. To meet other people out. I did not want this for fear of losing all of her energy, all of her energy that was steered towards me – replaced with the mass crowds of that notorious meat market. Besides, I hated Raffles with its door girl, always a dick; it's dark and it's cramped with tenuous branding. Your bank account could be cleared with one round.

I said for her to come to 'mine', just across the road on Thistle Grove – I didn't mean for sex as such. If it happened, it happened. It was more to pull the night in a slower direction. Red wine and a few lines, sitting on the sofa with her long legs draped on me as we watched Indie movies. She said that she would rather venture to where the crowds lay in waiting… and so in a way, I had no choice.

And so, we approached Raffles, with Coco more sober than me and the hordes of good-looking men and women huddled in the smoking area. I saw that a man with broad shoulders and no collar took the eye of Coco. I wished then that I had worn a T-shirt for the night, not the slim-fit shirt that made my arms look like wavering trees swaying in the wind.

We went inside and this second flirt of Coco made me want to rebel; there were girls in there that, with my shirt on, thought I was a Chelsea establishment. Coco faded from my left, probably to check out the man outside and so, I talked to the girls, offering them an expensive shot which they consumed without hesitation. I started to get close to one, pseudo-grinding and they asked if the girl I was with was my girlfriend. I told them no, not realising that Coco had cleverly returned and snuck behind me. She was listening in and I heard her mumble, 'You little slut!'

She said to me, 'Come on, I will get you a drink,' and aggressively pushed past the girls, reinstating that she must have liked me somehow, in some form, in some way. But this was what I was afraid of; all of this, the crowds, the other men and women – the pretentiousness of the establishment that tries to take you to a higher place. A fantastical world where there is only glitz and success but, in fact, it does the opposite: it takes you to a grinding and intimidating reality.

I know that I have done enough bad things in my life to go to hell – perhaps not Dante's deeper circles where they are engulfed in a frozen lake until the end of time. I know what my punishment will be. I will wake up in the fire and heat and brimstone and will have to go to this club every day for the rest of eternity. Begging the door girl for entry. The door girl will be my Virgil, diligently guiding me into the depths of the crowds.

The magic moments of Coco were soon to be lost in time. I knew it, perhaps she did too.

We managed to have a drink and she was shocked at the price. I told her this, I warned her that it would end up like this. That it would be maligned and embittered, that we would spend too much and remain unenlightened by the overrated experience. She wandered off once more and I had my suspicions where. And so, I bought the girls another round, but this time, I had ran out of money. Not only that, but my phone had died so I couldn't transfer, and my card savagely declined in front of my new friends.

I felt ashamed that I had promised them a drink. I told them to wait there, right there. I told the barman to wait there as I was paying and although I was drunk, I was a man of my word. So, there I went, heart pumping as I exited the club and saw a glimpse of Coco speaking to the broad-shouldered boy, smoking a cigarette and laughing which made me sprint in anger, faster, and even faster down Beaufort Street, past the pink-rosed trees as I closed my eyes and said to myself: 'I am a man of my word.' I got to the Sainsburys on the corner, carefully crossed the road and ran onto the country like pathway of Thistle Grove. I saw that staff from the hotel were smoking on Scatty Alice's bench as I said hello while getting the keys and entering. It was then I realised, I stupidly realised that I could have asked the club for a charger.

I swiftly fumbled for the charger while tapping my toes. I wanted to get back for the girls to prove something to them and myself but, deep down, maybe I wanted to see what Coco was doing with the broad man – Tammy. Tammy kept intruding my thoughts.

The battery charged to ten percent and I made sure to transfer my funds that were supposed to make my dreams come true, heavily compromised in this warm and strange night.

I tried to do a line from what was remaining but there were only remnants. It makes me run back to Raffles with the XXs 'Fiction' blaring out of my headphones, knowing that this would likely drain the remaining battery:

'Fiction When we're not together, Mistaken for a vision Something of my own creation'

I couldn't remember how long it took, the run a blur as I was not in the present. My mind occupied with what lay ahead.

I got back in with ease as the door girl recognised me from

before. Coco was not outside. I went in and looked for the girls and they were not at the bar but I eventually found them, they were surprised that I came back and did not want to engage. They tried to shuffle away as I explained that I was ready to pay the bill. The age-old bill that could not be left like that. They stated, 'You really could have got away with that, you didn't have to come back.' As if my return created additional lameness – they would have preferred a cocksure man who left them with the bill and exited in mystery.

I started to walk out and but then saw Coco, her hair radiant when mixed with the dark red neon's of the interior. She was getting close to the broad-shouldered man and she didn't message me for the rest of the night – I went home and slept while sobering up and tried not to think about it, tried not to think how they were probably shagging at this very moment while the girls at another destination were still laughing; laughing and fucking while I grasped the pillow in a small comedown. Deep down I knew, I knew that I would lose her in the club where all promises are broken. An institution that reflects your social weaknesses like their mirrors on the dance floor. I put on Florence, the new song: 'Too Much is Never Enough' followed by 'Falling' as I started to doze in relative peace, forgetting to be grateful for where I was sleeping tonight. Coco had made me lonely. All of it had made the loneliness breed. Tammy.

I woke in the morning to the feeling of anger. Promising myself that I would not text her back if she texted me, praying that the guilt would eat her up and spew her out into her West London residence; although I spoke to other girls, I was angry and if I had let myself, I would be upset in a form that was not socially acceptable for a man. Lo and behold, she did text me, asking if I was okay and why did I leave her at the club? Only a millisecond past and I fell for it… an immediate capitulation without thought or reflection. I folded and I texted, knowing deep down that the capitulation would not serve me. Knowing that it would undermine any remaining respect she still had. 'Hi ,sorry… are you okay?' She did not reply to this, in fact, I did not hear from her at all. I saw her social media a week later, showing how she had returned safely to Austria, smiling and frolicking with her snow piste friends.

I made sure to go back to the cinema that day for "Suicide Squad", this time I was sure that I watched the entire film, nobody would stop me. I switched off my phone and there were only two people at the back. I watched in silence and reflection. I knew that I had to switch off the phone because if Coco called, I would be sure to go running to her.

AUTUMN AND WINTER

Chapter 15

Intern Part 2

'Never do coke with an intern, they may not be twenty-one.'

Only me. I thought of these two words and their most relevant meaning: only me. When I was a child and managed to smash three dinner plates on the same day, my father said, 'Only me.' When I would say something quirky and irreverent to my mother she would say, 'Only me.' Only I could be sitting in a private members club with a nineteen-year-old intern, not knowing where I would sleep that night.

The facades of the twenty-first century; if we appear okay to the rest of the world, that is the priority. We look for the positives and we enhance them until we are blinded by their light.

The intern was still cheerful and had done well on her lists of journalists and fashion personalities. The range with the celebrity had picked up serious traction and we were getting approached by sustainable blogs and articles, to the point where we had to reject. And we sat together, still closely but we were happy with the set up. She was glad not to be paid, just to be a part of something that she believed in - I was glad that I could provide that to her.

But she was eager to have an office environment. As charming as the working in the H Club was, there were always members walking past and the sales-driven waiters were a constant interruption.

I repeated the same: that I was doing renovations and it was better to do things here – that I would take her to come on a photoshoot, that this would be great for her. She wanted more days a week, but I couldn't tell her I worked another job – it didn't align with the image.

She would brush against me and I would not know if it was inadvertent, or acutely timed.

Female attention was sparser than usual and I couldn't say that I didn't like it, it would be a lie to say that I didn't like the young energy next to me. It was Inquisitive and energetic and different to Tammy's weary and worried ways.

We could rely on sales regularly but I could easily spend it as soon as it was received, especially with the constant moving and the split with Tammy. The margins, my penchant for class A, having to eat out, travel here and travel there and other miscellaneous meant that my money was not going up, in fact, it seemed to just dwindle. Some would read this and think, you have a salary coming in and other income – where was it going? To be honest, some of the time, I did not know. I could easily clear seventy to one hundred pounds eating in the evening, staying out and trying to find somewhere to stay by spending on a person of note. In many ways, it was cheaper to live in a flat share, unless you wanted to be one of the homeless on the brink of death. It was too late now, I was already there, within the depths of Ironside... just do not try it yourself.

People have their passion and perhaps I do underneath all the flack. Perhaps that would be my next thing to figure: my focus. Many of my friends didn't have it either, the lack of direction was collective and we could blame it on arts cuts, student debt, or austerity, but the main stress must have been us; our lost-ness was our sole responsibility to resolve. Getting high and drinking and fucking at any given opportunity would not help us to move forward. Blaming the state while on a grappling comedown would not help us achieve our dreams. What would help us achieve our dreams – consistency and focus – I felt this now, well, I felt glimpses of it. But I knew it would be a long road.

I thought of Solus: whenever Solus was out, she mentioned an app idea that she was going to develop. She would grab a party-goer by the wrist and say slowly and highly: 'I have the greatest idea.'

They would say, pretending to be interested, 'Oh really? What is it?' And her eyes would get wider.

'Oh, I can't tell you! It's to do with dating but until I get it copyrighted, sorry hun it's not that I don't trust you, it's just that you could easily steal it.'

The party-goer, who didn't care about the app beforehand, is left more confused. Solus mentioned it a lot, but I knew that she would never even attempt to complete that app. I knew it, our friends knew it, and most importantly, she did. Lack of direction could follow us like a lingering smell and surrounded us when we were together. The smoke and the drink and the snort clouded the smell of our lost souls for a night, but it would be back in the morning – more pungent than ever.

Eventually, my intern informed me that August had ended. If she could not go full-time, she would have to go with another job. It wasn't about pay – it was about fullness. I had no choice but to let her do it, pretending that there would be the possibility of her doing full time later in September, but I couldn't be too sure. We agreed that we would go for a final meal, of course at a vegan restaurant, almost like a date to say goodbye. She had done some good work and I was sorry that the work could not be there for her in the way that she wanted. It did teach me something: you can fake it until you can make it. You can make a concept seem far grander than it actually was, purely by having a digital presence. My intern thought that we were huge, getting into digital magazines, having emails and working in the day. The offset is that there must be constant progression.

And so, it would be, in the days of late summer, we attended a vegan restaurant on the left flank of Regent Street – she said that she had seen a guy friend the night before and was a little tired. I shouldn't have been, but I was afraid that they had slept together. She arrived late but I was glad to see her – her young and vibrant eyes that shone at the smallest of excitements. She tapped her leg, smiled and expressed with the upmost immediacy.

We sat and drank vegan beer while we started our food but she was more detached than usual, not as playful. No showing me her tattoos or inadvertent brushes, and I had a sneaking suspicion that it had something to do with the male-friend. I didn't help the situation; I had bought a forty-pound bag two days ago and dropped a bump while waiting. I always had a cheap bag with me, I worried about money but... always a bag. It's something I couldn't seem to correlate, something that I did not want to.

'Look, he's got a shirt on and everything,' she said, saying that I was taking this more seriously than her, more seriously than I should be. For her, now, it seemed to be a formality. Something that you do when you finish a work placement when really what you were thinking about is the next step. For her, the next step was a full-time step with another clothing brand.

We finished our mains and she was excited by dessert. I tried hard for her not to see my thoughts: a persistent niggle that desserts would add fifty percent to the bill. I ordered another beer and planned our next destination, if she would even come, I wasn't so sure.

I paid the bill which was over a hundred pounds, but she agreed to come with me into the depths of Soho – she was keen for another drink or two and I had the perfect place. A speakeasy with an Italian theme on residential premises. It was called Trisha's – an institution for people in the know, shrouded in photos of famous Italian Americans and Scorsese film actors. The outside area was where you could smoke and meet the strangest of strangers. We walked there so I could show her the cobbled streets of the area, through Carnaby and into the bustle of the Soho lights and restaurants; I did not trust people who did not like Soho.

There were drunkards frolicking and drinking outside. Transvestites handing out leaflets, strip bars with door girls and it was beautiful. I worried that the duration of the walk may be too much for Noda but she did not seem to mind. 'I do a lot of walking; I like to keep fit!' I decided to see what else she did.

'Yeah, it's good to keep healthy. I try to keep it healthy, I only drink sometimes.'

She nodded and agreed, 'Yes, yes.' And so I continued:

'Yeah, I don't really dabble in anything else, only on occasion, I mean do you do drugs or anything?'

She was firm with her answer, 'No, no, I do not do drugs. There is no point!'

I nodded to her. 'Yes, I agree, I agree.' I then stood back and checked myself: I was trying to groom my intern into taking cocaine — and this was not acceptable.

Why would I? Perhaps it was because cocaine pretended to be your friend, but in reality, it can make you more lonely. You beg for others to join the lower vibration. Now I see why Solus's eyes glowed incandescent with rage, why she hated it when I said I didn't want it.

We got to the bar and I told her to get behind me as the man at the door was temperamental. Sometimes he would let me in, sometimes he wouldn't. You would have to give him a certain energy, a smile and a slight submission. So he knows you know that he is in charge. Never beg him, but never expect. And this is what I did – the perfect balance. He let us in with a welcome and a smile, but Noda was unsure. I don't think she was old enough to appreciate the grit and destitution of the place, an almost ironic set-up. She would probably want known bars, trendy bars, sleek vegan hangouts to post on the socials and to tell her like-minded aquaintances; I was Gen Y and she was Gen Z.

We sat down at one of the few half-broken tables and she had a vodka and coke, me? A bottled beer to negate the costs of the vegan meal. Beneath the dark red lights were a couple directly opposite. They were kissing passionately and rubbing it in our platonic faces - to the extent where it unnerved me and made me angry. Why? Because I haven't kissed a girl since Coco and that was mitigated. They seemed so passionate and I wanted to be a part of it, a part of something like it, and I wanted it now. There was a dark, sexual energy about the girl. The passionate ripples were reaching the feet of our table as she kissed and stroked the man's leg.

Noda was talkative, but it was difficult to concentrate with the noise and the dark red lighting and the kissing and frolicking and…

I saw the couple leave to go outside and I needed a cigarette. Noda didn't smoke, so she said that she would wait for me and guard the table. So, I went outside alone in the small smoking courtyard where the characters congregate. No more than three metres square and when you looked up, you saw the lights of residential towers. The conversations they must have heard; some obscene, some intellectual, some noncoherent.

I saw the couple and they were smoking. I decided to do the same. I lit up, pretending not to be entranced by her aura. I tried to remember that I had a guest, my sole intern, alone and inside the bar but for now, I needed to be right here with the drunken strangers of Soho square.

Suddenly, the man went in for more drinks, leaving me a window to talk to the girl. She caught my eye but I saw another lecherous man in the shadows to the right, scanning the situation in predatory silence. I don't know how it happened, but I got talking to her while her man was by the bar and the situation soon turned to cocaine. It was as if we sensed it from each other, the dark side of our minds and she flirted with the idea as I told her that I had some. She protested, saying that she shouldn't, but I did. So, I proceeded to go to the bathroom. She speedily followed.

It was then I who stalled. Her danger, which I recognised so acutely, was out in full speed and was intimidating. As if the speed of her danger had made me slam an emotional brake. I stumbled as I reached into the pocket for the bag. 'Erm… we better be careful in here, if they see two of us.' Why? Why would I say that now when my forbidden fantasy was tangible and right in front of me. Because the temperamental bouncer may oust us? Or because I was unsure of Noda's whereabouts.

Suddenly, she heard determined footsteps which panicked her – she assumed it was her date and she scarpered out of the unisex toilet. I exited in silence as if nothing had happened, as if this were as normal as going to the loo itself. But I waited for two minutes before I left and saw that she made the right decision. The loud and speedy footsteps she heard were her date who she was now re-united with. He hadn't the faintest idea. He did not know this girl in the slightest. This girl that was sure to cause his heartbreak within the year. I looked at him smugly and thought highly of myself as outside dwellers swaggered past. 'I have just taken advantage of you, you and the rest of manhood.'

Noda pinched me on the arm. 'Where have you been?'

I mitigated. 'Oh, sorry I just bumped into an old school friend.'

She asked, 'The one kissing the guy?' And I wondered what she had already seen.

'Yes, that one.' She paused and looked in suspicion and asked for a cigarette. I said of course, as long as she promised not to get addicted.

We left and she reminded me of how she needed to get up early, so, we had one last drink on a club on a cobbled road towards Dean Street. She was leaving but I wasn't too concerned; my mind fleeted towards where I was going to sleep. Something, a little something thought there was the distinct possibility I could stay at hers. It was a long-ball as there were convoluted logistics, this included speedy seduction and a valid excuse as to why it would be better to go to hers. Not to mention, although her parents had paid, she may reside in a student style studio.

She left and ran to the tube towards the lights of Piccadilly... I weighed my options once again. They were: the tent or the tent. Too late to call a friend and I didn't feel like seeing them. I had some white in the bag left and so there was only one thing to do. I texted Solus as she wouldn't answer if I called. The text said something along the lines of, 'I have some, can I come over,?' She replied abruptly and surely 'yes'.

Interlude

Winter is Coming

I arrived at Solus's and she answered the door in nightwear. She yawned as she beckoned me indoors and her grandma was still watching TV. 'Hello, John!' she said; very warm, very friendly. Not pretend or compulsive but genuine - the grandma was pleased to see me.

We went upstairs and Solus' lace lingerie left her tanned and toned legs bare. She was sexy, there was no doubt, but Ritchie, well, I didn't have many rules but permission to shag the girls of my friends was one.

I swiftly made the thought leave my mind and Solus seemed tired and bored, but not bored for what I had for her. 'What you got?' she said while yawning. Plate and a straw already organized by her small bedside.

I poured the remaining onto the plate and she made the all-familiar cackling noise. 'Nibble nibble.' Then, she swayed her head from side to side and clapped and then sniffed a medium sized stripe. She remembered she had some cigarettes and that her grandma had noticed the smell when she smoked out of the window. And so, we stepped outside the front doorstep. Solus put on a large coat, I left mine inside.

We stepped out into the cold, a surprising cold for the time. 'Brrrr!' Solus exclaimed while puffing on a fag. 'Do you watch Game of Thrones?' she said.

Of course I did, religiously and routinely. Well, I did when I had a television.

We said it together in sync as we giggled. 'WINTER IS COMING!' I put the jest aside and thought what that meant as Solus noticed me shaking.

'Are you okay?'

'Yes,' I said. 'It's just I didn't expect it to get this cold already.' I looked at a rare sighting of stars as the sharp cold pinched me. I was worried about something and I knew what it was. The tent – the tent in this weather would be an entirely different game.

Chapter 16

Financial Counterattack

"What happens when we die, no don't ask questions just make
sure you survive."
– Wolf Alice, 2016

The summer was over and my finances had dwindled, almost into obscurity – eight hundred pounds of savings; that was nowhere near the amount needed for a deposit. The City was three days a week and so I decided to take another marketing job.

A lady that I had known for some time and had worked under before; neurotic, unpredictable, but I could work with her again doing business development on a freelance basis. One to two days a week to help me bump my incomings. It would take time away from doing the business, and I had the pressure of the celebrity range, but I would have to work it out.

Belinda agreed to pay me a hundred pounds a day, so an extra one to two thousand pounds a week. This was satisfactory if you didn't think about TFL costs to get to Hackney, minus tax, minus no shops nearby and I couldn't prepare food.

At the time I did not realise that I was going the other way, the other way from why I was doing this in the first place. But I was. I was working for the man as much as I was when I had a flat. But I would have to work as much as possible as quickly as possible to get a deposit before the weather turned colder and colder. I remember what the man had said to me at the sleeping bag shop with concerned and wide eyes: 'The cold goes through your bones.'

And so, I started, a real trek from the Bocage to Hackney. A walk or bus then a tube then over ground and another walk over a bypass. My role was to approach certain health and beauty companies and see if they needed rebranding. Belinda was obsessed with the Swiss, and I needed to get people into a phone meeting so she could discuss their options. Simple enough, and my experience gave me enough to handle the high intensity. I was put into my own room, it was a small office with three rooms and I was in one, in solitude, while I rang the Swiss and others and asked about their health and beauty capabilities. While I did this, I tried to counter-attack the money I lost from the rent scam by emailing an ombudsman. In the end, it was to no avail. The money I was offered back by Barclays was a hundred pounds, one hundred measly pounds and they made out that they were doing the favour.

It wasn't clear cut. If you are willing to give one hundred pounds back then you are admitting that there was some fault with the bank, and thus they should give me all of my money. All of my well-needed parents money that I would have to return. An amount significant, an amount that was transferred by them that I thought was secure because it went into the Barclays bank account.

There was a new girl that worked in the Hackney job and to call her beautiful would not be enough: five foot ten, long brown hair down to her shoulders with a modest temperament. I wondered what her first impressions were of me but, when I returned to my small office, I wasn't sure I wanted know. I managed to get a whiff of myself, the familiar stale armpits that permeated the room. The results of another late morning from missing the gym after the stale and damp tent. A result from travelling and walking without showering for at least 24 hours.

Suddenly, Belinda paid us a surprise visit and entered my office. 'Oh, it's stuffy in here, shall we open a window?' I couldn't work out if this was subtle or not, but from then on I had the window decidedly open, at all times, without a doubt, and whatever the weather.

The work was easy enough and I would start the arduous trek back to central London, to eat, usually in Pret, do laptop work for my business and then to the long night to the tent. The weather was already more severe and, with my new work intensity, I had to be sure not to lose my mind. I would have to realise why I was doing this, that it was for the bigger picture – not for the very present.

At times I would lay on my back and look at the top of the canopy. I would think, would the girl at the new workplace want a man like me? A slightly older, more experienced man? When she asked to see my place, I could get in a hotel and say my flat was being renovated. Then I thought about Ritchie's Mum, what she said about people who are homeless and don't quite need to be. That they have deep social issues, potentially psychotic. Perhaps that is the case.

What was my mental state? This was re-enforced one night at the Bocage. I had carefully set up the tent, placed down the wet roll mat that needed some drying and held it down with my rucksack that was weighted by my laptop. Phone to one side and quickly into the sleeping bag, socks off and apply the headcover. I heard two voices behind me, behind the exposed rear wall and I was not shocked because it was inevitable that this would happen. I knew it, I was just surprised it wasn't sooner. They were close – so very close. And I made sure that I was still so the only sound they could hear was a small bird chirping to the left and a wakening exhaust on the main road. So close, but still they didn't see me.

Man one: Where is this guy, man? How many did he order? Two?

Man two: Two, yeah.

Man one: Can't believe all this shit for two, man. He knows Dee, yeah?

Man Two: Yeah.

Man one: I'm gonna have to have a serious word with that guy, you know.

They were drug dealers, and they were right next to me, the camouflage tent was disguising me as was the darkening night until…

Man one: Mate, check that out, in the bushes there… Look!

Man two: What is… Oh my, what the fuck?

Man one: It's a tent, bruv. Who in their right mind would do that?

Me and my mental state would. To my surprise they seemed to wither away and retreat, they could have easily thrown something at the tent or set it alight. But they were too shocked.

And this was what it was, I would work my City job, tent, the new job. Tent. Business development on the one, digital marketing on the other. Tent. I was paid fortnightly by my new role, and monthly by the other which meant a constant stream. And, altogether another eight hundred gross on average. My business, well, that would have to take the backburner until I had generated wealth and plugged the deficit.

The issue was my weakness. Perhaps every Londoner's weakness. The problem, my weakness, was my need to socialize.

Because London is inhabited by millions, but you feel you are all alone...

Other weaknesses were my need to drink, shout, take a line, feel dizzy, kiss a randomer and maybe sleep not being myself. And so, with extra funds going into my account, and the extra work I was doing, the need to release would be more. It was a time when I should have been more frugal. A time when this would have been the perfect opportunity to not spend or socialise.

Another issue was the increasing cold, with the weather and constant travel I was finding it easier to hire the odd room in a cheap hotel. Things could only get worse and I thought to myself, the only place, the only place I would be able to sleep for free would be the dread of the haunted office in the City, in the room, down the dark hall and I would still have to wake up at an ungodly hour to not bump into the incoming staff.

And so I played yo-yo with the elements and did not plan my dwelling too early. I would creep, check the coldness in the September air and if too cold, I would find somewhere to sleep or to party, much like the summer before it. The good thing about the summer was that everyone was partying, wanting to be in groups, wanting to feel each other. The incumbent autumn had changed people's minds. People would get home and snuggle, they wanted to hibernate with their close ones, away from the greyness and harsh noises on the City streets. This meant that my options were narrow, and thus, improvisation.

The improvisation soon led to the inevitable: the office. I tried it again after walking from Covent Garden, down the Strand past the hordes of homeless and a number three bus to the City. I sat at the back and look at the sights towards Fleet Street, down through London Wall and the great St Paul's until finally my destination: the silent road of Cornhill to the right of the royal exchange. Down the narrow path to the right of the road into the office. The door closed before me and I hurried to put the lights on. I ran, sprint-ran up the stairs as they darkened behind me. I ran to the second floor, past the loo and to the room where I locked the door and clicked the lamp. To my relief, I could hear strangers outside, drunken and bantering – thinking the humanity will keep centuries of bad spirits away.

Inevitably, I needed the loo and so I crept in the dark hall to the toilet. I washed my face and braced myself for the journey back to the room. The experience soon brought out the past, the scared infant; the infant who was scared of the long dark hall of my childhood home – scared of potential ghosts, of the large glaring portraits on the wall. Hearing my parents argue while the television murmured in the background.

I went back to the room, used a small cushion from the chair as a head piece and used my long coat as a duvet. I was foolish to let my skin touch the office carpet, but I managed to slumber, better than the tent, though the floor reminded me of its hard surface when I attempted to turn. I dreamt that night:

I was in my family home, perhaps I was eight or nine and I ran in the garden, then I ran on the road outside when I was not supposed to. I went inside and the house was suddenly dark and empty. The furniture had plastic sheets on them and my sister was in a car but there were two cars in the driveway, both driving away – one with Mother and one with Father. My sister looked out of the car window as she drove out with Mother. Father, in the car ahead, drove away without looking back. I looked around at the empty house once more and I woke as my alarm rang from my mobile. It was seven a.m., later than it should be, and I had to move before some of the early birds started to enter. It was then I realised that the night wasn't as bad as last time. It wasn't haunted by a ghost and I was in a room with four walls. I would do this again, especially as the weather continued to bleaken.

There was also Nayarra, my dear friend. A friend that I knew if I got stuck, would let me stay at hers, unconditionally, without regret but of course on one-off nights. She would usually have a guy, always muscle-bound man that would need to come over so that she could have her fill of rough sex – that was Nayarra's vice.

Nayarra was Nayarra, not a fraud. Those with numerous ideas but never execute. She was a high-flyer in architecture, worked full-time, wore work suits and went to after-work drinks. She collected a salary and had flat-warming parties whenever she moved. When I could afford it, I would pay, when she could afford it, she would pay, she didn't mind about money so much with men, perhaps until she wanted to get married – then they would have to be secure.

Her birthday parties were notorious, as were her Halloween parties, all in a house. A civilised and captivating working crowd. She would tell us about Brazil and how they all eat copious amounts of meat, and how her brother would play with the South American bulls. It sounded masculine, it sounded determined, it sounded a little like Nayarra.

Chapter 17

Nayarra's Party

"We are all in this together."
– David Cameron

I got up from the tent to a minor shower in the gym, but not enough to mitigate a lingering smell of damp. I managed to pick up another jumper from Scatty's, cleaner than the one I was wearing, but I wasn't entirely sure that I hadn't worn it before. And so, I went to the office in Hackney where they seemed to leave me in my room and I hope it wasn't anything to do with... I made sure that I kept the window open.

Nayarra pestered me. 'You must be there at a specific time, so that you can meet this person.' All very well but I would have liked to have nabbed a full shower and some kind of pre-nap. Where? To be honest... no idea: perhaps Oakley Street, perhaps sneak into the other office and have a nap there. It seemed to be okay the last time. Another option was to ask Solus if she wanted to arrive with me and I could sneak a nap on her bed. Perhaps I could quickly book a film in the cinema, drape myself across the dark floor (providing it was not too busy) and a quick shower at the gym.

I finished late in Hackney and there was the pressure to get to the party. I didn't get to the gym; my phone lit up every five asking when and where I was, so I headed straight towards Sands

End to Solus's – I had ordered beforehand; it would be rude not to.

I arrived at Solus's already tired. I walked past the gran and said hello as usual. Solus smiled and took me up to her room. I wondered if Ritchie was coming tonight, so I gave him a call and he told me that he would later. When I was on the phone to Ritchie, I heard a female voice near in the distance, but I did not mention this to Solus.

I did not get the bag out straight away, instead I jumped on her bed and started to nap, stating to her that I had cocaine but I would save it for the party. I could hear her rustling by her wardrobe which kept me awake as I tried to rest. Finally, she found what she was looking for, it was a spray can of deodorant that she not-so-subtly sprayed around the room. 'Do I smell?' I asked.

'Erm… maybe it was just getting a little musty.' I did not want to ask Solus to shower at hers, for some reason, it felt as if it was crossing a line.

I had noticed that this jumper, the best I had, had a slight rip in the shoulder and this time it did not look like a fashion choice. But we made our way to the party and Solus was gagging for a line. Nayarra looked at me. 'Come, come on you have to meet her.'

She looked at me again with a puzzling look. 'Are you okay? You are looking a little thin.' Then she put her finger under her nose – the compulsive action people choose when they have suddenly smelled an unpleasant odour. I quickly went to the bathroom before meeting the mystery guest and looked in the mirror – I noticed that my face had thinned somewhat, gaunt and a complexion that seemed deficient of minerals – I had the rip in my shirt, but I still thought I could pull everything off. A quick bump would help me to do the chat and rounds and… everything social.

Solus found me; her tiny nose could promptly sniff out drugs in any bathroom in her proximity. She knocked on the bathroom door and crept in with astute self-awareness. 'Hello, you…. do you have something for me?'

I poured powder straight onto the mantle by the sink and she rolled a five-pound note. I realised for one flash of a moment that I had hardly seen Solus with her own note. I could hear Nayarra in the hallway, talking about me to the person I was supposed to be introduced to. 'He has a big crush on you,' she said. 'He watches your videos and knows who you are.' Nayarra's intentions were to set me up but to make sure nothing ever happened. Why? To probably keep me for herself. Not in a sexual way, just as a friendly possession for when she may need. For me? On the whole, I was fine with that.

We did a line and went downstairs. The congregation of people were mainly in the basement, listening to rambunctious house music and pouring make-shift cocktails. Nayarra had returned down there and acknowledged me as soon as I entered – and that's why I loved her. To her, I wasn't quirky or an outsider, I was wholeheartedly one of hers. She ran and grabbed me and left Solus to talk to strangers, then, she took me round the corner to finally meet this girl. I did recognise her – she was a singer from The Saturdays – the blonde ethereal one that dated David Gandy. She was here in the basement of Nayarra's flat. The reason? She was friends with Nayarra's flat mate – a female footballer with a penchant for pretty girls.

I was given a cold beer and I put on my smooth voice. 'Hi, how are you?' And she didn't even look at me, as if she was half creeped out, and half disgusted by something.

It was then that I felt movement on my skin and scratched while talking, this fuelled the coarse atmosphere. She didn't fancy me at all, in fact, she was likely repulsed by my presence. I asked her, 'What are you looking for in there?' and she answered.

'Ah just getting some ice.' She was hoping that was the last question. Hoping that my flea-ridden body would go to the other side of the room with the masses. Nayarra's pre-speech did not help but I was a millennia away from the aesthetics of David Gandy.

It was only when Nayarra grabbed me that the other reason was set in stone. 'John, I love you but you stink,' in a not-so-subtle, Brazilian way. She took me upstairs to the bathroom where she pulled my jumper and almost gagged. Solus had tagged along behind us, giggling, and Nayarra started spraying me with deodorant. I told them to wait, first I must wash the armpits and so I did, both of them watching in shock and awe as I used the handwash and created a soapy lava between my fingers. I washed thoroughly under my pits while Nayarra wanted to get back to the party.

'Come on, let's leave him to it.' Solus followed out but paused, turned around and said in the firmest of voices, 'Excuse me, can I have the bag?' I looked in the mirror and pondered which was more embarrassing: a celebrity that was physically repulsed or two of my friends giving me a hose down.

When I was in the basement before, it was sparser. Now it was filling with a variety of frolicking humans. There was a secondary space: a small drawing room where I would watch movies with Nayarra and it led to outside where people would smoke and talk to the equally debaucherous neighbours. There were four flat mates, but the flat was on three storeys and I saw the celebrity giggling with the footballer on the stairs. A random man towering above them – trying to get in on the conversation. One leg on the stairwell, bent by the knee while he leaned with a beer. I thought to myself, this could be a good time to… try again? Perhaps I should tell her that I have purchased David Gandy underwear? And, although expensive, they really are comfortable and temperature sensitive. I glanced over and I could already feel that she sensed me. She didn't even need to look at me and I knew it – the coarse and unwanted connection that she hoped would dissipate as quickly as it came. So, I went outside for a smoke, pretending that was always my intention and Solus joined me.

Solus hadn't bought her coat with her and she shivered with her reclining fag in her hand, and again we read each other's minds: 'WINTER IS COMING' and Nayarra's muscle man arrived outside as we smoked. Solus slowly turned towards him and found it hard to conceal her attraction.

'Hello, is Nayarra here?'

'Yes, she's inside.' We firmly shook hands and his name was Alejandro or Alejandra or something suitably Spanish. Solus checked his firm ass when he walked in and, although he was entering, Nayarra had promised that I would be staying there tonight in the small drawing room.

I walked back in with Solus, did a line and partied as we tried to steal the tunes but Wolf Alice's 'Silk' was vetoed for being depressing. Brazilian beats resumed and I saw that Nayarra was re united with her muscular lover, they smooched while he grabbed her and lifted her up, showing her pert Brazilian butt to the entirety of the party.

I missed that – the Tammy-shaped hole was gaping, Coco had burned me and now I was stuck with Solus whose intentions were clear – to obtain snort whenever and wherever possible. Ritchie called soon after and told us he was on the way, though, he sounded more than drunk. Not the merry kind of drunk where you know you would have a good time with a friend, the unpredictable murmuring drunk where a darkness had taken him – usually it went this way with Ritchie.

They say that alcohol being called a spirit stems from Middle Eastern alchemy – alchemy to transform a material – and they would say that a material could be a volatile substance. They would use alcohol to distill things, to separate substances: there would be liquid and vapour and the vapour would apparently hold the essence, also known as the spirit.

Some say that if you consume alcohol, it is a distilling process within itself. The alcohol separates you from your essence, just like other materials, so, your essence, or your spirit is separated from your body. Sounds far out, sounds like the holistic bullshit that is sprouting from everywhere in this age of information, but it seems logical when you have to view the likes of Ritchie on alcohol.

Suddenly there was an argument – the female footballer and Nayarra. Something happened but I was not sure what and I was not sure who would win in a fist fight. Both so physically adept, it would be close that's for sure. I drank beer and watched the conflict unravel which left the party polarised: Nayarra's team (including Solus and me) in the basement, then the scouse footballer, the celeb and others upstairs. I am still not sure of its origins, but I went out to have a cigarette and heard the footballer shouting in anger, she saw the back of my head, paused and stated:

'And that creep tried it on with *****!'

People with her were laughing, but nervously to reassure her.

171

I ignored it, smoked a cigarette and went back inside to the tension and separation and I really hoped it wasn't Nayarra's birthday. I hadn't purchased a card and she seemed dispirited by the footballer's acrimonious tones. I thought I should say something, to encourage our side of the fence but all I could think of, all I could think of was David Cameron. David Cameron and his speech when he started severing public services. I turned around, put my arms out and said, 'We are all in this together.' Nayarra looked up and smiled, the others laughed but not with me, only to themselves.

Solus left to see Ritchie instead of him coming to the theatre of conflict. Nayarra's crew: Charlotte and her boyfriend, Eve and many others – decided to go to another destination. To let the situation dissolve rather than simmer and boil over. This left the footballer, the celebrity, and their crew with the flat. For me it looked like a concession, but it was a good idea.

We were told to travel to Charlotte and her boyfriend's house. He was in finance and drunkenly drove some people in a Mercedes to the Battersea apartment. It was cute and clean, and Charlotte loved her boyfriend and the vast funds he received in Canary Wharf – Charlotte bragged about how they talked about marriage and moving into a bigger place before they had children. Eve, her other friend was also trying for the rich men. And there was me, the pseudo artist, pseudo-city person, unshaven, poor, and itching with an unconfirmed Anthropod.

We had more drinks and lines, but Charlotte's boyfriend was reserved. 'Please, guys, no more.' And Nayarra decided to return to the house of conflict. I had no choice but to join her. In fact, we all went back except for Charlotte and her boyfriend. Solus, for some reason, came back to us after an argument with Ritchie and Nayarra was good enough to give Solus and me the spare room – me on the floor, Solus on the bed. This time, she groaned in her sleep as if she was reliving a struggle. 'Stop, get off me please, just… stop!' Followed by demonic breathing. Almost vocal as she exhaled.

I tried to sleep through it, I turned around and tried to drown out the noise pollution with a cushion but then, suddenly… I felt a large weight on the bottom of my legs. It was a warm feeling, as the cotton of the garment touched my lower thigh. I looked up and saw Solus's grey and distraught eyes. Did she want to talk? Fuck? She looked at me inquisitively, then angrily as if I had done something to annoy her. Then, she shifted her weight off my legs and crawled herself back onto the bed.

This time she was silent, this time she seemed to be at peace and I also managed to get some sleep in the cramped room. I got up earlier than Solus, I made sure I went straight to the gym and took a shower. I scrubbed and scrubbed and thought of the celebrities face. The lack of desire to shower is apparently an autistic trait and I thought about the girls at Scatty's, although, this was more than likely to do with homelessness: with the homeless, it's harder to get into a routine, and sweat and grease keep you warm.

Just in case, I stayed in the shower for a long period of time, scrubbing and trying to enjoy it. Creating a soapy lather and destroying the dirt in every crevice. Destroying the itching. Destroying the bugs, destroying the awkwardness of the night. As I continued to scrub, I thought of the disgusted glare once more. Perhaps she told her celebrity friends of how she met a bathless creep while trying to chill with down-to-earth folk. I continued to scrub. Such was the duration that a muscle-laden man violently knocked on the door. 'BE RIGHT OUT!' I shouted with a lack of fear and relative displeasure.

Interlude

Office on the Weekends

Drew had warned me about the office on the weekends.

As the days grew colder and people shrank away from extensive social schedules – I would go there on the weekend. I would go to H Club but the spiky haired marketing gurus would obtain the seating before I arrived.

If I did arrive early, they would soon distract you by arriving in hoards, pressuring the space and the waiting staff around it. Drew had experience. 'Buddy, I did this when I was moving flat – It's weird that shit, you know. Do I use the office microwave? Do I sit at my own work seat?' I saw what he meant and I tried to not sit at my own desk. Many of the times I would use the room that I would sleep in on the second floor, sit at the desk and watch something on my laptop, eat and place the remains safely in the small kitchen upstairs.

I felt safe in there, but only in the day. There were still the odd creaks and noises but overall, in the day – okay. It was the night that started to bring the horrors, all after I thought it was OK again and it was just my imagination.

There was one time, when I thought I was in the safety of the second floor, in the day, having a nap. I felt uneasy, there were constant rumblings outside, but I tried to reassure myself that people wouldn't come into the building on a Sunday... why would they? Suddenly, I could hear the large door downstairs open, it opened via an electric tag and made a huge buzzing sound – it buzzed with definition, I was startled and suddenly upright. I made sure I remained quiet and slowly folded over my laptop. Then, I heard two people talking as they strode up the stairs. Okay, they were in the building, nothing I could do, but the likelihood of them coming into my very room…

Suddenly I heard the lady say to a man, 'If you just wait here I will check the room,' and she entered, finding me rustling around, trying to pack everything as she looked at me with surprise and resentment. 'Hi, hi,' I said. 'Sorry, I will just pack up.'

'No problem,' she stated. 'You work here?'

I told her that I did, she told me that she used to but now lives in Norfolk and hired the rooms for consulting.

As I tried to build rapport, her tone changed. She didn't seem to respond to what I was saying – avoiding eye contact and blatantly wanting me to leave. She had seen some clothing leaking out of my bag and thought that something was not right. Well… she was right that it was not right.

Chapter 18

Visiting Mum

"Never lie to your mother. And if you do, never assume you got away with it."
– Unknown

I had a weekend that I would rather forget which included three grams and copious amounts of beer. I managed to sleep at Solus's on Saturday but we were rudely interrupted – her father burst in the room in the dead of night. Solus was asleep but I pretended to be. He shuffled and shuffled looking for something, violently stomping around and fumbling. Solus stated that she often did drugs with her father, but this raid was to confiscate them. When he stopped near us, he paused and towered over me, no words, just silence and the potential threat of violence. If I woke, I was not sure what would occur so I pretended to be asleep. So there he was, towering over me – in the dark. Then, he leaned over to throw the duvet neatly over Solus. He paused again and left the room. Now the stays would be even rarer.

I wouldn't say it was the last time I stayed there, her Dad would stay at his new girlfriend's, occasionally leaving me with a safe window to slumber. My sleep was not a smooth one that night or indeed the following.

I skimmed some snort from Solus which I had given to her anyway and I used it as I slept in the tent. Wet once again –

Sunday night – wriggling and writhing as I micro-dosed to not stay awake: I hoped it would elevate to a high but relaxed state. This, rather than a quivering hyper wreck; a wreck that wouldn't be able to sleep without the danger of Xanax. I thought it was working as I embraced my sleeping bag but then... then the pattering rain and increased heartbeat made it hard to settle. Around me, a shivering dark and murmuring on the main road. There were no stars out... just dull cloud amongst the black and pattering London rain.

Not much sleep and my eyes showed it as I caught my reflection on the gym mirror. A quick shower and shave and I was off to see her, a restaurant near Notting Hill and she was buying. It was fortunate that the meeting would be out and about, that she didn't want to see the 'new place' that she gave me money for.

I arrived, looking as clean as possible and my sister was there also. It wasn't that I didn't want to see my sister, I just didn't want to see her at this very moment.

I came in and the mood was sour, they had been arguing. You see my sister had ran off with a girl who didn't love her, had no prospects and pretended to have a modelling career. I could see Grace's fake tears from a mile away. 'Mum, if I wasn't gay this wouldn't BE A PROBLEM!' Voices were raised and people tried not to look but our family didn't care about that. It had always been that way, one way or another – shouting or resentment in silence and my sister was setting up a classic smokescreen. Positioning the guilt that her sexuality was a problem. And it wasn't. To detract from the real problem, to detract from the fact that her girlfriend was a cheating slut that drained my sister's money and subsequently, my mother's. Grace stormed out but not before saying, 'Hi, John, speak to you later yeah?'

My mother was visibly upset – a rare sight to see, but Grace had always been the favourite. I remember as a child, 'Be careful, John, Grace is the sensitive one.' I remember when Grace swore at a neighbour for backing into our driveway, the neighbour complained. Mother said to the neighbour that I put her up to it, because Grace was too sensitive for the repercussions.

Mother shook herself out of it and looked me in the eye, smiling. I quickly averted by turning my face to the side. Usually people would stop looking after a second, but I could feel my mother, still glancing, as if it were a double take. Suddenly she became colder:

Mother: So how are you, how's your flat?

Me: It's great Mum thanks so much for the help, I will definitely start paying you back.

Mother: Worry about that next year, get yourself, sorted, established.

Me: Okay, thanks.

Mother: You look tired John, worn out, what have you been getting up to?

Me: Oh, I have just been working hard.

Mother: Okay, well looks like you need a meal, what would you like?

Me: I'll get the lentils with greens, please and thank you.

Mother: I used to have this friend in the seventies, maybe it was early eighties… she used to do a lot of drugs John – cocaine to be specific, it was when it really started to come in the scene.

Me: Oh dear, not good.

Mother: Right, you see I could always tell by the eyes when she was using, you know these dark circles and blank pupils.

Me: Okay…

Mother: You aren't on drugs are you, John?

Me: Me? Drugs? Oh no I am anti-drugs, I don't believe in it, don't have time really.

Mother: Not to mention you cannot afford it.

Me: Yes, I bet it is fucking expensive!

Mother: Language, John, your nose is all snotty. Did you want a tissue?

Me: No, I best go to the loo and sort it out.

I went to the loo but made sure I wasn't long – otherwise she would think I was racking a line. Her suspicions were astute but I wondered if there were deeper origins. Perhaps it was my sister, it is the kind of crass and undermining thing she would do. To slyly plant a seed into my mother's head for her own advantage, I can imagine her: 'Does John take drugs, Mother?'

Mother, falling for the bait: 'Why do you ask such a thing?'

The idea that she could tell by the bags under somebody's eyes must be pretence; as she would walk the London streets, streets where cocaine has a market of one billion pounds, she would be in for a shock.

'She's doing it? My word, he's doing it!' It is nothing short of an epidemic and I will shrug it off. Firstly, by pretending that I do not know what she is getting at – classic ignorance. And I will deny until the ends of the earth. The main thing will be to evade. Mother has known how I lie, ever since I stained her favourite dining table. Her spontaneous reaction of anger was shocking and unjustified but, as unpredictable as she was, she had been there of late, she had been a gem in a sea of rough and blank stones.

I returned to the table with my large fake smile from cheek to cheek. The smile I practice before interviews, for parties, the one that Tammy hated. Some said it was menacing, as if I was in intense pain and was trying to conceal it in public – perhaps they

179

are not wrong.

We sat down and things were more relaxed, she bought up the drug question one more time and I swore to her. Then, other questions:

Mother: How's Tammy?

John: She is great.

Mother: Any wedding bells soon?

John: You never know…

I tucked into my food with a calculated orange juice when my sister knocked on the window. I hadn't seen her for months and she didn't bother to come in but that was fine by me. Mother got up to leave. 'Listen, John, I better go and talk to your sister – if I can't get back let's catch up in a couple of weeks. I will be in London a lot more at the moment, are you okay for money?'

As she asked, she was already in motion and I made a rule to never say that I needed money. This rule was heavily enforced after the scam – the scam that already wasted some of her funds. I was only taking money if mother physically shoved it in my hand, which, if I am honest, is what I thought might happen. 'Oh no, Mother I couldn't possibly.' I would say and she would reply with, 'Take it, take it,' but this time, this did not happen.

Before she left, she told me that Father was coming to London very soon. Very soon indeed. But I knew this already because he texted me. I remembered it in the peripheral of my mind, but didn't mark it as urgent. I marked it as 'To be confirmed.'

Chapter 19

Drugs Gone Sour

"I thought that love was in the drugs, but the more I took, the more it took away. And I could never get enough."
– Florence and the Machine, 2016

Autumn and me were drifting; I had the two jobs and, as predicted, it made the business suffer. It would have been an idea to hire a new intern but my days consisted of working, travelling and finding somewhere warm to stay. If this was not an option, then just like summer – it was the tent. The suffering of the business made me feel off-centre. As if it was a dishonesty to what I was supposed to be achieving. My mind knew it and made my conscience bug me at inappropriate hours.

My staying in the office had increased from sporadic to regular. As usual, I made sure to wipe the area clean when I had finished, removed all belongings and sprayed with an air freshener that I bought with me. Ready for whoever would use it throughout the day.

I got comfortable with my life. Some may say that would be a good thing but this was not a part of the exercise. The exercise was to grow, get abundant and to get a flat. Instead, the office as accommodation had given me a false sense of security. My thought process was deceiving me. 'I have free accommodation, I can do what I like; I can spend, take drugs, get drunk and sleep in the four City walls.' The idea of saving soon became less urgent in this strange period. I thought I would trick time by using the office and its free accommodation, but trying to trick time was a hopeless endeavour. Humanity can do many things: it can defy gravity, it can cure disease, but trying to surpass the constraints of time by taking too much of it? The epitome of foolishness.

And this was the issue as I made my mind slow down. I took the foot off the proverbial gas when it should have been firmly held down. I almost felt that I had already made it, and so I would go to one of my respective jobs, drink at H Club and sleep at the office or a rented room if money would allow. It was only an issue when I worked at the office in the day only to sleep there on the same night. The office people who worked late would interfere with my routine. So, I would leave for hours in the evening – either to Brick Lane or restaurants nearby to eat and drink and return when the sky was black.

Drugs increased without my realisation – they crept up on me like any other evil. Like water in a flash flood that suddenly emerges and, before you know it, you are up to the neck; you don't know how it happened, but it was always in your psyche.

Solus had been frequenting the New Forest with her mother. That's where her mother lived and she was happy and healthy there. She would return, fresh faced with a smile from cheek to cheek. One night, Solus had returned to London and I thought it would be fun to see her, well, perhaps not fun, but human contact had been sparse since her absence.

She asked me with her lungs full of clean air, 'Let's do something wholesome!' I had realised that through this time, the entirety of it – that I hadn't visited the Countryside, not even once. Mainly because Mother would realise I didn't have a home, and because the sheer thought made me panicked and nauseous. This City, this evolving metropolis had me in its vice-like grip, my emotions rigidly attached to its grey interior. To leave it would be impossible. Even for a weekend.

We decided on the cinema but I had a baggie in my pocket that would usually delight the fiend. I purchased the tickets and we crept down into the smaller screen. I can't remember the film, but people were sparse and we were left on our own on the dark back row. When we were in the light, Solus told me that I looked like I had been partying for a month – she pointed to the bags under my eyes while I pulled the small clear bag out in the back row and dipped my finger. This time, she didn't make the weird nibbling sound. This time it was: 'I suppose I better.' We sneaked a bump in the bag, once or twice even though there were others in the theatre, but Solus, well she soon became irritable. It was as if I was forcing her. Me. As if she didn't want to do it and asked if we could leave, which we did. For once, for this very once I felt as if I was leading her astray, as if I was the bad seed. All the times I felt made to get drugs or she ordered without asking and now… it had come to this; inevitable karma, and the devil does not take cheques.

At this moment, my life choices were not for her. The tables had turned in the depths of the New Forest which had centred her… at least for a few weeks. I did a couple of lines to myself on the way back to hers and she slept suddenly in her bedroom. She hadn't told Ritchie that she was back in London, and neither did I.

The next day was Saturday. We had spent Friday night in the cinema and in bed with me on the small floor, shoes firmly on in case her father paid a visit. That Saturday, I slept in the office and later saw Solus on Facebook she was with Ritchie having a wholesome couple's evening. Drinking tea in his flat and watching the television. All they needed were woolly jumpers and a dog in the background.

I would have asked to stay over but I didn't want to intrude. Instead, in the morning, I left the empty office after trying to disinfect – trying to clean it to not leave a trace of human scent. I needed to get out of there. Out of the office and somewhere where there was a congregation of people and the only thing I could think of was… Brick Lane. First, I ordered from The Forty Man who had no location jurisdiction. A twenty-minute wait and I was bagged up including the stuff I already had. I was still coming down from the night before, and the night before that – but I wanted to continue, to carry on the party until I physically couldn't.

I walked down the cobbled roads towards Brick Lane and smelled the curries and other food stalls, the trendy couples with Dr Martens and tight black jeans. One guy was talking to his friend, woolly hat on with a coffee in his hand, leaning on a wall with his leg raised. Checking his hat and routinely shifting it to obtain the perfect angle, to fit in to the trend of the area. I wondered if he knew that Shoreditch lost its edge a decade ago. Old Street, a great example – once full of ambitious new bars and heaving with youngsters. Now? Boarded up and full of signs for residential property. 'We are all in this together.'

I bought vegetable curry from a stall to maintain my relatively new vegan ethics, and then, to a bar on the lower end of the lane; a bottled beer ordered and a line in the small loo. I started to text anybody who would be up for a party and would travel East.

Niccy: Sorry babes I am on a date.

Drew: Sorry bud it's Sunday I got a biggie tomorrow.

Solus: No response.

Ritchie: Oh my word, you still on it? Solus said you were snorting all week…

Plum: Hi, babe. (No other response).

Coralie: Not East babe.

H: No response.

Oli: Where you, East? Ahahah nutter, how rank.

Nayarra: Ahaha, John, you crazy.

Various others were approached, as well as people I found hard to tolerate. No bite to be had: my only chance of a social mix would be to meet randoms, randoms who were already out on a Sunday.

I went to another bar, past the graffitied bridge and on the left-hand side. It had a main floor and a basement with a pool table and I had another beer and hoped that I didn't look high. There were two girls in the corner and I smiled at them. I couldn't work out if they smiled back or refused to acknowledge my gaze, so I went to the empty downstairs for another line. I don't even know what I was sending in the texts; smiling to myself and sweating, thinking that I have found out the hack in life: I am high on a Sunday and chilling with beers and I didn't have to work tomorrow – I had a business, albeit with margins that were super narrow but I still did. Freedom I thought, we were not supposed to do this…. but I was and there was just the small issue, the issue that there was nobody to share the glory.

I moved towards a hotel bar on Shoreditch High Street – sparse of people. Only the frequenting Essex types with their short skirts and tans were braving a darkening Sunday. I thought to myself, *Is this it? Is this the great metropolis on a Sunday? A few people in the corner, dwindling and nonchalant. Everyone anticipating the insipidness of a Monday morning.*

I saw a girl by the bar; petite and svelte with the classical cheekbones that you see in the magazines. I spoke to her with relative ease and she was inquisitive.

'So why are you talking to me? And why don't you look me in the eye?' she said with a Polish twang, and I soon told her about "The Game", the speed seduction book which maintained her intrigue. She was interested in my approach, how I came and spoke without hesitation. She told me how she lived across the road, and so, we went to her place so promptly it made me nervous.

She wasn't lying: a tucked away cobbled mews, just off the high street and up some balcony stairs to which I nearly lost my footing – the state I had become had made me lose balance to even walk in a straight line and we sat in a living room as her flat mate entered. A shirted, overweight man with an inebriated face. I wanted another line, and usually I would feel the situation but... well, this was a different kind of day.

'Do you guys do coke?' The girl was surprised and I was aware that I was jeopardizing my opportunity to be intimate; some people think cocaine is a great attracter, but many times it can do the opposite: people have already had their high and talk too much. If they don't do it at all? It can be an unabridged turn off.

The flat-mate's answer was different and showed the extent of cocaine's boundaries. East was the same as West. 'Actually I have got my own, did you want a bit?'

Immediately, I said, 'Yes, please,' and the excitement of the buzz trespassed over any rationale. I asked the girl, cross-legged in the corner, if she would join.

'No thanks, I don't do it,' and she looked at me with a mix of perplexion and disgust – perhaps she thought I was a drug addict. She had only just met me and, as I thought of this, I thought to myself - perhaps she is justified.

The guy bought in a plate and we nailed a long white stripe with a five-pound note. The girl watched in the corner, twitching her foot with confusion but I didn't care what she thought anymore. I had a plate of free snort in a flat in an exotic part of London. After a while, when bantering with the flat mate, I realised that I should spend more time with her. I went towards her, jokily dancing as she tried not to look my way – she took a second look at me. 'Are you okay? You look a bit ill.'

'Yes, I'm fine, I'M ABSOLUTELY FINE!' I blared at her with unnecessary decibels.

She invited me to their kitchen so we could drink alone and she yawned on the way there. She took me in, leaned on the laminate and showed her slender legs through her tight jeans. She took out a bottle of Polish Liquor and said: 'Oh yeah, I am getting tired I will have to go to bed soon, but we should try some of this first?'

The thought of being thrust out into the street was not appealing. 'I could stay here if you want? I won't try it on or anything... I... I have work to do tomorrow too.'

She hesitated and started to shake her head. 'No, not tonight. So much to do, but come drink!' And there was no way back to it. I could ask again but the insistence would surely create a sinister vibration. And thus, I would have to retire when she said.

I had a shot of the Polish drink and it was strong, so strong that it made my legs quiver to the extent it was an effort to stand. Then, she opened another bottle of a different concoction and we had a shot while I thought to myself, 'Why are we doing this before bed?'

'It's good, huh?' she said to me, and she seemed completely

187

unaffected by it as my eyes started to jade and blur. She yawned once more for what must have been the twentieth time and said she was heading to bed.

Me: Oh, are you sure?

Her: Yeah... I will see you again.

I asked her for her number and instead she said to add her on Facebook. Then, she looked at me weaving unsteadily with surprising amusement. 'Do you do drugs a lot then?'

I mustered all the concentration I had and told her in no uncertain terms, 'I DO IT WHEN I CHOOSE'. She went to hug me and I tried to rub my hands down to her legs and buttocks – it wasn't that she wasn't receptive, but she didn't encourage it.

'You know, I have never taken somebody home so quickly before; it was good chat about the game, have a good night.' And with that, I was thrust away, down the balcony stairs and into the darkness of the small mews – I staggered towards the bright lights of Shoreditch High Street. From there, I knew that there was only one place to where I could physically make it. It was, yet again, the City office with the ghosts of past times.

I swayed onto to a bus, down the Bishopsgate stretch and sat downstairs which I did not normally do. There was a child in a pram this late at night and the smell of fast food was overwhelming. So, I ran outside to semi-puke and get some air. Eventually, I entered the office and ran up the stairs to the second floor, my heart double skipping to the point of danger but I still scooped a key from the baggie as if it was going out of fashion, as if it was cool to do this on my own... very much on my own.

I turned on the lamp and laid down on the carpet. Almost immediately I could hear the elusive clanging and creeping that this building was notorious for; different floors, different noises as I imagined the ghouls of the attached cemetery congregating to enter the office and eat me. This time, this time though, I was so high that I couldn't give a fuck – my reactions speedy and my demeanour cocky. 'OH FUCK OFF GHOSTS!' I shouted while laughing to myself and hitting another small bump. As if I had an imaginary audience and I was making them laugh; my imaginary friends in the room with me, frolicking and getting high.

I could hear a clatter on the Cornhill Road and I looked out. It was the transvestite with her cardboard box, talking to herself and smoking a cigarette, at this time of night? How? It must be so cold, so… lonely. I thought in my head that I should go and speak to her – but I didn't. I thought that because I at least had the thought of it, that should be enough. I hoped the warm vibration of my thought would travel to her in the colding air.

The building went quiet, and something came over me as I went to dip the key in the bag: I couldn't have another; my body couldn't take another hit. And then I suddenly felt a fatigue, not so much a physical fatigue, my body's reactions were still faster than normal, especially in the arms and the foaming mouth. A mental fatigue it was, as my mind started to crawl down into a stark reality. Any gratitude towards life started to slowly peel away, layer after layer, and I knew the inevitable outcome.

I laid on the floor and started to grip it. I started to feel hungry – I started to feel that I could not stay there on that flat floor tonight, I would not be able to wake up in time. I looked at my phone and saw that nobody had called me back. I realised something worse: that I had fucked my schedule and I should be working in Hackney tomorrow. I frantically open my laptop and emailed them to say I was ill, and wouldn't be able to go in.

Then, I look for last minute rooms, even Airbnb's, there weren't any but there were some cheap serviced apartments back near Old Street – still eighty-nine pounds for the night but a full apartment. I conjured strength and managed to get upright but my body was shaking and my mouth was twitching to what seemed to be my heartbeat. Fast and relentless. I paid online and hoped it wasn't a scam. From then, I don't remember leaving the office, and I don't remember walking to the apartment block, but when I got there it was simple enough. I showed the lady my reservation and she told me where to find it.

And so I did – and it seemed as though me and the reception lady were the only ones in the building. Because the building was as quiet as the night, as was the mini street off the Commercial Road.

I went into the loo in the apartment and managed to conjure up another bump. Why I did this? I will never know; my nose seemed to reject it as I sneezed across the sink and I violently chucked the rest of my stash down there. I vowed to myself to never do it again while looking in the small mirror.

I needed a shower, but I sunk into the large white bed and was surprised at how large the space was. Large wooden beams and a high V-shaped roof. If only I was coherent enough to appreciate it, but soon enough, it all started: stage two or stage four or whatever stage somebody with better medical knowledge would dictate. I lay on my back, heart pounding so hard that I wouldn't be able to sleep. So, I had to lay there, wide awake and feel the self-inflicted mental strain.

I had been there before but this was strong.

I started my breathing exercises, breathing regular and constant; regular and constant but it was inevitable, and the mind went there anyway.

At first, discombobulation and confusion. How long would I feel like this? How long would I be in total panic? The heart wouldn't stop, it wouldn't slow, if anything, it increased in speed.

Probably because it had just ingested and registered the last of it. The brain was irritated and the lack of gratitude intensified: 'I hate the City – that fucking office – I hate this fucking space!' Whenever I thought of warm faces, it revealed their dark energies and created a rush of anxiety. Solus: her face turned into the demon nun from the film I watched with Nayarra, then, into a black blur and my body and mind would recoil. The same for Ritchie, Plum, Coco, H… anyone, anyone except for Nayarra and Scatty Alice.

My mind announced my loneliness and I felt as if I was sinking – slowly sinking. I could see myself falling into a black mass below, and I would reach my arm out to the surface that looked like glistening water. My hand struggled to reach it – calm and rippling and dark. Whatever it was, I was being dragged down by its weight. I could see what was above the water although the water was shining and moving. I could see a new flat; I could see my friends clean and sober, peering down at me. I could see the business and its exponential growth but they are unattainable – especially as I was sinking and sinking further into the black.

My mind sunk further into a flatline. Any hopes or dreams were nulled by negativity and fear. 'You will never make it this way, it is all hopeless.' Then, after a struggle, time stopped completely. I was in the present – fully in the pain. My mind let me know that there was nothing for me in the future. I had already failed and the only thing left was… stillness and silence.

I lay there accepting my fate when there was a knock on the door. I was shocked and it gave me a jolt that enabled me to get up and answer, it was the receptionist, flustered and curious. 'Hi there, I was just checking that you are okay? We heard screaming and some loud noises.' I told her it was fine and it wasn't me, it must have been from somebody outside – some crack addict perhaps, and I was too intoxicated to hear or acknowledge.

I drank water from the kitchenette tap and sunk back into the bed, intermittently I blacked out but did not realise until I was woken by screams and shouts. So, I dragged myself out to the window to see if I could spot them, but I could not see anybody spare two younger girls walking home from a drinking hole. Their demeanour and lack of energy made me think that they were not the culprits, that they were upstanding citizens whose only crime was staying out on a Sunday. And so, I swayed back to the bed, slurring the words, 'Shut the fuck up!' to the rest of the road. The dark thoughts continue to alter my state. The shivering, the heartbeat. The pain. My mind leaking guilt about the money I spent to feel like this, forty a pop, fifty, sixty pounds to be in a bed, quivering in fear and broke.

I blacked out once more but woke violently as my chest crept out above the mattress and, before anything else, it curved as if I was possessed; I could hear something departing my mouth. I couldn't decipher it but could feel my warm and tainted breath exiting my body. I needed to say something else and I was unsure to whom, maybe it was to the musted air, or to the outer and expanding universe but there was a compulsion. And I struggled to say the words but I managed as a desperate whisper: 'Help... me! Help me please!' And it was then, it was then that I realised:

I realised that all this time, I was the one screaming.

Interlude

Crazy Girls

Aphrodite or later, Venus, was the Classical goddess of beauty and passion. She was a goddess, born from the depths of the sea as the waves stirred up the water and then laid calm to announce her presence. She was created as Cronus severed the genitals of Uranus and thrust them into the Brine. A foam formed, creating an image that would be the antithesis of male symbols. These biased, male symbols of order such as the sun, symmetry, or Mars.

I know of such women, women that live in the wild as if they themselves have been created by sea broth.

I have always been entranced and fascinated by them. By women who appear confident and wilfully party with the upmost imagination. It's not sexual, though Freudian. My mother was emotional, wildly unpredictable but had an over-arching energy of love. She went for the wrong men, she was sociable. She created an energy of success even if it wasn't there. Much like these girls. These girls who front with smiles and positivity, who take the party to the party. Tammy would say, 'You do have a lot of female friends.'

I would ashamedly say, 'I know, yes.'

She would return, 'But really… you have a lot of female friends.'

There was a plethora. I have tried with men and failed as,

inevitably, they will try it with your girlfriend. This is not speculative. It's a fact. There will be physical altercations and there is the perception that you are liaising with somebody just like you: shirt and jeans, mobile on a phone cover, chasing girls. Trying to make money, trying to be better than the man next to you.

These girls, these specific young women. Ethereal but dark nymphs with their zeitgeist clothes and long hair. Their zest for sensual simulation and social congregations. High heels or don't-give-a-fuck trainers. How men look at them – as if they rule the world.

I became attached to it, more so than ever when homeless. Their wild movements that could occur any day of the week. Their activities filled with the upmost deviance and imagination. Their aesthetic beauty.

I seldom ever slept with them. This type of person would not be girlfriend material for me unless you are okay with being profusely cheated on and her attending when you least expect it. You cannot plan with them, not really. In fact, you only and staunchly set a time and date when you know they won't turn up. That way, if you are tired, you will not be pestered.

They always see the beauty in things, even in a rubbish-lidden street scarred with congestion. The way they take a photograph on their mobiles – it is particular. It captures London's vast and complex atmosphere. As if every street is different in the moment, and the constraints of time move outward and slowly. Cities and places aren't well constructed areas with limits, they are not road maps and marked roads and landmarks. They are places of symmetry and beauty, just like them.

Similarly, they can become sensitive to a situation, if an area is too bungled, stressful – they implode. They have to feel released and to do what they want – when they want. The antithesis of how society is run.

. They can have bankers, models, millionaires, married men and they have them all. But who they end up with ultimately shadows who they are underneath. It justifies their cynicism of the world though it makes them feel safe. Ultimately these are men with no real prospects: drug dealers, men who already have kids, men with no money.

This story is also dedicated to these girls.

Chapter 20

Sober Life

"You can't stay sober today on yesterday's sobriety."
– Various

I had been avoiding Solus but spoke to Ritchie, mainly via text. We had developed a penchant for fake gangster talk. Threatening people that we didn't like, pretending that we were in the Gomorrah television programme. 'Let him see the fishes!' Gomorrah, what a prodigious programme and stripped of all theatricalities; pure and visceral drama. It was what it was without any decoration and Ritchie loved it. Unfortunately, these messages would come back to bite him but that is another story that I will tell not too far away in the future.

Ritchie was in Ibiza with his friend Matt. It must have been a strange holiday: just the two lads frolicking in the sand, holidaying in a location that some of us could only dream. I could imagine them comparing their sun-kissed skin as they swam in the refreshing saltwater, perhaps laughing, perhaps touching. Ritchie was well prepared; he went sober two weeks prior and got his asshole waxed. 'A back, sack and crack to be precise.' Why would you do that? Unless you were expecting something – we teased Solus as much as we could.

'Maybe he is confused?'

'Does he always do you from behind?'

I had been on a sober streak for three days and the downer in Old Street was still fresh in my memory. Although I had been avoiding her, Solus had been kicked out of her house and texted me about it. She never told me why she was kicked out, but with Ritchie being away, she would need to scrape and scrounge for a roof in some form. It happened regularly with her, her dad would return to the house where her grandma resided and oust Solus for some reason or another. "Okay, Solus. I can hang but I am sober at the moment.'

She seemed excited by this. 'Oh my word, me too! Let's do something sensible like the cinema or something and find somewhere to stay?' She had been sober of sorts since the New Forest, since she rebuffed my offer of class A in the darkness of the cinema.

We would need somewhere substantial to stay, worst case, a hostel or Airbnb but that could not be last minute. I couldn't handle the tent that night, I really couldn't. I had seen more hostile nights, but a fear had gripped me and my brittle mind could not compute. Perhaps the stint of sobriety had created some sanity in me. Perhaps, I could finally see my situation in its aberrant reality. I had slept in the tent the last few nights but I was acrimonious, fearful, and without the two drinks before bed, I was colder than usual.

It was getting late for the cinema so we met at the Kings arms and had an orange juice each, we tried to partake in civilised chat, almost like a new age. 'Yes, what's on at the cinema at the moment?'

'You should come to H Club more, Solus; Covent Garden is great!' We needed to find out where we were staying, so I made Solus call her father. He didn't answer and Solus pretended to cry. It was as if she thought her father could see her forged performance directly through the phone. Solus had trained as an actress, went to one of the top drama schools for two terms and left in obscurity. Another mystery that I would have loved to unravel at some point, but not right now.

We decided to go to the Swedish bar where I had met the Viking girl not long ago. Again, a soft drink each and free popcorn – texting other people simultaneously through the maturing night. We were doing so well, being sober and healthy that we decided to get something to eat. She insisted on Sophie's Steakhouse but I was being militant with my veganism. She ordered meat and I had a salad. Of course, I had to pick up the bill and I suddenly noticed something about Solus: she binge-ate her food and lots of it. Lots of hearty expensive food, gulping it down at great a pace for her almost midget size. Then, she abruptly went to the loo for quite some time. I thought she might be snorting but I knew she wasn't. She was out of money and supplies and I do feel she was taking sobriety seriously. Ritchie's rumours maybe…? And I had noticed that she had strange eating cycles, sometimes not eating at all for some time then, all of a sudden, binging followed by a long stint the loo. It could explain her physique, it was ultra-svelte and muscular with not an inch of fat. Abs and definition that would reflect off dim lighted bars and clubs. She seemed to always wear knee high boots, but that is a separate thought.

Solus was apprehensive when returning from the loo. Peering at every human body towards its entrance, checking what they maybe thinking. I made sure not to ask her questions, for tonight, we needed each other's trust and positivity. But we moved from the Steakhouse, still not knowing where we would stay in the progressing dark. We walked past the homeless man outside Sainsburys, Scottish and cheery and you could tell he had a great heart. Not like the aggressive ones who sigh when you give them the lowest of change. He had his pot and you could place money in, or not, and he would smile convincingly. Solus gave him a pound which was the most money I'd seen her spend in some time. I didn't tell him of my situation but I noticed that his sleeping bag was wet and wafer thin; If I ever got out of this mess, I promised myself that I would give him mine with its luxurious thickness and silk-like feel. This is only relatively speaking; nothing could halt the intense and isolating cold at four.

Solus and I decided to go to Nam Long, a Thai restaurant that turns into a late-night bar. We walked through the Thistle grove and past Scatty Alice's where I went through the side entrance to change my top. I left Solus on the path smoking a cigarette and hoped that Scatty did not see her. Scatty hated Solus with a vengeance. The last time she was there, the time when Solus decided to overdose – she had tried on some of Alice's dresses, purposely taking photos and putting them on Instagram. Potentially, I would have asked Alice if I could have stayed that night... potentially, but not now that I was with Solus... there would be no chance. Scatty Alice's new strict instructions were, 'When I go away, John, and you stay, Solus is never allowed in the house.' I grabbed a shirt that was half ironed, even though Nam Long at night could be full of the well-to-do types, checking your every appearance.

We walked down the dark path as it was now, full nightfall. Solus told me how she had been getting into Florence because of me – especially the song I listened to late at night: 'Falling' and I listened to her adulate while I smoked a cigarette through the narrowing path – cigarettes were safe in the sobriety manifesto.

We arrived at Nam Long and it was heaving with a certain demographic, the energy was ripe and full of posh delinquents. I knew the bouncer and he dutifully nodded as he let us in to the main, narrow bar. From the windows I could see many girls, smoking and joking in alcohol fuelled unity. As we entered, our resolve changed – with everyone around us, frolicking and drinking and having a good time. It was like the crowd was congruent in their statement. The statement that everything was going to be okay when you party. In fact, that it was a good thing. And so, Solus and me decided that we would have one drink – just the one, solitary alcoholic hit to align with the flow of the establishment. She decided on a flaming Ferrari, I had a beer and you only had to guess who picked up the bill. We sipped it and didn't feel guilty because we felt that we did well with our two or so days. We were almost sanctimonious in our previous purity, sniggering at the concept that everyone else had probably been drinking all week. We thought that we had made our point to ourselves and thought that we could return to sobriety whenever we wanted to. We would have our drink and return back to sobriety tomorrow.

Suddenly, we were drinking quickly because we knew the time was finite; Solus's dad would not answer and I thought the only place that we could possibly stay was in the Oakley Street building. Solus had suggested the crack den but, for me, never again. With the needles and the wide eyes by the crackling fire, I would feel colder there than in the tent.

At the bar, a man approached us, an older man with who was already merry: 'Hello, people!' he said to us and Solus was unhesitant.

'Hello!' and he beamed at the response. I couldn't decipher if he fancied Solus, usually men would; she was wearing a tight black top that accentuated her breasts. A leather skirt with black tights and knee-high boots, fitting for the sleek and elitist environment that surrounded us. The man proceeded to show us something.

'Guys, guys, look!' He pointed behind the bar. 'It's the owner, look!' The owner looked at him smiling.

'Hi, Edward.' he said.

'Me and the owner are really good friends.' He looked Solus up and down and said, 'Let me get you guys a drink.'

We thought about the sobriety, the one drink, but we also knew we needed some forward planning. This guy was extroverted, largely harmless, and most likely lived in the borough. There was also something lonely about him, as if his extroverted chat hid his desperation and futility.

The plan is always to pretend that you don't want to stay at their place, or at least that the thought didn't cross your mind so when it does happen, it was as if it happened organically and spontaneously.

Solus started to talk idly in the man's ear, almost as if she was flirting but it had the opposite effect – it seemed to repel him into indifference. He was an old Etonian that was now in oil. Oil was against so many of my millennial morals but my need to survive superseded it. And so, I tried to take his number, but instead, he made me add him on Facebook. It showed that trust was not whole, and the night may still be a long one.

For some reason, he maintained at close proximity and wanted us to see something. Solus said she was going to the loo but he jokingly grabbed her before she managed to get away. 'Guys, check this, CHECK THIS OUT!' And he opened the palm of his large hand to reveal the largest ball of white I had seen – bulging and almost iridescent among the shadow of the rowdy dwellers. The two drinks I had already and the buzz and live energy of the place made me excited about the drugs. But Solus, well, she was clever as she pretended to be nonchalant, unimpressed. She was almost self-entitled, as if she deserved a snort for the time spent with him. 'Well, can I have some then?' she said abruptly while amending her short skirt, and he was taken aback.

But he responded, 'Well, yes! Yes, of course!'

She took the wrap not-so-subtly, smiled and strolled down the dark, winding stairs. I gave the man a look as if to say, 'She's crazy, but harmless,' and we tucked into another drink. I felt bad and paid for this new and should-be-forbidden round. My reasoning was to warm him, and then, we would be more likely to stay at his elusive abode. 'Where do you live, mate?' Perhaps it was too abrupt of me; he seemed to sense something and sipped his drink slowly.

'I'm living with my sister at the moment, it's... complicated.'

I didn't pry too much and kept up the energy by looking around and smiling. I found it hard to smile but I could of course imitate. The one I have mentioned, the same one that Tammy hated. She could spot it from a mile away. Somebody would say a joke and I would place it on autopilot, the large creepy mouth opening from cheek to cheek, held longer than necessary.

Solus returned and I asked the man if I could have some, he said yes. And so I did. I went downstairs and snorted a large one while flushing the loo so nobody could hear the sound of sniffing. There seemed to be excess coke residue on the wood above the basin, somebody even left an empty baggie in the aloe vera plant. I flushed the chain again after urinating, skimmed a bit for Solus and myself and walked out of the cubicle only to see the man urinating.

'Hello! Can I have a bit, young John?' and I gave him his

own bag. 'See you upstairs!'

I went upstairs and noticed that there were some girls, highly attractive – dressed elegantly, some with slick hair and the bold red lipstick that seemed to be the taste du jour. Solus with the blonde hair and fake-tanned skin would not get away with that look, a different look, not better or worse… but different.

Solus asked where her drink was and suddenly recognised somebody through the glass exterior. 'Oh my word, it's that guy!' She turned around and sipped her drink towards me to hide her face. Now the man who we were hanging with was interested.

'Yes, I know him too, he is one of my dealers.' Solus smiled and nodded sharply in recognition. 'What shall we do, say hello?' the man said.

Solus told us fervently not to. 'No, no don't. HE HATES ME!' Perhaps this was the man she gave my phone to, or another dealer in London that she owed several thousands of pounds with. The man indulged himself in the crisis and drama while the tall drug dealer man clocked us through the glass, looking over, cautiously but looking. The man with the drugs started to talk.

'Look, I live across the road. We should go there into hiding – don't kill me though.' I was surprised by the revelation, considering he had said that he lived with his sister. He insisted on getting us another round and then we left. Before we did, while we were sipping our drinks, the drug dealer man from outside entered the bar and whispered something to the indifferent bar staff. The bar staff looked at us briefly and then carried on serving their drinks.

After our drink we started to walk with the main man, it was west from the bar, down the dark but beautiful Old Brompton Road towards Earls Court and Solus skipped as we walked. Smiling like an excited child. She knew the amount of drugs that he had – I was a little more cautious:

I still remembered Old Street.

Suddenly, the man received a phone call. As he was talking on the phone, he looked at us and then went back to his conversation. He was walking ahead and finally he looked at us. 'That was the bar we were just at, they warned me to not take you to mine?'

Solus soon interjected. 'That fucking guy, it was that drug dealer!'

The man didn't respond to Solus but continued. 'They said that you were bad news!' To be honest, Solus and myself were probably bad news. In the grand scheme of things, it was an accurate description. But for the life of me I did not know how they knew that; it was definitely the dealer stirring trouble and definitely something to do with Solus. The man continued. 'You are not going to mug me and kill me are you, John?' I would have taken offence if the image wasn't so comic, but I decided to lay out the truth.

'Listen, I don't know what they are going on about – and if you aren't comfortable with us coming to your flat, we completely understand we don't have to.' I tilted my left leg away from him as if to walk away. Solus looked at me with piercing eyes as if to say, 'What the fuck are you doing, it's getting cold!' And we started to walk again in silence.

As we walked in silence, there seemed to be a mutual recognition that we were going to his, until he turned again, a suspicious energy that consumed the air. 'Are you sure you guys aren't going to kill me?' Bizarre and offensive. I felt that I did not want to beg to stay at his, and if we did, it would probably make things worse. The whole reason I was in this situation, or at least a part of it was my disdain for begging. I did not want to beg to

204

my parents anymore, to the government – to any friend, hence why I was here, wandering endlessly. Physically uncomfortable, beyond uncomfortable at times but in my mind – it was better than relying on another fickle being.

I got firm with the man. 'Listen, nothing is going to happen, if you would prefer, we can leave, or we can go to yours and have a good time?'

He smiled at me with that idea and seemed to ease: 'Come on in, kids!' We got to his on the Redcliffe gardens and down into his dark basement flat. He changed from suspicious to excitable. 'What drugs do you guys want? I have every type!' He went to the kitchen and poured the gak he had from Nam long onto another pile that was mounded on his chopping board. I was grateful but recognised the rough wooden grain of the board was not the best surface. The man and Solus lit up a spliff and the smell consumed the room. I despised weed and snorted a line from the biggest mound I had ever seen. The sobriety that we were so proud about was well and truly over. In fact, it had plummeted to a new level; a copious amount of drugs and drink in major variety. Everything illegal and toxic was so abundant that we asked to invite Tonny, as Tonny loved drugs and Solus was always trying to impress her.

The man took off his top and sang to eighties music bare-chested, frolicking around and smoking a rotund spliff. Solus trying to join in, took her top off and exposed her breasts to the man's indifference. Wasting energy when there was no need. There was no need to try and hustle him – we were already in the flat. Tonny came unusually promptly and her large blue eyes bolstered when she saw the large mound. It was a fun moment for us, on an impromptu night of discovery. Whatever we wanted was ours for the taking.

Tonny tucked into some coke by scraping the fine powder around the wood-base and then Solus and the man took an enormous one, to the point where I tapped his broad back and gently told him to be careful. He leaned back and his large eyes bulged in ecstasy. 'Yes, yes, my friends!' Solus showed the man how to pour cocaine on a cigarette while Tonny showed her confusion as to why I was drinking.

'I thought you were going sober for a while?' I remembered that I told her I couldn't party two days ago for that very reason. She could see that the idea was well and truly sunken. That the partying had us locked in its vice-like grip once again. In fact, sobriety maybe hindered us from safe- ish shelter in the future: it alleviates anxiety, makes people with potential housing lose their guard, and makes for a convivial homeless experience. I have said it before:

Now I know why tramps drink at night.

They smoked and giggled while me and Tonny stayed near the white mound, snorting as soon as any affect from the previous line wore off. I asked them to put on some of my song choices but they did not listen and, after ten minutes, the man told us he was feeling tired and went to his bedroom. He kindly let us stay and said we could stay anywhere in the party room. Solus and Tonny decided to move on and they went to the den of all iniquities… They skimmed a large amount of what was remaining from the mound and took it to that place. They offered me to go there to which I wholeheartedly declined. I would never go there again with the needles and chairs and eighties crack cocaine. A frequency so low that it stripped the humour out of life's calamities. As if you are looking in mirror that enhances your imperfections and negative idiosyncrasies.

I decided to sleep on his sofa I put my bag next to me and

206

used the sofa cushions and coat as covering. The sofa was large and comfy and before I went to sleep, I skimmed some of the mound for sparser times. I hoped that he wouldn't notice how compromised his stash was. Due to his state I doubt he would, and even if he did, he probably had a brick stashed away in a safe or trap door. I could imagine him skimming it for times just like these. I dimmed the lights and started to doze on the sofa when I heard somebody come back into the room. Quietly they creeped. It was the man and he said he was looking for something. I foolishly turned around to see him walking around, in only a T-shirt, his cock peeking out and flapping around in the dark. There was an energy about him that made it seem contrived, his movements speculative and calculated. I tried to not acknowledge by pretending to be asleep, my head turned towards the inner sofa, no movement from my body until finally he went back to his bedroom. I modified my set up by putting my bag near my back area in case he tried to rape my asshole.

I found it harder to sleep and soon, he came in again. I didn't look towards his direction but I knew the cock was there, flapping around near the bottom of his T-shirt. He was doing the I-am-looking-for something routine and I hoped he noticed the bag by my ass. A strong and silent code, a code stating that, 'I am not interested.'

He was creepy but I could also feel his heart. That he was potentially exploring his sexuality, perhaps for one of the first times and I felt that he would never use physical force. He was like a lost puppy and the smile he gave me at the bar now made sense. My coked-up brain worked all of this out within what seemed a millisecond in passing time.

He finally retreated and left me to sleep, I felt relatively safe, and I am not sure why but I slept some. I imagined that Tonny and Solus would still be at it, snorting skimmed coke and smoking crack by the crackling fire and I vowed to myself to return to sobriety just like the last time… but it didn't happen.

I woke up in the morning, fairly fresh. No huge coke downer or depression but needing a shower. I went to say goodbye to the man by quietly knocking on his door. He said to come in and he was in the bed, tucked in his duvet, lying on his large back in reflection. 'I just wanted to say many thanks for having us, I have tidied a bit and perhaps speak soon.' He looked at me with a certain vulnerability, almost trying to work something out and I knew what it was as Ritchie, well, Ritchie did the same. He was worried if I was annoyed that he was floating around in just a T-shirt. So, with subliminal messaging, letting him know that everything is going to be okay. I looked him in the eye, a rare occurrence for me, and put my right thumb up in awkwardness. He let out a small relief-like smile.

'See you later, John, take care.'

I walked out the flat, wondering where Solus and Tonny would be now.

A few days later in the City office, I decided to look up the oil man. I took a look at his Facebook wall while sipping a coffee and noticed something was different. It was filled with RIPs and blessings. His sister, who I could see was friends with somebody in the office, had written a three-paragraph commemoration. It looked like the man was dead, actually fully dead. Not somebody said he was dead but he wasn't, this was the end. Final. And my concern moved to a major point that the bar staff may have thought that he was killed, murdered by not other than Solus and me.

That night after work, I ran to the Nam Long restaurant with the hope of showing myself so it didn't seem that anything was untoward. When I entered, it was the same bar staff of the night in question, and they looked at me with a mix of suspicion and disappointment.

'Hi,' I said to them, to which they paused, nodded and said hi back. I asked them about the man that we were with.

'Edward?'

'Yes.' They remembered of course, as they were the ones who warned him about us. 'Do you know what happened to him? I looked at his Facebook and…'

The main waiter continued to wipe the bar. 'Yes, he unfortunately died.' And I asked what from. 'Blood pressure, yes from the partying and everything they say.'

Shit. Blood pressure, I suppose he was older but… these toxins, all of these narcotics, it is true what they say: in the end, the result will always be something like this.

Plum's theory was wrong and one day she would find out herself. I am sure you would believe me if I said of the people I hung around the most in this book, a while after these events took place, two became impregnated with low-life drug dealers and were reliant on their stash, one of those developed a serious auto-immune disease. Another would have to go to narcotics meetings for the rest of her life to stay sober and I myself continued an on and off struggle. Cocaine is not something that you can do and leave as perceived; it sticks to you like wet druggy mud. It will find a way to find you again, and it will, unless you repulse it with the upmost aggression.

Chapter 21

Whip Girl

"He hit me and it felt like a kiss; I can hear violins... give me
all that ultraviolence."
– Lana Del Rey 2014

I had been interviewing all day, not so much for an intern, but for a remote candidate who could send the occasional email. I interviewed in the H Club and Solus came over to say hi and assist. I hadn't seen her since the death of the basement man and our failed sobriety. To be truthful, we avoided the thought of it, and carried on with our lives that were now, almost the same as before: frolicking and looking for angles.

If I mentioned it with Solus, she would say, 'Ohhh... nooo!' in a laboured form of sadness, but what she really meant was: it's inconvenient – do not mention it again, especially in public.

The candidates flowed into one of the drawing areas on the second floor. Me and Solus had a drink by our side, one beer and one wine but no cocktails. A few came. All female, all eager and it seemed to put Solus at unease. She seemed to feel threatened by the beauty and drive that some of them had to offer. One beaconed out from the mass and Solus knew she was my type. Tall and athletic but with unflinching femininity; neat hair that clipped the middle of her neck.

She interviewed but I wasn't sure she was suitable, though,

she was intrigued by us and seemed to stay around after the interview, potentially curious as to what happened next. Next though, maybe something that she would regret.

There was a dead silence and Solus got aggressive. 'Okay, that's the interview then!' I walked the girl to the lift and told her how I was going to move to Chelsea for an office, how we had all these plans. How I was trying to be as successful as possible.

I re-instated the fact that I was the member at H Club. Retrospectively, looking back, I wish I had taken her number, not for interning but potentially for dating although that would not be etiquette, and the moral boundaries were grey.

The issue was, my mind was preoccupied with Solus and what she had planned… I knew that she was grooming me for this weekend but there was a caveat – Scatty Alice had let me stay for the weekend so I didn't need Solus, in fact, Scatty Alice had said that I could stay the entire weekend with the usual rule that Solus was not to attend. Alice said that Tammy could stay, but at this stage, we were so estranged that I didn't even tell her. I didn't tell Solus either.

Ritchie, Oli and Henry were meeting up at the Builder's Arms and Solus asked me if I would go. It would be good to see the guys but I was less than eager. I wanted to hang around and perhaps talk to whatever girls would let me and take them back to the comfortable basement den on the Thistle Grove – it wasn't long before Solus bought up the subject, the subject of drugs. It always tends to be after the second drink; no more, no less.

Solus: Shall we order then?

Me: No, I'm not doing it at the moment as I said I had the worst comedown.

Solus: You have done it since then so we may as well, remember?

Me: I thought we aren't supposed to talk about that. No and it's expensive, I can't be bothered to pay to feel like shit.

Solus: Well, I think it's my turn to buy so it won't come out of your pocket – my treat.

I paused for a second and thought of the consequences, only a second or two. My body said no but my mind said it was a winning situation.

Me: Okay.

I had broken it again, less than a week but felt like a lifetime. And at least I wasn't paying for it, so, in that sense I had kept my word. We sat in the comfortable couches in another reception area and Solus was frantically texting – most likely the boys on the Kings Road.

'This wine is disgusting, babe – do they have anything else?' She said while typing furiously. Then, she left for ten or so minutes. 'Right, okay, so I am going to pick this up!' She went out to meet the dealer but again seemed to take a lifetime. I took my laptop out and proceeded to do some much needed business work: checking out the candidates and saying yes or no, making notes and checking sales and then... she returned.

I was indifferent about the coke; I was rather enjoying the beer and the laptop but Solus snuck it to me in a wallet and placed it on my lap. I did a line and gave it back, the issue now? The issue was now I had a taste for it.

All of a sudden, Solus decided to create conflict. 'When are you going to get some new clothes, John? You don't have to behave like this.' I took it on the chin until she insisted I bought her another drink. I shrugged and hesitated... and then did. She told me how she bought the coke and, therefore, I should buy the drinks. This, in turn, led to a debate – I explained how I bought everything, all the time, in the vast majority of situations which made her storm away into the nearby lift: 'I'M GOING TO LEAVE. YOU CUNT!'

Now I knew how Ritchie felt when he told me she would create an argument out of thin air, purely for the purpose of destination. And I knew exactly where she was going.

Solus went with the boys and I didn't fancy seeing them – it would be harder to chat to girls with their statistical noise and competitive flexing. And as the loneliness crept in, I decided to call Tammy; I let it ring and ring to voicemail twice and left a text message: 'How are you?' I could see it was delivered but she did not respond for the rest of the night. After this, I capitulated and went to see them. It was Solus and the chaps: Ritchie, Oli, Henry and herself and as I got towards the Kings Road they were already inebriated. Oli was in a cuffed blue shirt moving frantically and animated. Solus and the rest of them drinking in good humour.

They were pleased to see me and soon, I got into the spirit. We moved to a secret hotel bar and I skimmed some of Solus' drugs so I didn't have to keep asking. Oli was volatile, shouting up and down the street and trying to antagonize random passers-by. The other boys tried to appease him while Solus found it amusing. I was indifferent and checked my phone – another sale, perhaps Tammy will contact me now. Perhaps she would, even if it was because she had no choice.

My mind flitted towards work: I could ditch this degenerate show and go and do some work at Scatty's and all of this self-righteous chat that never quite happens but you think it and feel superior and then… Oli spotted a homeless man outside the hotel bar and I notice there was a police van nearby. The homeless man asked for some change.

'Oh fuck off, you cunt,' said a slurring Oli.

The homeless man hit back as Oli started to sway somewhat: 'Oh, you fuck off.'

Henry and Ritchie kept track of the police car that was definitely populated and Oli decided to retaliate; a fruitless task, an immature approach. 'WHO ARE YOU TELLING TO FUCK OFF, YOU DIRTY CUNT!' And Oli, in his drunken state, his skinny legs swaggering, tried to kick the tramp as the boys tried to hold him back, and I wondered why the police had not seen this as Solus let out a theatrical squeal. I looked to my right and the night had taken hold of the City; a Lamborghini screeched by. There were a block of flats named after Nell Gwyn, the original Chelsea girl. There were many shirted men and elegant women.

The boys lost interest in holding Oli back and he managed to kick the tramp, square in the face. Now I remembered when people asked me why I hang with the girls, it was because the men held the same insecurities, only they had fists. After a spray of crimson red exit the tramps face, the tramp tended to his bloody nose. He was unperturbed, took some of the blood into his hand and spat it at Oli as the boys half-heartedly asked him to stop. I looked at the tramp, bloody-nosed and used to the adversity. It was as if I had known him for a thousand years. His eyes had seen what I had seen in on those windy black nights.

'Oli, leave him be.'

Oli was confused. 'What the fuck, why, John? He's disrespecting me!' As Oli tried to push past me, I swung him to the floor.

'LEAVE HIM THE FUCK ALONE, OKAY!' And the guys pulled me off.

I could hear Solus, softly and inappropriately singing, 'and it's ultraviolence….it's ultraviolence.' She hummed to herself, as if it was a default. As if this was a drilled routine when she saw violence. As if she had seen it regularly in her past.

I pulled Oli back up and fixed his shirt in place. 'I'm sorry, Oli… but he's out of bounds.'

And I left them, and walked through the side street as Ritchie and Solus shouted, 'Where the fuck are you going?' I liked Oli, but his darkness and trauma could shroud the brightness of occasion. I do not know what happened to him as a child but, for a West London boy, he was decidedly erratic.

I decided to go to the bars in the area of Alice's flat: the Swedish bar where I met the Viking actor, and then to a side pub – nothing was happening. Stupidly, I ordered drugs because I had a taste and thought that would give me the balls to approach. I stocked Alice's fridge with bottles of prosecco just in case but the night was dead for a weekend. People sprawling in and out of Maggie's or the overpriced pub on the corner, but they were preoccupied or waiting for a taxi. I took some time out to see if what I was doing was predatory, for me it wasn't. I was looking for girls to hang out with, maybe shag, and I would be honest about it. Honest with them, and honest with me – a natural exchange.

I walked back towards the Sainsbury's and I saw the homeless Scottish man looking more gaunt than he did. He recognised me and we exchanged words; other people seemed to know him and said hi too. Two other tramps seemed to appear regularly, one with a sheetless duvet, brown with dirt.

I saw three Ladies walking and I approached. 'Ladies, hi, sorry to approach out of the blue, I have a flat across the road, prosecco, and wondered if you wanted to party?' Two of them promptly declined and I noticed that they were all a little older than me, mid to late thirties – potentially a reason for their sensibilities.

One of the girls accepted excitedly and she was the most attractive. The one I would have chatted to anyway if I had the choice.

They warned her against it, 'He's a stranger, why would you do that?'

I let them bicker amongst themselves with the thought that if I tried to argue my case, it would make me look desperate. More lecherous and needy which is the fastest way to a lonely night. Meanwhile Ritchie was texting me, 'Oi you forkin cunt, I'm gonna have you whacked. Solus is still with us lol – we run Chelsea. You should see Henry he's chatting up all the girls, killing all of your crew! We own it now.'

The girl decided to come and the girls asked her to text her as soon as she got to the flat. I was considerably drunk and gagging for a line and walked the girl to Alice's. She had long blonde hair and a neat physique but even to this day I am not sure of her real name, certainly not the surname. I know that the first name begins with an M: Miranda or Melanie or...

We got to the flat and walked down the stairs, she asked if the place was mine as Scatty Alice's photos consumed the stair area. 'Yes, it is. I'm renting but I have to move very soon.'

'Oh, it's wonderful, aren't you lucky?' she said.

I responded, 'Yes, yes... I'm very lucky.'

We drank the prosecco that was now chilled and I was glad I did it. I realised that I must always do that, just in case. Just in case it happens in the closing moments like it does so many times. And if a party does not happen, at least I have spare ethanol.

We drank and I tried to kiss her on the lips to which she teasingly denied – she worked in marketing in some form, for Harrod's or some luxury brand along those lines, but I switched off after her first diatribe on how everyone was being underpaid in this town. The issue was, I still was gagging for a line, the sobriety from before was all but lost. Not even glimmers of it could be felt; rather than Old Street, my mind was back to Lacrimosa.

Hours had past and instead of asking her, I placed some on a plate and racked it accordingly.

'OOOOH!' she screamed. 'I'm supposed to be off the stuff!' and I felt that I had to ask her why. 'I get a little crazy when I do it, yeah, my parents had to be involved.' I remember her telling me her age, mid to late thirties and wondered why her parents were still in the picture, then again, when I am that age, as things are going, mine will have an undeniable role in my destiny.

I didn't tell her to have any, I didn't even point to the rolled-up piece of paper that lay in her direction. She just came, knelt down and helped herself to a generous proportion. She rubbed a bit into her gums and we went outside to smoke by the bench. She took it upon herself to give me the inquisition.

'So what do you do, John, clarify for me?' Usually, I would skip the issue but I could tell that I wouldn't get a kiss tonight if I didn't - and so I laid the career glossing on as thick as the line I placed on the cigarette.

Me: I'm also marketing in the City.

The girl: Oh, are you in finance?

Me: Yes… in a way…

The girl: Oh wow, big money then.

Me: Can't complain.

I puffed a cigarette while I said it, she fell silent, and I could see that she was relatively impressed. Not so much about the money, but that she had verified this slightly dishevelled looking man in Chelsea. He had a good job in her mind and had a wonderful one bed in the most exclusive borough in Central London.

We went back and had more prosecco and coke and smooching commenced. She had a muscular but slender body, immaculately toned to which she told me was from teaching Pilates on the side. I was starting to get tired, genuinely and so I pulled the bed down from the wall in Scatty Alice's sitting room.

'Ohh… bed so soon?' She stated, disappointed and wanting to stay up. I promised to stay up for another hour or so, much to the struggle of my brain and I realised that I was, yet again, wasting a night's sleep in the security.

We kissed and started to strip and she let me do cocaine on her pert breasts. It continued to change in that direction, you see M, or Whip Girl as she would become to be known, was very sexual. She had seen Scatty Alice's equestrian collection in the corner and told me to collect the small riding whip. She asked me to whip her while she was naked and then to fuck her from behind. I said I would do as long as I could tape the whipping to show my friends – not only would it provide humour, it also provided a safety blanket; other people would be shared in these quite bizarre requests. A necessity I thought, in case she would murder me in the night.

She snorted a line as I proceeded to whip her with the riding whip, videoing on my mobile. Her naked body glistened in the dark light and she smiled with an air of gratification. At first, I half-heartedly whipped her naked rear and then, I hit her with firmness. I apologised immediately but was soon told it was the perfect amount of thrust and spank. She swayed her head in

218

ecstasy as I hit her firmly and I could soon see the red stripes across her pale skin. A different ultraviolence to what I had witnessed a few hours ago – it was voluntary and elegant and she was in her carnal element.

I moved across to get the condom from my laptop bag. I always kept one, just in case, and I paused for a second as I realised that this was the first time I would be shagging since Tammy. We started to have sex and, as I was on top, she made me strangle her which I did, softly, but then she briskly grabbed my arms to create more and more constriction.

'Yes! Yes!' She grinned with a strange smile that confirmed to me this girl was eccentric and likely had secrets varying in quality. Secrets that I did not want to know at this moment. Secrets I may never want to know. The sex was good, and we stayed up finishing the remnants of the bag and smoking a cigarette outside which was now, worryingly cold.

I tried to show her the art of putting coke on a cigarette, but she exclaimed that it was crack. I told her that it was nothing of the sort, that crack was a substance that was created differently. I told her that crack was a derivative of cocaine in powdered form, it is combined with water and baking soda. I told her it was a sore subject. She left in the morning, early, to teach Pilates and I wondered how, how in the state she was in did she manage to do that.

We had exchanged numbers and, as I could not remember her name, I named her 'The Whip Girl', or 'Whip Girl' for short. The whipping video was sent out en masse that very night and I still have it to this day. Soon enough, I was to see Whip Girl again.

Chapter 22

Hackney Office

"Hackney at certain epochs has given itself suburban airs and graces, before being slapped down and consigned once more to the dump bin of aborted ambition."
– Iain Sinclair 2009

I looked forward to going into Hackney, what a dichotomy: 'Hackney' and 'look forward' in the same sentence. It wasn't the shitty transport links, sporadic corner shops or pseudo-Shoreditch residents I was looking forward to. I was looking forward to seeing Monica. Monica and her long brown hair. Her elegant clumsiness that made me wonder if she knew how attractive she was. She wasn't hyper intelligent, more a type of intellectual intelligence that you would expect from an Oxford graduate. Overall, her cognitive package made Oxbridge seem overrated.

I nearly went to Cambridge myself; Classics. Went for a taster tutorial but the lecturer repelled me with his pretences. 'If you haven't read the Odyssey, you are but only half educated.' Ended up in London: English and History.

I did the tea in the mornings, she would have a herbal and I would make sure to hand it to her first. The boss wasn't in – hardly ever was but she made the great plan of me having to work closely with Monica, she helped me to source business names of fat cats. The boss must have thought I was a happy-go-lucky asexual, one that would never semi-fall-in-love with her precious assistant.

Monica would speak calmly and passively and was the very opposite to what happened in South-West: she wore blue nineties denim jeans that were oversized on the waist, followed up with Dr Martens and a black necklace. She walked clumsily, without trying to enforce sexuality that societal standards had placed upon women. I believe that the other assistant was into her – they would always chat and joke and I would shrug it off to the fact that they knew each other before my arrival. It's hard to be a part of the 'in -jokes'. Nothing to do with the fact that they were a few years younger and were a part of the East London thing. Their humour would probably be deemed down to earth.

They didn't seem to mind that the park opposite, whatever it was called, was effectively derelict. It stank of dog shit and there were hooded drug dealers moping around on bicycles. I almost approached them myself, to see if I could get a deal before returning to the sleekness of South-West. It would be cheaper here… everything was cheaper here.

They seemed to be comfortable, this was their London experience. Ours was something quite different. We didn't feel right unless there were models walking the streets, expensive cars revving, and people acting as if they own the world and the small, tailored dogs that have jumpers on. But it wasn't ours really. Really, none of it was. It was just a part of the escape – all part of a gloss that we thought made us something special, but, if I didn't shower for a couple of days, I stank just like the tramp on a Hackney Street. This had been proven.

Some people work and then they party at the weekend to escape. That's their let-loose. The friendship groups and their cozy flats with rugs and flat mates make their arduous role in the office, most likely the service industry, seem relevant. They are hyped up by their friends who have similar jobs and they discuss workmates with each other and bosses while drinking wine and maybe a bag and that's their assurance.

Ritchie told me an alternative. 'I work to fucking get away from it all!' He told me that he goes to work in property to escape. To escape Solus with her secret eating disorders and shagging around, to escape the flat mate who is reportedly shagging his sister. To escape cocaine and bickering and spending money on toxins that store in your body.

I thought about Ritchie and thought, 'Yes, you maybe correct, for once in your life. Your philosophy may well have a spark of intellect. I sometimes need work to escape – to escape the frantic energies.'

This new girl in Hackney was part of the escape. Another girl that tended to be further away from my grasp than I even knew, but the dream was still there. That we could run away together in a one-bedroom flat – I would pay most of the rent of course but she would pay a bit and learn from me and my business ways and in the evening we would… As I was thinking this, she coughed and seemed to have a look of disgust on her face.

'John, I am just going into the other room, okay?' I thought to myself – the smell of sweat couldn't be emanating from me again, could it? I made an effort to wash in the gym that morning with my own shower gel and a clean towel. I looked across to my armpit and saw an ever-growing patch of wetness. There was a smell of must as I went towards it. Not only that, but I started to itch again which would be due to sleeping in the office. I used my coats to separate myself from the carpet, but recently I had started to use my roll mat. I kept it in the clogged-up shower room they had on the vicinity and would pull it out at night. I remember turning in my sleep and my face touching the dusty carpet. The carpet, ridden with flea type things or something that made me itch. And now, what could be even worse, is that the roll mat could be compromised. So, I went to the loo and sprinkled myself with water while sneaking a look at Monica to see if she was mentioning it to her assistant friend.

She was laughing with him, Sam, completely in the moment and for once I prayed, just prayed that she went into the other room to hang with Sam… rather than my acquired scent.

I heard them talking about Brexit and how Monica's parents were Polish, she said there was much prejudice around in these strange days. Sam was equally perturbed at the result, and I made sure that I did not even mention the way I voted. They continued and I felt I should at least try to justify the leavers with something, with some sort of substantiated advice.

'Well at least the house prices will not be so high now.' I wasn't even sure what I meant by that. I suppose what I meant was that Europeans would not so easily be able to buy the housing which was easily counter attacked by Sam.

'The housing that you are talking about, the ones inflating the prices are bought by Arabs, Russians and the Chinese.' So, I myself had got caught up in the leavers confused immigration rhetoric. Monica was detached from the conversation, and I am sure I did not do myself any favours.

I opened the window as wide as it could be, even forcing it and used the roll-on that was in my bag – back in the day, one shower a day would be sufficient, but now, with all the moving around and the grease, bugs, anxiety and alcohol – body odour was intrinsic. Monica's beauty was hard to explain. It was a type of reassurance – that the world isn't just ugly. That there are grey areas: there are ugly things and there are beautiful things. Monica was a beautiful thing.

On the way from the office and towards the tube station, headphones in: MXMS, Delooze, followed by Florence. I see a billboard over the large motorway or bypass that you have to cross to get to the Hackney station. It was a man, advertising his underwear including socks – a large picture of him with a part of his collection and he flashed a watch from his side. The successful man on the billboard, while I walked across a grey crossover onto a packed train towards somewhere I didn't live.

Chapter 23

Whip Girl Meets Solus

"Recent figures suggest that up to 1/3 of millennials may never be able to own their own home and have no other option aside from renting property their entire lives – while 1/2 will rent well into their forties."

–   ABC finance

I set up the tent in the bocage, as comfortable as possible and a night I didn't mind; my phone on full charge and next to me. I had my softening drinks and the road was quieter than usual. I settled, feeling accomplished as I had done my work in the day and the business in the night and I had not spent money in the evening on accommodation.

I sunk into the sleeping bag and roll mat as much as I could. And with everything, when you don't need them, that's when they come. A vacuum that the universe creates but nobody understands why. The phone announced itself – twice: one call was Solus and one was Whip Girl. I hadn't seen Whip Girl since, well, the night she made me violently whip her and acquired her name. This time, she wanted me to go to a party with her friends towards Hammersmith.

'Come meet my friends, lots of free drink!' Solus also wanted to meet, even had her own drugs. For once.

I thought it would be an idea to merge the two.

'Hey, Whip, do you mind if my friend Solus comes?'

'Ha-ha Solus? What a cool name.' She checked with her friends and we went to Hammersmith. I had to pack my tent up and Scatty Alice was the other way, so Solus offered to take it to her grandmas along with my sleeping bag and bag and they were both happy to see me. Solus's father was luckily away.

I left my stuff and Solus's grandmother, still up, decided to wash them. 'I am gonna wash them for you, John!' I told her not to, but I did not want to offend her. And off we went, to Whip Girl's party in Hammersmith. A wonderful one bedroom that her male friend and his Australian girlfriend had apparently purchased. They were in finance and you couldn't help but be intimidated by their success. They asked me where I lived.

'Oh, Thistle Grove in Chelsea.'

'Oh, Chelsea! Nice! Do you rent or…?'

My response: 'Oh yeah I rent… at the moment.' They nodded, satisfied with the comment and I decided to take a look around as well as go to the bathroom. I added some spray on my clothes that had a whiff of wet grass.

Whip girl found me, kissed me and I was glad I had brushed my teeth in the gym before heading to the bocage. She grabbed my hand. 'You must come and meet my best friend!'

'Hi there,' I said, and was wondering what Solus did to her cocaine. The girl said hi and offered us prosecco with the rest of the poncy Hammersmith cunts. I noticed that they had champagne in the fridge that a select few were drinking and the rest of us were left with the prosecco. The sanctimonious chat about buying a place had fucked me off and I wondered exactly how old they were.

Then, they bought out cocaine and I wondered is there any corner in this town, any corner whatsoever that has not been affected by this stuff. Probably not – across the City – 2.7 million pounds a day.

They gave us a line and Solus joined in but I wouldn't let her get away with it – I knew she had more. Whip girl's friend tried to talk to me, but I couldn't remember her name and was more concerned about how I could get to the champagne, and even more concerned if Solus had listened to me when I begged her not to get her tits out.

Everyone relaxed into conversation and I decided to take the bottle out of the fridge. I felt somebody behind me nudge and it was Solus. 'Yes, please.'

I poured some into the glass and told Solus, 'I want a fucking line.'

She sipped her drink and said, 'You just had one of theirs.'

I don't know if she was aware how personal this became, but I was irate. 'And now I want one of yours… come on for fuck's sake!' I didn't really need it, the buzz from the last still had me elevated, but this was about principle.

I could see that people had branched out onto the balcony, of course they had a fucking balcony. And so, Solus took me into the loo where we did a line and then she skimmed half for me and wrapped it in a receipt. Seemingly satisfied that I was begging for her drugs.

We got back to the main room and people were asking who drank some of the champagne. Then, I heard somebody say it was 'them'. Before we knew it, and very abruptly, we were asked to leave. I think they wanted us to leave anyway; I was giving them the snobby I'm-better-than-Hammersmith subliminal, purely because my dirty clothes were stored in SW10.

And thus, we left, Whip Girl came with us and suggested that we go to hers. She didn't seem embarrassed by the fact we

227

were told to leave, even when we were exiting and her friend ran after her. 'Wait! Wait!' She called out whip girl's real name: Miranda… or Martha. 'Are you going to be okay?' suggesting that me and Solus were dangerous which I thought was ludicrous until my mind drifted to Nam Long and the man in the basement.

As we walked down the stairs, the lights shut off and we used the phone light. Solus and me giggled. 'What is it they say on Harry Potter? Lumius!' Whip girl looked dissatisfied. Confused as to why two people approaching their late twenties were quoting children's films, but nobody can deny that these books get dark towards the end.

We got to Whip Girl's and we skipped past the flat-mates, into her room where me and Solus got the coke out, we proceeded to snort a line on a silver tray that Whip Girl had on her dressing table. Her flat was in one of the brown builds in West Kensington but, considering there were two flatmates, it was eery and quiet.

The sitting room was always empty, partly because Whip Girl congregated in her bedroom with its feminine perfumes and neatly tucked-in duvet that faced a wall-mounted TV. After the line, we were high and joyful and were still smirking about being kicked out of a party. Whip girl started to smooch me while the three of us lay in bed. She tapped me on the head while she went to the bathroom with Solus and they returned in nightwear, namely, skimpy shorts and a T shirt.

Me and Whip start to smooch again and I felt bad for Solus though, at the end of the day, it was accommodation; Whip Girl gets what Whip Girl wants.

Our high state made us progress into a sexual state despite Solus's attendance. We got under the duvet and I stripped off my trousers. Solus, a veteran of threesomes, tried to join in as I was taking off Whip Girl's bra and started to nuzzle her breasts. Then,

I felt Solus lift the duvet only to see my naked rear. 'Oh jeez, okay!' she exclaimed.

She crawled up the duvet cover and in a strange, mechanical movement, placed one of whips breasts in her mouth. Then, she released the breast from her mouth while making a popping sound with her lips. Whip girl wasn't into it. 'Babe, stop, Solus stop. I love you, babe, I'm just not into women.'

Solus seemed indifferent and Whip had an idea. 'Why don't you give me and John some private time and just go in the kitchen for a bit, if you keep quiet, you can take the plate with you.'

Solus ran towards the idea. It left me and Whip on our own and I appreciated the time we had together; the drunken, high intimacy – riddled with excitement. She got out from the bed, revealing her trained physique as she dimmed the lights and put on a candle. I thought to myself, this is romantic and nice; fifteen to twenty minutes of love making and back to the drugs with my de facto best friend. Then, sleep, not too late I hoped.

We got back under the covers, kissed and caressed and I thought I needed to get a condom, but Whip pushed me on the chest and whispered, 'Wait'. She made me stand upright which was frustrating – I already missed being horizontal in the warm bed. She reached for the cupboard and took out a riding paddle and a riding bat. She asked which one I wanted to use and to be honest I was looking forward to conventional, missionary sex but this was her house. And this was her way. She let me stay in the warm; the least I could do was whip her until she was satisfied.

I chose the riding bat because, marginally, it looked more friendly. She got back on the bed and bent over on all fours, her face grinned cheekily, and I knew this was her favourite position. And there, stark naked, I whipped her on her bare ass until there were red marks. She groaned in pleasure, but quietly so to not disturb her flat mates or Solus, who seemed to be engulfed in the stealthiest of silences. Whip Girl wanted more: 'HARDER,' she kept telling me. 'HARDER,' her dissatisfaction could be seen on her shadowy face. 'FUCKING WHIP ME!' she said with eyes that would not look at me, as if to hide the unnecessary anger that were in them. And thus I tried, indeed I did. Although it went against all my instincts – I struck by swinging my arm upwards and the struck down with what I thought was all my might. But however much I struck, she seemed to be able to take it and I realised it must do with the design of the bat until I accidently hit her lower back – she raised herself up off the bed and down again, still on all fours.

She had her fill and dragged me onto the bed, threw a condom at me and we proceeded with missionary sex. As we touched, I could feel that she was still shaking for the excitement of being beaten quite thoroughly by horse apparatus, and she groaned as we started to fuck slowly. I wish I lasted longer but my concentration... it was jilted by the fact that Solus had all the coke to herself, and I could still smell the grass on my skin from laying in the tent not-so-many hours ago.

We climaxed... or at least I did. Whip girl rolled over on her stomach and smiled and I hope she was satisfied. I needed sleep but there was still coke left. Coke and the fact I did not have to work in the City tomorrow.

We beckoned Solus who came in with the tray and a rolled-up receipt. She tilted her head up towards us and smiled in the candlelight. 'You guys are so nineties.' To this day, I do not know what that means, and to be honest, neither did she. Whip Girl put on her small shorts and joined us for a line. As she came to the tray, I saw the reflection of my triceps on the mirror, made golden by the flickering light. Solus was directly left to me holding the tray, still tranquil, head tilted. Whip girl to the left with her tight shorts and firm ass. I looked at this in the mirror and I thought that this could have been painted by Da Vinci, but more likely, Caravaggio.

Later, we went outside for a cigarette to not rile Whip Girl's silent, most likely sleeping flat-mates with the smell of smoke. I had on underwear with no trousers, just a long thin coat and the cold hit me. It hit the girls too, but it meant more to me. As I saw my smoky breath evaporate towards the red bricked buildings on the other side of the street. 'Winter is coming!'

Solus looked at me and grinned while smoking a cigarette. 'WINTER IS COMING!' she said.

Whip Girl looked at us. 'Winter is coming? Winter is fucking here!'

Solus got a call from a guy, I couldn't tell if it was Ritchie but she scarpered into the black night, leaving me and Whip to sleep by ourselves. Whip stroked me and tried to conjure another round of fucking but I couldn't, physically or mentally. I gently shrugged her off and turned around so that I could appreciate the sleep in the warm.

Chapter 24

Meeting with Father

"Nothing haunts us like the things we didn't buy."
– unknown

He made sure that we didn't meet near Notting Hill. Instead, he met me in the City in a bar towards Aldgate – probably one he remembered from the eighties. It was slick but had a traditional bar set up. Something that you would see in Sweeney Todd with glasses hanging upside down, waiter in a waistcoat and brass or copper finishing's on the beer taps.

He was in good spirits, telling me that he met my sister yesterday and that she is finally trying to get her career together as a lawyer or something, and that she was looking to move in with her on/ off girlfriend. The girl who had cheated numerous times but had a large family house near Warwick Avenue – if I mentioned it in a protective way, I was jealous.

He asked how my mother was, but I wondered why he didn't ask her himself. I said she was fine; I think she was fine anyway. I did not ask him about his new family, I believe there may have been two other daughters, whether they were his or not was up in the air. One was, one wasn't and from what I gathered, it all got a bit messy. Although I was young, I could remember something; the arguments and Mother leaving, sometimes driving away and coming back. Shouting. Acrimony.

My father leaned back on his chair, tapping his toes on his leg that was crossed on the other. Revealing his jet-black socks.

'You look a little ill, John. Are you taking care of yourself?' he said as he yawned and looked at the time.

'Yes, sorry. I'm just a little bit tired, work is crazy.' I faked a yawn and I am not sure why but he yawned back at me as a response.

'Good, good, it is good that work is going well. That's how you progress, more money etc.'

This made me remember that I owed him money for the 'flat move' and I made sure that I was explicit in telling him, 'Oh, Dad, about the money… I will pay you back as soon as I can.'

He told me not to worry – to pay when I can. He looked down and paused as he said it, as if he was continuing the conversation but the thought went elsewhere. 'Yes, always try and keep healthy, you know, do your work. Get up early and stay away from drugs, this town, this City has a lot of drugs.'

I kept my head down and nodded with all the sincerity that I could muster. 'Yes, yes, of course.' And I thought that he must have had a conversation with my mother.

He asked about the new business and seemed impressed. 'Online fashion, eh? Highly creative.' He crouched in and said quietly, 'It is all about multiple income streams, keep going!'

'In fact, winter is coming and I think you will need a proper coat, a treat from me to you. I'm going to put some money in your account.' He looked me up and down as he said this. Inquisitive and analysing.

I put up resistance but was indifferent. 'I have your details, going to give you five hundred big ones, as I don't know when I will see you again.'

'Oh, you really don't have to do that' I replied.

'It's fine, its fine. It's a one-off, and you don't have to pay this back, just make sure you buy a good coat, a Burberry or something.' I smiled but knew that Burberry coats cost over a grand. I wondered how much money he had and how much the other family got. Then again, it was not up to him to make my wealth. I was over eighteen, the responsibility was mine.

We left with a hug and I walked a little bit, wondering what would happen next – perhaps another visit in six months. Suddenly a text from him: 'Very nice to see you, the money is in.' And it was five hundred pounds. A five hundred pounds where he insisted that I paid for a coat, but it would be a good bumper to put me on the road towards a one-bedroom flat – would take weeks off the campaign that could sometimes prove tumultuous. I knew, with the confusion of the gift and my very nature: I knew that I would not spend it on either.

I soon changed my mind about the money, I was excited. Because I was going to go straight to Solus and the others and was ordering at least three grams, then I was going to get a maligned Airbnb. The short-term thinking was exceptional. The plans that I had made had scared me to the point of wanting to escape them. As if I knew in my mind I probably would not be able to achieve it, or that I would at some point achieve it, at some point eek my way through it like I usually did. This was just as fearful.

Before meeting Father I had a scare at the office: one of the account managers had decided to come in at an ungodly hour and type away at her computer, right next to my chosen bedroom on the floor two. I knew the lady; she was the type of person who had a knack of interrupting whenever you were just about to concentrate on something. That was the only time she would interrupt – it would never be when you are ready or receptive, it was not within her nature. It wasn't even as if she was a bad person. It wasn't as if she even knew it, but she was attracted to people's energy when they wanted to be left alone. Perhaps it was something that happened in her childhood, perhaps it was something else. All I know is that I had to lay low as I had woken up two successive nights and she had been there. The first time I tried to sneak out and she heard me. 'Hello? Hello?'

I had to let her know I was there. 'Hi, only me sorry, was working early and they told me to check the computers.'

Brenda: Oh thank God I thought it was the ghost!'

Me: The ghost?

Brenda: Yes, there is a poltergeist. (She smiled enthusiastically) Or at least I believe there is – It's worse in the summer. I used to work here early all the time and sometimes I just knew I had to get out of here, an energy, you know?

I remembered the lifts and wondered if it was my imagination. Brenda was a little kooky but both of us had felt something; the office, though convenient, had far too much history. The second day, the day directly after this one, Brenda was there again, six-thirty a.m. Around the time I had to wake up. The door was locked but her shuffling made me anxious. This time, I snuck past her open door and tiptoed up the stairs to my actual desk, turned the computer on and sat. Soon enough, Brenda trounced up and down the stairs shouting or squealing. 'Hello ? Hello?'

I revealed myself. 'It's me again, Brenda, did you want a cup of tea?'

'No I'm good thanks, you start early these days, John!'

When I hit the desk, one of my co-workers entered within fifteen minutes. I knew her well, did the payroll but she started to give me tasks until she realised that I wasn't supposed to be in

235

today. 'What are you doing in today, John?' I had mixed up my days and I walked out of there, down the narrow side-path and I could hear the drunken transvestite talking to herself on my left. I got a coffee with the kind man and left towards Chelsea, to the gym.

And so, with the five hundred pounds I did not feel like the tent, I was still scared of hostels and I wanted to relax in luxury. Relax and shake off this extra money from my memory. I rented a flat in Chelsea: a one bed with a luxury feel, small but neat. One hundred and twenty pounds for the night plus two grams from the forty pounds man that was two hundred down already – short term thinking, but immediate highs. Highs that excited you and let you escape but at the end of the day, they will drag you down lower. For now? It didn't matter. I had loosened my timelines, thinking to myself that this way of life wasn't that bad. Sometimes it was, sometimes it wasn't – just like a norm in a flat with four walls.

I booked it with Airbnb yet again, even though I had been scammed with them before, and even though they had not even messaged me about the scam. Ever. No effort had been made to rectify my loss… I still booked. And, of course, it wasn't the first time since the scam.

Solus was ready with the upmost alacrity, she came to see the flat as I entered for the first time. Quite close to Sydney Street in a little muse that tucked off from a car park. But I wish Solus had come later as the lady who let us in was more than beautiful. An older woman, voluptuous and softly spoken. As I tried to make a connection with her, Solus would interject into the conversation with a loud briskness that annoyed the lady. She asked me if she was my partner and I told her in no uncertain terms that was not the case.

236

She told us that we could not have any other visitors, we could use the small outside area but had to be quiet. I wondered what my father would think of all of this, no coat as of yet – he wouldn't be angry, just disappointed. As if I had truly lost my way in a world where many were. Mother had messaged me asking me 'how it went' and I said, 'it was fine,' protecting themselves from themselves. A Swiss bank of parenting and children. I didn't mention the money to her, although, I wouldn't put it past the man to use it as a power trip.

Fuck it, it was only five hundred pounds, five hundred wonderful and disposable pounds. It was as if he was setting me up to fail; not enough to buy a house but certainly enough to have a lavish weekend with friends. Living in luxury, living in the now. Living temporarily.

Solus and I went outside for a smoke, I looked up towards the sky and saw the same star or planet that had come out first, before all of the others, resolute in its appearance and, notwithstanding, the occasional cloud. Thank you, Father, for the information.

I remembered that I promised to see Whip Girl at some point. I called her and told her to come over, she thought it was a night enclosed in romance but I told her that this was not the case. I told her that Solus would be joining us, in fact, she was already here. Solus met the Forty Pound Man and I bought the two while she contributed with a small bottle of gin. I suppose I thought this was a thank you for letting me stay those times. The drinks flowed but the flat was small and the bedroom adjoined the main room so, really, it was studio. We were cramped and I started to think we would have been better off at Whip's. But with Whip I had to keep the Chelsea illusion, just a little glamour so she didn't realise the situation.

She arrived but arrived late, wearing tight leggings and a bottle of vodka in one hand. It seemed the Forty Pound Man had cut the stuff – we weren't getting high and so we drank and Solus suggested going for a walk. At first, I thought she meant she was going on her own, but she had decided to take Whip Girl with her instead. So, I would be left alone as the pseudo snort and cramped energy made me anxious. Strangely, Oli and Ritchie were down the road and Solus planned to see them. Perhaps it wasn't so strange, it was all contrived by Solus.

Ritchie called me on his mobile. 'Oi, you forkin kornt, get Solus over here, do it before I get you whacked… I run this town!'

Whip girl said to me that I should come. I hadn't seen the boys since the kicked tramp and I didn't feel like gratuitous violence. My thoughts drifted to Tammy when she partied with Oli the last time, handsome Oli with his long dark hair. The indignity of her wanting to run off with him – the indignity of her denying it. He was a handsome guy, his specialty being confused and pretty women. Tammy could be described as one. Whip girl was almost definitely one as there is a look in her eyes. A look of vulnerability, as if she has been transported back to when she was a child. A mislaid pup that had been left out in the wilderness. Her irresponsibility gave me relief. As she was older, it was as if I wasn't the worst – I was not supposed to be the immediate adult. She was supposed to be by default and sometimes she would be. She would frequently tell us to keep quiet or grimace at our dissolute gossip.

Whip girl and Solus strutted towards Chelsea Manor Street where Ritchie and Oli were stationed. I was not sure what the boys were doing there; Ritchie lived in the depths of Fulham in his mum's flat and Oli at his dad's, an Ivy-Laden house somewhere towards Notting Hill. Solus said they were shacked up and partying in one of the gated ex-councils hidden on the road. Hidden in shame from the large townhouses that were either side of them. It was strange that they did not invite me, although the etiquette was missing, the rationale made sense; too many men in a small setting wasn't good for sexual conversion. 'Bring that girls, bring that girls Ciro!' said Ritchie over the phone. Ciro was my nickname from the Gomorrah series, one of the dons of the camorra clan; the quiet one, the smart one... the strategic one.

I thought to myself that I would not worry about what would happen there – c'est la vie, if Whip wanted to run off with another guy I could not stop her. The issue with it? I would not be able to sleep at hers – the new man would surely take the priority. She was a rare find; she knew how to party, was pretty and had a flat. I am not saying that she was in love with me, this would be a gross miscalculation, but the caring was there. She chose to hang with us - us the reprobates. People that made her feel young and alive but would ultimately do nothing for her. In the end, we would likely drag her into a deeper and older hole of unwavering loss.

I napped off the half-dodgy gak and through the gin. I remember wisely that, whenever there is a comfy bed, never waste the opportunity. I also remember from that fateful night in Old Street. The night when my mind entered seventeen levels of darkness – to pace myself with the drugs. Even if you are partying, if there is a gap in the socializing flak I must drop through it like a societal kamikaze. And that is what I did, nodding off, maybe waking up to take another sip of gin but then nodding off again, pacing myself, restoring energy. That was until there was a knock on the door, a familiar frantic knock that I remember from Scatty Alice's that night – Solus was back and so was Whip.

There was a relief in seeing whip, returning to me in one piece but I was worried that they had bought the boys with them. We were only supposed to have two people and we were already three. I cautiously opened the door, Solus smiled and walked right in – I could see the familiar melancholy in her eyes. 'Where are the boys?' I asked.

Whip girl mimicked me. 'Ooh… the boys!' as she flopped her hand.

Solus shrugged it off. Dunno… they just weren't there.' Perhaps they got what they would perceive as a better offer. Perhaps Martha, perhaps Coralie… I hoped it wasn't Coralie.

And so I was left with the two girls, a cramped but good night and in my semi-high state I remembered I would have to buy a coat of some form. I would need evidence that the money spent was spent on a coat, even if it was a ten pounds from a thrift store. I was a strange human; I went to great lengths to avoid the feeling of owing people, blood relatives almost included, but when they do give me something, I fuck it to extreme proportions. Either that or I become resentful and suspicious and subsequently, revenge spend.

It was strange that I didn't hear from Ritchie again that night. Out of curiosity I tried Oli's line but he was not known for answering calls; every time his phone rang it was as if he had seen a mouse sprint across his sitting room. He wanted to kick it away and carry on. Text or WhatsApp only, and he will reply when he has the time to, usually when there is snort.

Whip girl was getting tired and let us know by stripping down into some hotpants. Then, she started to stroke me on the back. It was time to be intimate, but Solus was there and she had just ordered a late night pizza. It came as we were yawning but I still managed to consume a few pieces, Whip ate a little but was watching her figure and Solus guzzled at a frightening pace.

'Oh, I'm starving!' Whip Girl looked at her, as if to say a lady shouldn't eat so much and Solus bobbed her head from side to side in her own consummate world. Whip girl went for a kiss but I was also entranced by Solus's eating.

'Drugs make people so hungry,' said Whip. I listened to this comment, watched Solus eat and quietly nodded with my eyes down. Solus then stripped into underwear, revealing toned thighs and her athletic body which I had seen many times before. Even though this was the case, it never ceased to amaze me. We all climbed in the bed and I was on the right side, Whip in the middle and Solus on the left.

Sometimes with snort, once I have finished, it gives me an unwanted but enhanced libido spike. It is horniness beyond reason and without morality. Fantasizing about people you should, and fantasizing about people should not. I thought about the artist lady downstairs, imagined if I crept out of the bed and successfully seduced her.

Suddenly, Solus left to the bathroom. It was a great time to try with Whip but she was, now, in and out of sleep. She took my hand and draped it round her body for a friendly, sleepy spoon. I looked at Whip's face in the dark and she was smiling, content, but not I. I had a violent erection that felt as if it was going to launch off and orbit the room. Then I heard the sounds, the all-familiar sounds that Solus makes in the loo after stuffing her face with food. Almost violent choking or gagging.

'Meewaaggh,' a small interlude and then once more, 'Meewwaghh.' This time it was enough to wake up Whip Girl's fragile slumber.

'Is she okay in there, is she puking?' I wasn't sure what to say about it, and if I was supposed to do anything about it.

So I said, 'Yes, probably.' Hoping there would be unspoken text. The subtext being that the excessive puking was because of her drug and alcohol intake, even though it likely wasn't.

I walked up to the door and checked on her. 'Solus are you okay? Solus?' I had a nonchalant tone, hoping that she would say yes, and the yes would mean I had done my bit.

There was a second of silence, an agonising silence and then, 'Yes, yes I'm fine!'

With minor relief I returned to bed, hoping that Whip would have had the same chemical reaction as me. That she needed ravenous sex while we allowed Solus to heave out her guts in the rented loo basin. This did not happen, in fact, Solus returned from the bathroom and joined us in the large bed that consumed most of the room.

My needs were still there – in the dark, a sexual desire beyond control and I looked to my left. Two pairs of toned legs semi-draped around the white mattress cover. Hotpants. Solus then moved and lifted her leg up, revealing the lower buttock. My mind was irrational; I took my hand and placed it on her arse. Perhaps trying to induce a threesome or perhaps to do something with Solus while Whip was asleep. At least, I thought Whip was asleep, she didn't move as I did this, but I felt an energy as if she was watching this in its entirety. As if she knew exactly what I was doing. Solus didn't move as I stroked my hand up and down her leg, my arm stretched across past whip girl and onto her, locking them in together. Solus was neither receptive or aroused by my hand and I soon stopped, realising what I was doing and who I was doing it to. I thought to myself, if they ask me anything in the morning, deny it. Deny it flat out like Ritchie who pretends he is sleepwalking or asleep like he did when he tried to spoon his flat-mate, thus, relinquishing responsibility.

Chapter 25

Ritchie Returns

"Gen X have pills and Prozac. Millennials have coke and binge-drinking."
– Vice Magazine 2019

We woke up from the Airbnb and I could instantly tell that Whip was distant. Almost certainly because I draped my arm across her to touch Solus.

Even still, she suggested going to hers. Solus and I thought it was a grand idea. She had psycho flat-mates but we could watch TV in her bedroom and drink once more. Hair of the dog. This wasn't before Whip insisted that we open all the windows because Solus had decided to smoke inside.

She made us tidy thoroughly and I checked the loo basin for traces of Solus's puke, it was immaculately clean, in fact, it was sparkling and I hadn't even entered to tidy.

We made Whip sneak out in her own taxi while I dropped the keys off to the attractive art woman – she didn't complain about any noise or extra guests.

We went back to Whip's and she offered to pay half for another gram. Solus, however, did not. Instead, she anticipated the resentment and negated it by being cordial: 'You guys are so great, you guys would make such a cute couple... both so beautiful.'

Whip girl chuckled nervously as I laughed to myself and tried to change the subject; me and Whip had an understanding, I was sure of it. For her, I plugged her into the social pipeline, or at least that's what she thought. First impressions: Scatty Alice's flat, then Solus who was friendly of sorts and I had the membership at H Club. For Whip girl, I was a fun thing that occasionally stayed at her abode, and carried out her strange sexual desires of being beaten by various objects. I feel that she knew she would need a proper man for a relationship, an older man, perhaps a man who embraced obligations with a wholeness of heart.

The snort arrived and we thought it civilised to enter a pub at close proximity. Eat lunch there and have a few drinks, play board games. Mainly, Whip wanted to get away from her flat mates who had already beckoned her in for a chat, leaving Solus and me in her bedroom, watching pop videos and swigging down the remainder of the hair-of-the-dog vodka.

We left for the pub, a derelict looking place on a derelict part of West Kensington and the pub seemed to be isolated away from any buildings. Whip had been there before, and when we went inside it was rustic and trendy. A wooden bar with a variety of ales. There was an outside garden that would have been pleasant if the heavy rain wasn't battering the wooden tables.

We sat down and pulled out the board games: cards, chess where some of the pieces were missing. Solus was looking at herself in the mirror on the wall by a dart board. She pulled up her jumper and looked at her stomach which was so toned there was not an inch of fat, in fact, there was not an inch of fat on her. Her waist was so small that it wasn't in proportion to the size of her head. This is what she seemed to want by the looks of it, by the way she pivoted her body and checked every angle.

Occasionally she would smile, then occasionally she would look disappointed.

Whip came back with a round of drinks and told us that she couldn't spend too much. To this, Solus exclaimed that I had obtained a small amount from my father and that I wanted to party with it. Whip Girl said her name in contrived shock. 'Solus!' I thought to myself that it was probably, again, time to impress Whip as I was sure it would be good to stay at hers in the future, so, I bought them lunch and a few rounds. Now, the extra cash was dwindling beyond reason.

We took it in turns to do bumps in the loo. When I look back at this, it is nothing but contemptible. At the time? We thought we were rock stars – using a day in the weekend to snort in an olden pub. We loved it, us three, at ease with each other. I could have stayed with them forever, at least at that very moment. The three of us, cordial and in an eternal loop. There by the wooden pub tables and the occasional old soak.

Whip had started to warm to me after last night but asked outright, 'Have you two ever slept with each other?' To which Solus placed her head downwards in a kind-of-shame emotion, and I knew exactly what she was doing. Making Whip think we potentially had for no other reason than to watch the world burn. I interjected.

'No, we haven't, I adore Solus, but we are just friends.' Whip girl looked at me as I said this and then looked away, as if to make her own conclusion.

Solus went to the loo to do a bump as my phone buzzed with movement, it was an unknown number but I answered it. It was Ritchie, and it was dramatic.

Ritchie: John, John!

Me: Hey, what's up? (Noticing the line was badly distorted,)

I'm just a little drunk in the pub here man…

Ritchie: FUCKING LISTEN TO ME! This is my one call, they have my phone!

Me: Wait, slow down. Who has your phone?

Ritchie: The police! The police, John! I am at the police station; I got arrested last night they strip searched me and everything, checked my asshole!

At this point Ritchie seemed to get emotional, forcing himself to cry. But I couldn't help wondering in my superficial state and penchant for irrelevant thinking – if he enjoyed the strip search.

Ritchie: Shit, John, I'm fucked. Oli, that fucking cunt. I need you to get me a taxi, okay? A taxi to wherever you are. I don't have Uber.'

I got him a cab from the West London police station and he was on his way to us. I told Solus when she had finished in the loo and came back wiping her nose. I saw the barman give her a stare, but with the exception of two soaks in the corner, we were the only ones in the place. I'm fairly sure he was thankful for the business.

Solus attempted a melancholy reaction to the fact that Ritchie had called me first. It made sense because, despite my flaws, I was still more reliable than Solus. Solus would answer, get dramatic and forget to send the address or elope with another male. She tried to get angry with me, as if to blame me that Ritchie called me first, not remembering that she was inhaling class A at the time.

Whip Girl asked who Ritchie was and I said to her that it was Solus's lover. 'FUCK OFF!' she exclaimed, for a reason I couldn't quite understand. I ordered another round and was sure to get one for Ritchie. A nice cold post-prison pint.

Soon enough, Ritchie arrived with a dramatic face, emoting his socks off. Solus ran towards him and they hugged but he didn't seem interested. He was more concerned about absorbing and emitting as much drama from this, and I could see his eye occasionally drift to whip girl. Solus stayed by his side for the majority of the night, as if to say, 'I am the most important to him,' but we couldn't care less.

It was an engrossing story leading to the arrest: Ritchie was with Oli, shacked up in the random flat with goodness knows who. They ordered drugs from a man named 'Daz', perhaps a commentary on the quality of product but it was Daz nevertheless. And Daz pulled up on Manor Street for Ritchie to meet him, not before taking two hundred pounds with him. Half of Ritchie's money and half of Oli's. Then, Ritchie went into Daz's car and started talking to Daz, I could imagine, trying to be cool and hanging with the dealer; talking about 'creps' and listening to grime. They were just about to do the transaction, Ritchie fiddling in his right pocket to pull the cash out when 'KNOCK KNOCK!' on the window door. Both parties knew they were immediately fucked. A plain clothed policeman asked them to open the door but the policeman was ever-so-slightly early. You see, the transaction hadn't been completed and, apparently the policeman was furious.

Policeman: What are you doing with all that money then, eh?

Ritchie: I was about to go clubbing.

They went to town on Daz's car, using sniffer dogs and those little UV torches. Daz was panicking and in handcuffs as they found substantial amounts in the wheel rims. They took his phone, handcuffed him and sat him down on the path. They arrested Ritchie also for a charge he was not sure about. Into the back of the police van he went. Then they took Ritchie's phone. These police were clearly angry that they missed the transaction and tried to compensate with legally blurred action.

When looking at Ritchie's phone, they pinpointed the Gomorrah based chats between myself and him. 'Yeah I run Kensington, this is my territory' – 'Yeah I am going to have my sister whacked' – 'Si is my head of security for when the police start knockin' on my door' and even more damning 'I run the international drug trade with Gennaro Savastano - we run it through London!' They read these messages, didn't understand the irony, and thought that Ritchie was the Kingpin, the brains of the operation.

That night, while they inspected his arsehole at the police station, they also took his keys and phone. They took a team to his flat and entered. Legally vague. As they entered, they did keep some kind of protocol - they were not allowed to go into any communal areas such as the sitting room where Si was in his panties playing X-box. exasperated, he pointed them in the direction of Ritchie's room, and, we assumed, continued to play on his computer game but not without taking the opportunity to snitch on Ritchie to his mother. Ritchie's mother owned the flat. If it wasn't for Si, his mother would have never found out.

They didn't find anything in Ritchie's room and went back empty handed, except for the drug dealer, Daz. Daz was in serious trouble. Arrested and estranged from contact.

And thus, Ritchie spent the night in a jail cell. He said it was awful, that he could hear wailing and screaming from other inmates. In my head, it sounded like a free bed and personal space, but he must have been shitting it, wondering if he would be charged. If they thought that he and the drug dealer were together – they could have pressed charges. The next day he was let free but they kept his mobile – against protocol, hence his phone call.

He was with us and he kept telling us how bad the situation was. I was only worried about the fact that they saw our messages and perhaps I was incriminated. Having said this, it was not the best time to bring this up. We just had to be there for him, do the occasional sympathetic look and nod accordingly.

This was the first time that Whip Girl had met Ritchie and she seemed intrigued by the no-holes-barred drama; in our circles we were truly lost, in our circles it was drama without end.

'So this is the whip girl? I have seen the famous video,' said Ritchie to Whip. Whip Girl smiled and appreciated the attention.

Solus took the opportunity to make me buy another round, which we did... I did. She also said that we should get Ritchie out of there. Ritchie couldn't face going home, so we decided that we would get him back to Whips, providing that we stayed quiet and away from the flat mates. Then, Solus took it to another level.

'We should re-order.'

This meant that the gram that me and Whip had obtained had already been consumed by Solus's unrelenting nose. Ritchie reacted to this with faux anger. 'Whoa, what the fuck. Did you not just hear me, Solus? I just got arrested for snorting and now you want to order?'

He smirked at the end of his outburst, not able to convince himself for the entire sentence. It was then that I knew, I knew we were going to order again and Ritchie was going to partake, even though he was released from the cell that very day.

Solus went to pick up the drugs that me and Ritchie paid 'halves' for. Luckily, he had at managed to re obtain his wallet from the station. And now ? Well he was buying drugs again.

We got to Whip's and we were lucky, of sorts. Her flat-mates were out which allowed us leeway to party a little, have some music and snort in the confinement of her bedroom. I had the idea of playing the song from the Gomorrah soundtrack, to ingest some bravado on what must have been a difficult day. Translated from Italian – it goes like this:

Released from prison yesterday, life begins now

Sitting on the back of a 600CC bike, wearing a brand new pair of white shoes.

I'm not going back there because she can't sleep at night.

I've got my mind on a Benz or a range rover.

As the song increased in tempo, I saw Ritchie trying to rap along to the Italian rhythm but there was melancholy in his eyes. Half–hearted, I saw that he was ingesting the events of the previous night. I wondered if Oli knew that he had been arrested… but perhaps he would not be interested.

Solus passed the silver tray around and, for some reason I was excited to rack the stripe up my nose. More so than the previous gram, perhaps it was because I had been drinking. Perhaps I was anxious about the phone. I did mine after Solus and Whip and Solus passed the plate to Ritchie. Ritchie made it look like he was hesitating, then, the standard capitulation and picked up a shared straw. Before he inhaled, he looked at us with a smug voice and said, 'Wow, yeah I need a forkin line to get over what happened!' and we laughed. Not because we found it funny – but because we were trying to encourage. We didn't want him to bring the energy of the party down. The party in the small bedroom.

Whip pulled me aside and started to kiss me while towing me into the kitchen. She bent over, lowering her tight leggings and underwear, revealing her curved and naked rear. 'Wooden spoon!' she said. 'Wooden spoon, there get it!'

I could hear Solus and Ritchie shouting in the other room but Whip was insistent - this is what she needed in life. For me it was drugs and uncalculated risks, for her, it was a thorough spanking. And so I did – I took the wooden spoon and started to spank her until her cheeks were imbued with red circles: 'HARDER' she would say. 'HARDER!' And so I did, conscious that they could hear us next door. Conscious that I could cause deep bruising. 'Call me by my name!' I still could not remember if it was Miranda or Melanie or… I had seen it on one of her debit cards but the mental block was unyielding. So, I called her Whip or Whippy as Solus would call her.

'Oh, Whippy, you are so hot!'

She thrived on the name, just as she thrived on the tape I made of her. The attention gave her a buzz, perhaps that's why she hung with us – there was always attention of some kind. Negative, positive, on the street… in the bedroom. She asked me to enter her which I did, willingly. Making sure I was aware that the coke made me teeter on the balls of my feet. And thus, we had sex on the kitchen mantle top and returned to the bedroom.

In my high state, I fisted my chest and shouted to Solus and Ritchie. 'I JUST HAD SEX WITH WHIP GIRL IN THE KITCHEN!' Whip revealed a smile but only a small one, as if I hadn't satisfied her fully. Thoughts to self: *I would need to double the efforts on whipping if I was to regularly stay.*

Solus and Ritchie did not react to my outburst, instead, Solus was crying in underwear. Apparently, they started having sex but Ritchie was boisterous and disorderly. And as I thought of this my mind drifted, my mind drifted to the irrelevant thought that he probably tried anal. Solus put on her jumper and Whip girl gave her a clement hug. Everyone did another line and Ritchie decided to flirt with Whip.

'So you are the famous Whip?'

She giggled at his question but hesitated with the advances – curious but hesitant. . She was curious because of human nature and likely because Solus had been with him. So many people are friends, but in my circles, so many would shag their friend's partners within a heartbeat. Perhaps it was control, perhaps it was visceral curiosity – but it was a stark fact.

Ritchie: Do you know John lives in a tent?

I shrugged off the comment, hoping that Whip thought it a euphemism for renovation.

Suddenly, they got closer and Ritchie was almost touching Whip's knee as everyone started giggling. I let it happen. Intentionally, I let it, as I wanted to see how far they would take the curiosity. To see if I could trust Ritchie when it came to it. To see if the rumours were true and he only got turned on with girls when they were other peoples. Perhaps that is why marriage is a doomed choice in this day and age. Perhaps this is why Whip Girl was still single.

Solus decided that she wanted a walk and I couldn't help but feel it was because of what she was seeing: Ritchie and Whip getting close. Teasing us with their unlikely chemistry. We hesitated in deciding who should go with her. Surely it should be Ritchie but I could see that he was already cozy. I tested again… the situation. 'I will go for a walk with you, Solus.'

Whip Girl paused, wondering how she should answer.

'You are going, are you?' And I could have changed this all quickly. I could have made a move, reassuring Whip that I liked her, defending my territory, but I did not. I wanted to observe human nature in all its brutality. To observe Whip Girl, observe her character when there is sexual choice.

Solus wasn't satisfied and she wanted Ritchie to accompany her, but Ritchie did not: 'I have just been to jail! I need to just chill!'

Through the awkwardness, Whip decide to assist Solus, leaving me and Ritchie in her flat with the remainder of the snort. We snorted on the sneak and laughed and giggled like boys although I never forgot the moment before. Although Whip and me had no inclination of commitment, I knew I would still blame her this. The elusive and lucid act of kind-of-flirting with Ritchie. Although she had shown me adequate affection, although she had let me stay at her flat, now, I wouldn't blame myself if I used her. There would, yet again be an emotional distance. Like so many before and I assume so many after. There would be an underlying resentment, minor but there. She would now never be a relationship choice…. then again… I am unsure she ever was.

Solus and Whip returned and joined in the festivities. Then, Solus soon left with Ritchie and they stayed at Solus's flat despite her grandma despising the boy. Whip girl yawned and stretched and struggled and I said I would leave. I did this for a few reasons:

1) Treat them mean and keep them.

2) She would need her own space and I did not need to stay that night.

This way I looked cool, a voluntary leave and I slept in the City office, two buses and an hour long journey but the views, the views can be outstanding; a brief peek at the glistening river by the dragon that forks the road towards Fleet Street. I told Whip vague things: 'I am staying near my mum's, sister's… whatever.' I am quite sure Solus had given her the real story in a mean-spirited attempt to socially annihilate, but it would be her word against mine.

I sank back into the offices second floor and locked the door ready for another uncomfortable sleep. A few things unnerved me as I started to shake the downer, a minor downer but still there. We were creeping towards November and I had not accumulated as I was still safe in the knowledge that the offices had a carpet and floor.

I started to sleep on the floor, making sure to keep the barrier between me and the bare carpet. To avoid another outbreak of the scabies-type pests that made me frantically itch in front of the blonde celebrity. I started to nod, more settled than usual. But I had noticed in life, when your brain starts to shut down it is like a vacuum: something will fill that idyllic void. And it did.

I thought I heard footsteps but tried to ignore it, remembering I was high and that the place was haunted to fuck. But then, it happened. Somebody trying to get in the door. At first it was a subtle noise, somebody trying to pull the door handle down, as if they had a sneaking suspicion that somebody may be in there. Then… they yanked the handle and I was relieved that I had locked the door. They shook the door violently, trying to get in and there was nothing I could do but to sit still. I looked at the time and saw that it was two in the morning. Suddenly, the door stopped shaking, but I could feel the pensive energy behind the wood.

Then I said to myself… I am in here, so what? I could say I got entangled in a party down the road. If it's a ghost? They could go back to whatever realm they came from. A tramp? Or another tramp, they shouldn't be there in the first place. For some reason, I knew that whatever and whoever it was, they had gone, at least for another room. And I tried to sleep.

It was the morning – that was the issue. As I woke up and realised that the space I used the most was now compromised, that somebody knew that I was in that room at a certain time and I did not know who it was. That this place was even less safe than usual. I checked the day, perhaps I should avoid the office on this particular night.

Chapter 26

Trump

"Well, Donald, I know you live in your own reality."
– Hillary Clinton 2016

Everyone was talking about the election. Who would win? The businessman or the female. Halloween had passed but the shops had already turned to Christmas; Oxford street was awash with blind consumerism. The sales seemed to start early these days and my business would need sales: Autumn, Halloween, Christmas, Black Friday, all to keep up with the competition.

I looked at the shops and looked for a long coat as my father had asked for a picture. His lack of trust re-enforced the fact that he may have spoken to Mother. I needed to make sure that it was long and black and, if needed, take out the label. And so, I found a shop with a clearance sale that was head to toe with cheap-ish coats. I found one that imitated the shaping's of Saville Row: forty pounds, reduced from eighty. I tried it on, it was loose at the bottom and the materials were cheap, but I could get it taken in. And so, I purchased it and pulled off any stitched labels before sending a photo. The lining was weak and thin. No chance of this being a real winter coat, but it was long and elegant and if I got stuck inside somewhere, I could use it as a blanket.

Then, off to Covent Garden. Wintery and Dickensian Covent Garden as I had obtained two discounted tickets to see "Matilda" with Stephanie. Afterwards, she would take me to watch the election at the Dean Street members club where I was shouted at by a Sex Pistol. I didn't care about the election. I thought my situation meant that I didn't have time for the bigger picture. Just my own periled foot in front of the other. Nobody else's. To me, politicians, the world, myself, they had already failed me. It wouldn't matter who took over, it's the same shit, just different days.

What I did like was the member's club. While everyone else was watching intently on the TV screens I would eat the free hot dogs, drink alcohol and try to kiss Stephanie.

We went into "Matilda" and she thanked me for inviting her. The tickets were courtesy of Father's now non-existent money and I thought this would be a great conquest. A Whip Girl but with a Dean Street Club membership. Older, with a flat in one of the northern boroughs.

To be honest, it was the only way I could get her on a date – it had to be something as elaborate as this. The theatre is the last resort and to this day it has never resulted in a sexual relationship. Only a magical, pure and friend-zoned night that is always more expensive than necessary. It was the second time I had seen this; the first time was with Tammy. But the theatre never worked. You see, you have to build a rapport with somebody, build feelers cognitively. Move onto kinesis and touch a hand but for some reason, I struggle with this. I struggle with the constant eye contact that you need and the laughing and the relating, accepting and building at a bar with a clean shirt on.... I would prefer to have my date in the dark and somewhere where they can't ask too many anxiety inducing questions. Where they cannot look at me because of the blackness and there is a show right in front of them. The theory is to connect with them through the art, mutually laugh and potentially, hand-holding in the aisles.

Then, you take them for a meal or to a bar and hope that a connection prevails, and that they are impressed with the way you wine and dined for a first date. You are cultured and sophisticated – and they will think that there is more of it and hopefully the endorphins will kick in and increase with the bubbly drinks you are buying them. Then, hopefully, you somehow manage to retire together in a building. And these days, that means their dwelling. Perhaps my flat is being refurbished and so we cannot go there. Anything. Any lie or nonsense to entice them to let me stay. We don't even need to have sex, just let me shower and nap.

We get a drink after an interval and sit down again. Eventually the kids congregate on stage and sing a song:

'And when I grow up I will be smart enough to answer all the questions

That you need to know the answers to

Before you're grown up.'

I listened to the innocent voices and glared at the stage and wished... Eventually, the show finished to a round of applause and I wanted to go to Palm Court Brasserie before watching the election. She wanted to go straight to Dean Street, skipping the dinner – she had had enough of just the two of us.

I thought I would message Whip Girl but she had gone to Cambridge for family, or at least she said that. Stephanie was entranced by her phone as we walked the cobbled streets up to Soho and onto Dean Street.

'Thank you so much for the theatre, it was great!'

'Not a problem,' I told her.

'Quite a few of my friends will be there, I think Amy Tez may be popping by!' And so, the inevitable friend fest – how would I…?

We entered the Dean Street Club, usually I would be excited but now? Not tonight. The interior was draped in American flags and there were no celebrities. Stephanie took me to her reserved table. 'I hope Hillary wins, will be crazy if she doesn't, do you agree, John?' I nodded my head but really I couldn't give a fuck. Trump was brash but whenever Hillary spoke, I knew she was a creepazoid. Just like this country, it was about the lesser of two evils and my hazed mind was indifferent and nonchalant.

Stephanie bought me a drink. 'Anything you like!' she said, and so, I got a daquiri to which her face tried not to reveal distress. She started talking to a group of friends and they talked about the election which I could not stand, at least not without cocaine and, if I was to stay in the office which seemed increasingly likely, I would need to make a plan of action. I wasn't keen on this idea from what happened not so long ago: the door being pulled and rattled in the middle of the night, so I was thinking that the tent would be the safest option – not to be said lightly. Then I realised I was working for the City tomorrow, I could wake up and already be there.

They were laughing and talking seriously about the polls while I wondered if it would rain that night. Then, I saw our mutual friend Rosie. She was giggling and laughing with a group at the bar and her face, as usual, was twitching and jerking not-so-subtly. I knew she would have a spare line and so I asked her quietly when she broke off from her crowd. She held my hand and dragged me into the large loo which was located in the hallway. Right past Stephanie. 'Hi Rosie,' she said as we entered the marble-based loo and Rosie racked a large one while shouting at me, shouting about something that happened so far in the past I wondered if it was a fabrication.

'Remember when you first met me, John? Do you? You tried it on with me like a fucking creep!' she said this while prodding me with her shaking finger and I was worried that she was going to punch me.

'I'm sorry, I'm very sorry,' I said to her. She said it was fine, stroked my shoulder and walked out with the bag.

I looked at the TVs and numerous news reporters. The polls and percentages and Stephanie laughing in the corner and I could not hold my resentment. Their issues and worries were concentrated so many thousands of miles away. Their pretentious comments and fake frowns were contrived as my struggles were immediate and at my feet.

I decided to leave for the office and walked up the Charing Cross road, onto the Strand with so many of my fellow homeless. I run to get the correct bus and see them collecting soups and preparing for the evolving night – they were not thinking about the election.

I didn't even say goodbye to Stephanie, Rosie or any of the others as I exited Dean Street towards the City. I arrived, but realised I hadn't packed my bag correctly from Scatty's, and so, already, it was a case of sleeping with the new coat while digesting the wonderful songs of Matilda. Civilised entertainment for a relatively civilized-night.

No ghosts visited me that night, no shaking doors or elusive energies but it was uncomfortable. My word it was; the hard floor and my exhausted brain from drinking and walking around Theatreland. Four hours sleep, a spray and opening of the window. A skip past Brenda in the other room: 'Working early, Brenda, did you want a cup of tea?' and straight upstairs where I started my work alone, or at least pretending to work but really I was working on my clothes business when I briefly saw the news:

Trump had won, the underdog and I was frustrated because all I could think of was I wish I had bet on the man – the odds were good and I could have remade some much needed money.

I got a look at my reflection on the laptop screen and it seemed the bags on my eyes were reaching the top of my lip. Surely it was the distortion on the screen, and so, I ran to the bathroom to see that bags of grey black were confirmed and expanding. I went to my desk and sat down as the other people started to steam in, surprised to see me here on time, with the laptop up and ready to type. I was listening to Wolf Alice: Wonder Why, poignant but damning lyrics for such a confined space:

What happens when we die?

Don't ask questions just make sure you survive.

I made sure they didn't look at my face. 'Have you seen the result, John? Fucking ridiculous.' they moaned to each other, fearing the future – just as people did with the result earlier in the year. Perhaps this was the start of a new era, an era that would get worse before it got better but I couldn't help it, I couldn't help grinning to myself as they panicked – panicked while they live in wonderful flats with other warm people.

'Trump is a fascist.'

'I hate this world!' and I kept grinning… to myself from cheek to cheek. They seemed so far away from the real and immediate dangers of this world, and I revelled in them feeling a little of the fear. I used it to fuel me working while my tired eyes dictated my face.

'What do you think, John?' I politely agreed and nodded with anything they said, but, in reality…I thought nothing.

Interlude

Love/Hate

"To walk alone in London is the greatest rest."
– Virginia Woolf

I spent the weekend walking around: Whip was still away and again I avoided Solus and her crack-drug ways. I moved from doing work at Café Nero to H Club on a bus, humping and moving, usually jovial movement but I was in a mood. People were everywhere and I had had no reflection to myself for quite some time; I was up from the tent or the office and immediately I had to avoid them… people. People bumping into me in Covent Garden, people queuing for loos… people shouting. People everywhere.

I seemed to be slower than the pace of everyone as they rushed with defined briskness. . . I decided to go back to the Chelsea gym to shower and workout, not before going to Scatty's to get some change in clothes. I got off the bus as somebody nudged me and the crowd behind me made me anxious. I walked faster into a run down the Thistle Grove as if to shrug them off like buzzing metropolitan insects - trying to track and sting me.

I got to Scatty's and could hear she had guests, so, I was careful as I hit the side buildings not to be heard. I could hear her in her flat from the small outbuilding, asking a male to obtain another bottle of wine from the kitchen. I promptly left and closed the large black door quietly. A lady with a pram blocked the path to the grove and the frustration hit me to the point that I wanted to fucking scream.

I saw the homeless Scottish man outside Marks and Spencer's who was still in a sleeping bag too thin for the nights. I walked up towards the gym, past many tall, self-entitled cunts that did not notice nor seem to care that I had a bag by my side. I could feel a larger vehicle creeping behind me, and then it nearly deafened me with sirens as it throttled towards the hospital two minutes away and this was the last straw. This was when I said to myself, 'I FUCKING HATE THIS PLACE!' London and its aggression and grey and cunty people with no remorse – but then I saw it as I neared the gym, a woman with the upmost beauty; nearly as tall as me; black leggings, Dr Martens, walking a dog while smoking a thin cigarette and I thought to myself – how? How does this place that enforced its concrete and skyscrapers against the laws of nature produce something so… angelic.

Her beauty contrasted the setting; her seemingly innocent nature worked against the concrete grain as she walked and sent out her unambiguous vibrations. It was then that I saw the faint sun peer from a cloud, I saw people laughing to my left side as a convertible car drove through with all the joy in the world. And I remembered, I remembered why I was here in the first place. And I don't think there was anything or anywhere else for me and I would go down… just like Virginia Woolf… and I thought this while I entered the gym full of sweaty work bodies full of intent.

The office had issues and the tent was getting colder, definitely colder. Those mornings, where the cold goes through your bones and right back out again until you quiver like a wreck and there is nothing you can do but to wrap as tightly as possible. You hope for a wave of warmth from somewhere, anywhere. Maybe the wind or the nearby street lighting.

Chapter 27

Investment

"You have a very short amount of time to make a first impression. If you've got a long rambling side deck... you're done."
– Naval Ravikant

Sales had dwindled but people knew I had a business. I have to say, they respected the effort. My friends, always looking on my website and asking for freebies while assessing my website and social media. Everyone with their opinions – in a world where we over value ourselves and our perspectives, it is to be expected. I would say to them, to the people who have no experience 'TO KNOW AND NOT TO DO IS NOT TO KNOW,'. Unless Stella McCartney herself would somehow locate me and give me inestimable tips. Or unless my brief and worthy acquaintance, Vivienne Westwood, managed to meet me again. To anyone else: to know and not to do is not to know.

H asked for one of our bracelets and bags which I obtained and, soon, she strutted around London with them. This was much to the annoyance of Tammy who hadn't got over the incident with the broken wrist. Tammy was talking to me a little more, mainly because of the business. Word on the grapevine - there was another rooster in the Country hen house, inevitably, someone in finance. She wondered why I was still doing this: 'Shouldn't it be over by now? It's nearly Christmas!' she exclaimed this on the phone while I tried to snuggle in the office.

Then H called.

H: John, John, guess what?

Me: What?

H: So I was at this party in Knightsbridge, Jez's, he owns the place. Used to own that nightclub in Kensington, you know the one…?

Me: I don't think so… but carry on.

H: Well, anyway, I had one of your bags on me and he asked where they were from, okay he was drunk on champagne or whatever but he wants to meet!

Me: Oh really? What for?

H: An investment, you dick, what do you think?

I agreed to meet with the anonymous man the very next day. Apparently, he wanted to move quickly, but, for me, it seemed to be too good to be true. Having said this, if there was a person who could consummate with all the characters and elevated stories, all the men trying to impress - it would be H. H and H alone.

As I lay in the office, I thought I'd better prepare something. I put up the long coat and rolled up the sleeping bag. I opened my laptop and prepared something basic. Basic figures of sales, the range with the pointy breasted celebrity and press and projections.

The next day I bought new shirt. All shirts at Scatty Alice's were compromised with damp and I could not iron them, besides, I was trying to avoid her. It wasn't an expensive shirt, just a pink non-iron from one of the large high street stores – I could have used the black one that I used for the BBC, but I didn't want to look like a butler.

I had my small presentation with my laptop and he wanted to meet, deep into the mysterious night. Late enough that many were preparing for the next day but H met me beforehand. She made me swig a bottle of beer with her in a bar nearby as she crossed her legs in indubitably short skirt. We went to Jez's, directly across the road from Harrods and his malnourished looking assistant opened the door. Not before H pointed at his car:

'Look, that's his Ferrari! See? He's loaded!'

We entered and Jez was waiting for us, and I suddenly remembered that I had heard about this guy – urban legends about partying. Niccy used to drink champagne with him until the early hours in his nightclub, now closed down, in rock-and-roll and mysterious circumstances. Too much partying I heard, too many free drinks for a plethora of models who would flock there at the weekend. No real money coming in to keep it afloat.

'Hi, so you are John, yeah?' he said as he sipped champagne from a metal goblet. Crossed legged. H now draped across him.

'This is the guy with the bags,' H said.

'Yes, yes. I know, I love your bags yeah.'

'How much money are you making at the moment?'

So, I gave him the presentation and told him there were sales weekly. I told him about Tammy to which he said, 'Oh, you deal with that, yeah,' and flicked his hand at me while he made sure champagne did not spill on his dark suit and flopped hair. That would mean that I would have to resolve the issue of my business partner, I would have to split it with Tammy and give H some.

He perched his leg on a brutalist coffee table, made of concrete or limestone and flicked through the presentation. It wasn't extensive, but he assimilated the information with lightning speed. I hadn't proposed any figures to him, but he proposed them to me: 'Okay, I am thinking ten grand, for a third by the looks of this, but I need to see more.'

I giggled, but soon composed myself. Imagine, ten grand in a lump sum. Imagine. Operation Ironside could come to an abrupt and fitting end. This, all of this, could be an abominable but fairy-like hallucination.

He said he would be in touch but I made sure that I didn't think too much of it. At this stage, the breaking of expectation would crush me and any remaining resolve that my withered condition could muster. I appreciated H for doing this, she didn't have to... but she did. Music played on a large but distant television screen: Twenty-One Pilots – Heathens.

'All my friends are heathens, take it slow.'

'Wait for them to ask you who you know.'

He looked at my trousers and boots as the waist-coated assistant passed me a goblet with champagne. 'Have a drink before you go,' Jez said forcefully. Slowly, he took a sip of a drink as his face turned into a grimace. 'You need to get some more clothes.'

And H laughed. 'He is living in a fucking tent!'

And I laughed, falsely, and perfected my contrived my smile from cheek to cheek. They looked at me and didn't say anything. The smile that is eerie, the smile that is a default. 'H! As if I live in a tent!' I said and Jez laughed wholeheartedly.

'Imagine someone crazy enough to live in a tent... you should get some new clothes though, yeah!'

He started to mock H. 'H will never make it in this town, she is jealous!' It was likely drunken, not mean spirited, but strong for friendship banter. And H's face dropped, only momentarily, as they started to argue. I decided to leave, thanking Jez and promising him a more extensive presentation.

In a fair world, in a world where I was not uncompromised, this business was undoubtedly worth more and I felt he knew that. But life isn't always fair and the men with the money, the one percent with the forty-five percent, they dictate the rules. The men at the top hold the cards and we have to play along to progress at any pace.

I left and walked through the glamour of Knightsbridge with the Lamborghinis and Chanel bags and wondered if I would be a part of the ostentation. If one day I would sit on a nearby street, smoking sheesha and parking my Porsche. Ten grand was worth ten million.

I tried to call Tammy. Then, I texted her the news when she didn't call - she replied when she wanted to: 'Sorry, busy right now... sounds good.'

Chapter 28

Kicked Out

'Time is the most valuable thing a man can spend.'
– Theophrastus

I tried to construct the winter nights: Whip Girl's on occasion and worst case, Solus's when her father was away. Nayarras, the office, Airbnb. Anything I could get. Scatty Alice had dropped hints to me, pretending to be inquisitive but really wanting to extradite me and take back her usurped space.

'Do you know how long you might be using the room? My Auntie might want to take the spaces back at some point... you know my bloody Auntie hates me it's all giving me this bloody headache and...'

I told her that I was in a rush and texted her later: 'time for a pay rise, going to pay you sixty pounds a month.' Usually I would bail when unwanted but this storage was crucial. Everything depended on it. Besides, she never used the space, the dank and dark unused spaces that she acquired from her Auntie. The Auntie that always threatened to expel her but never did. She waited a while to text me back although I knew that she read it – and so I responded with another text.

Me: Sixty pounds a month and I leave by February.

And to this she replied promptly.

Scatty Alice: ....OK.

The biting point was here, when friends make excuses because now they resent your presence.

I realised that I had been doing this a long time, perhaps too long, to the point where people did not care. Perhaps I thought that this could last forever; forever adventuring between adrenaline and uncertainty but it was misjudged. I had been stuck in my head, stuck in my dreams of what could become but the inevitability of time had caught me – and time is always a stark slap in the face.

This was re-enforced by Ritchie who I encountered at the weekend. I had purchased more shit-kicker boots as they were necessary for the increasingly hostile terrain:

Another night in the tent made me slip in my work shoes. They became mud-smothered in the morning which put me into a panic as I travelled to work. Frantically scrubbing them with the wet grass and tissue as I quickly took my wet tent towards Scatty's. So, I purchased new boots in town, and these soon became dirty. Not even from tent living but from walking to and fro, hitting the occasional puddle or random shit from the wet pathways. Practicality was rapidly being replacing aesthetics and my trousers were a great example.

My work trousers were beyond comfortable. The more I used them, the more they became a part of me. They warmed me when the weather wouldn't. The more I used them, the more I didn't want to take them off – the more they became merged into the campaign. I used them all the time, washed or unwashed – until the human grease became a lubricating comfort.

I was walking aimlessly one weekend, waiting to meet Ritchie when I decided to take a piss on a side-street. This was commonplace for me as loo rules in the area became draconian, and I increasingly lost a sense of self-awareness. Unhygienic for certain, but conventional for all variants of tramp.

I could piss in Oakley Street or the gym but the power of time would occasionally catch me. The side-street piss avoided the pain of having to run to a lavatory. It was convenient and rebellious at the same time.

I finished my business and saw a girl on the narrow street. I had to go towards her to get to the main road and, usually, when a woman is confronted so, they would avoid it by pretending to use their phone. Or they would move to the main road without eye contact but she, well, she stood there, unperturbed. Looking in my direction. I felt the compulsion to say something, and so I did: 'Nice face mask,' and before we knew it, and I don't remember how, we were talking. And I was taking photos with her and her face paint as she had returned from a party. She was supposed to be meeting a guy she was, well, seeing. But instead, she came to the downstairs bar with me where I was to meet Ritchie. We smooched in the dark as her face-paint rubbed on my lips – I believe it was a cat or a tiger... but now our impromptu kissing obscured it to smudges and shades.

Ritchie arrived and was confused by the girl in the face paint, especially as she was holding my hand. He had known me long enough to not ask questions. So, he sat and ordered a drink and was cold to the girl whose name escaped me. She left soon after and we exchanged numbers. I told her that I would text her... but I did not... and neither did she.

Ritchie looked me up and down and was unimpressed, almost physically, turning his nose. He looked at my shit-kicker boots that were all muddy and the weird and worn work trousers with stains and lint and said, 'Oh my forkin word, what do you look like?'

'What are those forkin boots?'

I found it funny, the fact that we were in an exclusive bar, albeit in the afternoon and I was wearing what I was wearing. The fact I managed to pull a random from the side-street while pissing up a small wall. It went against the order of things, of Ritchie's things – where appearance was everything and fitting in meant safety and respect. Where you worked in a job from nine a.m. until six p.m. and you got drunk and high maybe once in the week and Friday night. Where you had a main girlfriend and you wear shirts while you hung and talked with the lads. Where you paid rent in a flat with a regular full salary.

'That girl with the face paint, what the fuck, John?'

If I was wearing a shirt, if I was crisp and clean with a Foxtons mini outside – he would have found it amusing. Distance between genius and insanity is measured only by success.

He came near me and started to speak quietly. 'Look, there is a room in my flat, going spare and you can have it if you want … for six hundred pounds a month, it's yours.' He beamed. And so, he offered a room in Fulham for six hundred pounds. But I would rather stay in a tent in Chelsea for the rest of my life. For me, that would be better real estate than a flat-share in SW6. Besides, he should have offered me it for free on an ad-hoc basis until he found another flat-mate.

I didn't see Ritchie and his disgusted face for some time after that – he briskly left while gazing at my shoes once more. 'I really need to get some new friends,' he said. And I smiled smugly, as the dull fashion-lighting revealed a bald patch on the back of his head. I smiled with the knowledge that he was only out because he could not find Solus, and that Solus was likely fucking someone at the exact time he walked outside.

After the weekend, I hit the City office. The girl in finance, the one who paid my invoices but was also in charge of maintenance, she needed a word with me.

'John, did you sleep in the office recently?' My instincts told me not to deny, and so, I kept it stolid and imperturbable.

'Oh, yeah sorry. I was drunk and… er, out and thought I would just sleep in the room.' She looked at me, smiling but inquisitively.

'It's all good, I thought it was you because you left a card in there… and some socks.' She smiled again.

'Yeah, it's just that Dan uses that room and he had a client in there, he said it stank of 'human'.'

She laughed it off to make it more comfortable as I awkwardly gazed out of the window to see that it was raining outside. I saw that people were dramatically using the small office heaters and I thought to myself: worse than the embarrassment of my smell consuming the room, was that I, now, did not have the office to sleep in. I was back on the street corner like the transvestite outside and the shaven Scottish man on the Fulham Road. It waned my quest for adventure. I knew how cold that tent could be – through your bones – that made you not want to shower for the rest of your life to keep the grease between your skin.

A cold that is meant to be unrelenting. Meant to be unbreakable. Meant to make you still tired in the morning craving for the relative warmth of the gym. Towels. I kept running out of towels. The gym had restocked some but you had to pay a pound and would have to collect them between nine and five.

Scatty wanted me out and the last thing she needed were dank towels consuming the space. I already avoided using her washing machine by cycling to Oakley Street and using the washing machine there. Two-pound fifty each time, and you had to use the exact change. There was no dryer, so I took them to a separate launderette and then, back to Scatty's. Again, I dried myself on the air hand dryer but I was never dry, so I used the under-tee that I wore to wipe my wet body. Then, I put that in a plastic bag and went to bed in the bocage. Still, slightly wet and colder than before but I had the two beers, special brew, that helped me drowse out the angst and cold. I wondered what the Scottish man's process was. It was obvious that he skipped the shower and went straight to drink. I didn't blame him for a millisecond.

I knew why tramps drink at night.

Perhaps he went to hostels and acquired warm cups of tea but I had seen him out late, extremely late. When I got the tent from Scatty's, his shaven head was still by Marks and Spencer with the emaciated sleeping bag and, just like me, a can of special brew. And I was the same as him now? No money – no home, improvisation. Unless I got to see whip girl where I could shower freely, before I whipped her on her bed, fucked, and fell asleep.

Chapter 29

Another Night at Whip's

"From Long Acre to the Strand on the one side, and from Covent Garden Market Bow-street to Bedford-street on the other, the ground has been seized upon by the market-goers."
– Covent Garden Market by Henry Mayhew 1851

Eliza and I drank upstairs and H Club was heaving. She soon wanted to go for a cigarette but the cold was intolerable, even for five minutes.

I invited Whip Girl who had been hanging out with Solus. They both arrived, and Solus immediately wanted to order while we were in the billiards room. This was normal for us but Eliza was reserved… it's not that she didn't partake on occasion, just not like us; she didn't understand the need. The over-the-top high and chatting of shit for hours only for it to go the other way. Eventually, Solus made me and Eliza meet the Forty Man. Solus bought one round of drinks so it was left to me and Whip to buy the drugs. The thought of Eliza not doing any gave me anxiety, so I decided to pay her part. My plan to make people pay for coke, my unspoken plan - was not going to plan.

Me and Eliza walked the dark, cobbled streets and she reminded me that the shop we worked in was adjacent. She wanted to go and see it. Trying to conjure happy memories of a careless past. Eliza hadn't evolved into office jobs, she was still a retail floor girl propped up by living with boyfriends. We went to see it and gazed at its exterior in silence. We remembered the carefree times where we thought our dreams would come to us, that we didn't have to thrust forward... we just had to wait.

I got bored of the shop so we walked towards theatreland, past the market square and we found it hard to locate the Forty Man. We talked about the column structures of buildings as I realised this was where I first met Tammy's family. Eliza said she was getting cold so I put my arms around her and, for a split second, wondered whether I should kiss her. She, of course, had a boyfriend, but this had not stopped her before. The coldness and anxiety of finding the dealer stopped me from making what could be a polarizing action.

The side-street seemed quiet and black compared to the market square but this place had history. I imagined the Victorian dwellers walking to and fro, the ancient market a communal space for a universe of classes and types. Eliza looked up at me. I had only known her for two years. It felt longer. She smiled, as if to say she is in a safe place. A safe place as we waited for a drug-dealer. I thought of this and I thought to myself, 'Am I helping her? Am I helping these people? Conversely, are they helping me? Are we assets for each other? All we do is drink and smoke and take drugs and I wish; I just wish I could drift endlessly with Eliza and others on cold, dark streets such as this. Looking for drug cars and bars and pubs but life's endless motion won't allow. Its trials and tribulations will split people apart. Some will progress, and others will be left behind based on their decisions. Am I ahead? Living in a bush I have named after a World War II battle. At least Eliza is consistent. At least Eliza has a pattern.'

We managed to locate the dealer. He got out of his car to

meet us behind the dimly lit columns that partially hid us. I briskly took the wrap and exchanged the cash and realised I had met him before – a friendly face and a friendly price. Eliza mentioned that he was aesthetically sound and I wondered if Solus had been fucking him. 'Say hi to Solus from me,' he said while returning to his expensive looking sportscar.

We headed back to H Club to boozing and snorting with even Ritchie threatening to join. Solus met an actor couple in the billiards room, got flirty and took their number. She saw them again... that's for certain: we heard a few months later that Solus had been partaking in elaborate threesomes at their Covent Garden flat; cucumbers were mentioned. It got late and Eliza said it was too late to travel to Forest Hill or wherever the fuck she lived and Whip Girl had the best time. Filled with adrenaline and drinks and company and I knew that deep down, she was companionless:

Whip Girl: Thank you, guys.

Us: What for?

Whip Girl: For making me feel young and welcome.

Whip suggested that we stay at hers and so, we went. All four of us huddled into her bedroom as she told us to keep the noise down. The two actors that Solus met gave her extra gear. And so, there was an ample amount of snort and Whip opened one of her bottles of red. Everyone was merry, started to dance and got into nightwear. Someone leant Eliza some small tight shorts, and the drugs or the fresh air that I get when waking up in the tent mornings made me libidinous. A tight rope; I was supposed to be with Whip who was equally alluring... they all were.

Suddenly, Eliza remembered she had work, tomorrow, first thing. She didn't have her work clothes and it was already three a.m. Whip Girl scrambled for black shoes in her cupboard and they looked for matching black trousers. Eliza started to try them, her sleek body out in the open and I could see that Solus was eyeing her.

She sipped wine and kissed Eliza but I could see Eliza was struggling with the constant hammering of drink and drugs. She shouted, 'Let's have fun tonight yeah!' with an unconvincing and swerved tone.

Meanwhile, I could see that Whip Girl had clocked me, was still clocking me as I gazed at Eliza, but I was careful by moving and caressing her toned shoulders. Then, I was not sure how it happened, but we all decided to get into bed. Somehow, Eliza's gym-worked buttocks ended up next to me and I couldn't help it: I gave it a feel; she didn't nudge me or jolt in shock, but she didn't encourage it. Solus was being Solus, getting up and talking to herself and walking around. She nudged Eliza and told her to go to hers so that she could give me and Whip some time.

They left and inevitably, Eliza didn't make it into work. Despite telling us all she was already on a warning. Despite the fact that she had been trying on numerous work clothes. She was like this in the shop before, with me, selling canvas shoes as we would arrive late and leave early. Was I helping these people? Or was I hindering.

I tried to hug Whip when the girls left but she recoiled. I now know that she must have seen me, she must have seen the sudden and inappropriate grope. And I thought to myself that this was maybe one of the last times I would get to stay there – and I thought that she was overreacting because, at the end of the day, we were not a couple. I knew my respect for her would change when she flirted with Ritchie but there were flaws in my theory, the main flaw being etiquette. I left in the morning and quietly said goodbye – she ignored my texts and I did not see her for a while. Within the space of a week, I had lost all indoor dwellings.

Chapter 30

Hostels and Harry Potter

*"It is the unknown we fear when we look upon death and
darkness, nothing more"*
– Harry Potter and the Half-Blood Prince 2005

I walked past houses in High-Street Ken and they were alight
with Christmas trees. High Christmas trees with uniform baubles
and neatly packed Christmas cards on the mantle pieces. I was
walking in the area because I fell asleep on the tube. And
subsequently, I missed my stop. I looked at a family with a kid,
they were in front of the father with his slicked hair and neat
Ralph Lauren jumper and I thought to myself: 'How much does
his semi-detached house cost? Did he pay for it outright? Does
he have a mortgage or did he inherit?'

I walked towards Scatty's where only the wind and the cold
were keeping me awake and I snuck in the side in case she wanted
a passive-aggressive talk and then, I collected my stuff. Sleeping
bag and mat in one hand, the wet tent in the other. Usually, I
walked to the right to evade a familiar face but I saw the bald
Scottish tramp to the left of me, he had moved spots from the
main road.

I, for once had a pound coin and some rusty coppers and I
approached. At this point, I didn't care if he saw me with a tent
and a sleeping bag and part of me hoped that he knew. I put the

money in his hand.

'How's it going? Are you okay in this weather?'

He looked up at me, friendly as ever, indifferent to the fact I had a sleeping bag in one hand and a tent in the other. 'It's killing us, man!' he said. 'We Cannae take it, I have friends who are struggling!'

I was sure to shake his hand and make my way towards the bocage. There was a single thought that stuck in my mind as the cold wind picked up pace through the road. How would he survive five a.m. tonight? And now we return to the beginning: I have decided to reminisce before I attempt some form of sleep. To discover how I got here in the first place - convulsing in the winter cold between two covering bushes.

Solus's grandmother has washed my sleeping bag and it has shrunk beyond practical use. Any movement in the essential head-cover feels as if my esophagus will rip out of my throat. I wriggle my body, as if inside a cocoon while the cold water creeps up into the tent floor and consumes the roll mat. The weather has a particular savagery and it enables me to construct four considerations:

One: never in winter.

Two: feet and hair clean and dry.

Three: never sleep on the bare ground.

Four: four a.m. to five a.m. is the coldest of times.

I slithered, looking for warm positions as I remembered the day that I came up with the idea. An idea that started a series of events. A true story that I hoped would help to make sense of a generation, lasted several months, felt like a lifetime, and was dedicated to the people who do it for a lifetime. A true story with many distinctions attached: elation, fear, incompetence, drugs, death, parties, destitution, dreams, and sex.

This time it was different. This time it reminded me that I could not take much more. The psychological safety of other dwellings had been eradicated. I woke up and had had two hours sleep but I had worked in the City. As I woke and rose, I slipped on the wet tent floor but this time I could not seem to grip. This was because I took my shoes off in the night to wash my feet with travel-sized baby wipes. I tried to support myself by pushing the tent roof while moving but I still slipped… and slid. It must have been a sight for the bin-man who was staring directly at me, right at the bocage in shock and awe, as if a large embryo was trying to escape its camouflaged womb.

I should have been startled but I did not care. I zipped up the tent in under a minute as he continued to stare and I walked right past him as he stood still on the concrete; I was safe on the upper ground but I noticed my Villiers-bocage sign had been knocked down by the wind. And so, I walked past him again to return and erect the sign – this was my space, not his.

But I knew that I would have to find somewhere else to go on Mondays; this bin person was sure to come and look again. I had no time for the shower, just straight to Scatty's to drop off the tent and straight to the City with such fatigue… such tiredness. I entered the rammed tube and I felt afflicted as I smelt my armpit. I crammed up against the people and somebody, not-so-subtly, hid their handbag from me. And the packed tube jolted as the driver stopped suddenly. It was then that I craved water – above anything else, it was water that I needed as well as fresh air until it became overwhelming. I decided that I would get off at the next stop, but the district line had gone past Earl's Court with a pace so glacial that I knew I wouldn't make it. I tried to get out of the huddle of the middle or I would puke all over the hoard and I... started to swoon...

I don't remember much, but I do remember that people had clocked that I was falling. 'Somebody catch him, CATCH HIM!' And I have never felt so moved by Londoners, and I started to think there was good in the world, that the world was not only the brutality and results. One of the women, well-spoken and commanding, came off the tube and gave me some water. She spoke to the nonchalant tube man who let the tube leave to avoid traffic. The girl stayed with me.

'Are you sure you don't need me to stay any longer?'

I paused and I thought to myself: 'To be frank, I want you to stay forever by my side, please do not leave me.' But I resumed speech and noticed that she was dressed in work clothes - I did not want her to be late. I told her to go: 'go free to the safety of your work.' I got into work and headed straight for the loos to wipe myself with baby wipes, and I used deodorant and the mouthwash that I left in the back corner. I headed for my desk, hoping for no strange stares and I sat and tried to work.

I realised that I could not tent it again, in that cold. The dread for the nights ahead consumed me but it was the cold, the cold in the middle of that wild night. At a time when nobody was up, when nobody should be up as the winds roar and there was a silence not familiar to a metropolis. That was the time when the cold decided to nibble and feast the bottom of your spine. I can still feel it, and if I think too much about it, I get the shakes. This was not as bad as the fatigue, the couple of hours sleep you managed re-arranges your spine, and the cold finishes the job. I went to the loo for ten-minute's sleep, hoping to not get noticed. I drank coffee until I had heart palpitations. I was jittery. I was around people all the time: walking, tubing, humping up hills and

I realised once again why the transvestite surrounded herself with the cardboard box. Four flimsy but vital walls. Her space… nobody else's.

As I fell asleep I received two beeps, an order for vegan pouches – Tammy emailed me: 'Woohoo!' I tried to send her a personal text but she ignored me. As the business money started to swell again, I had no choice but to spend money on accommodation. And I had no choice but to revisit the idea of hostels. I would avoid the sweat-induced rapists in Earls Court and try something different. There was one near to the City, by St Pauls cathedral that would be useful when needing to work. The other was in Holland Park – a smart looking hostel, mainly for international students. It had a garden space and a restaurant and was twenty-five pounds a night. I suppose I still had Solus's, but this was only on occasion.

Tonight, I was more than lucky. Tonight, I was going to Drew's to drink red wine and watch "Harry Potter" as he was eager to show me his place in the depths of Wandsworth. There was something wholesome about watching Harry Potter in winter. Not the first ones, for they are juvenile. "The Goblet of Fire" onwards – and that's what we started with. I had a tour of the flat and his face was buzzing with contentment. This small space, more a studio than a one bed, it had made a man out of him.

'You will sleep here, buddy,' and he showed me the sofa in the joint sitting room and kitchen. I was especially grateful, because you could almost see the cold through the windows. We put on "Goblet of Fire" and lit a cigarette.

'Jeez, Draco is such a cunt isn't he? Even his face is like, cunty,' said Drew as he took out a bag of cocaine… more bag than coke. 'Yeah, I nearly didn't get this place buddy,' he told me.

I replied, 'Oh, how come?'

And he told me the story: 'I had a mortgage broker and they kept asking for documents and documents, and, although I earn a lot, I am freelance which they do not like. So they rejected it.'

'Wow,' I thought, 'What an arduous process.'

But then, he told me how the broker managed to force it through last minute. Drew was in finance; Drew made more money than anyone else I knew and he said, 'Months and months, buddy.' And I thought to myself, as I peered at the tiny space that he paid hundreds of thousands for, this will likely be my destiny.

We smoked out of the window and drank superior red wine and I thought how much this guy had been a gem. We got to the "Half-Blood Prince" while taking intervals of Coke and wine and I tried to concentrate this was my favourite; Snape and his origins and Tom Riddle as a teenager: 'Oh just intuition…' we said in unison. The scenes became still, quieter. Less airy-fairy. Drew seemed entranced as the TV light flickered on his face and the erratic flashes reveal his minor gurn.

You knew that the series was reaching a crescendo and that a climax is coming. All the fun and games and three hours of childishness had to come to an end. Now things were getting serious….

We watched Harry Potter perform *Sectum sempra* on Malfoy and cheered and laughed. At the same time, we were shocked by its graphicness.

We only made it to the end of "Half-Blood Prince" and called it a night. I sleep on the sofa and in the morning, Drew made me some dim sum with his dim sum maker which was his prize possession. He left me to return to Central London and pointed me towards a street where there was a bus stop. It was then I realised how remote we were, the bus stop had one bus and nothing seemed to be arriving. It was okay for Drew as he had a scooter, so the fact that there wasn't a transport network did not concern him. For me, I felt uneasy in the area. It was quiet and residential and reminded me of the countryside. My new metropolitan mind tried to run from this image.

I had no choice but to get a taxi. He said that I could stay anytime while I sort myself and he meant it. I also knew he needed to get on with his life, without me, getting involved, sleeping on the sofa and sweating out his new real estate purchase. Besides, how would I get into work?

The next night, I booked the Holland Park hostel with its relative sleekness: surrounded by the park itself, it had its own courtyard and fizzy drink machine booths where you place money in a slot. The place was clean, didn't smell of human, and the people consisted of young and attractive backpackers.

I was surprised about the set-up of the room. It was unisex with various bunk beds and chatter. I had a bottom bunk where the most sensuous Australian girl had hoisted her bare leg above it, showing her underwear. I wondered if it was contrived, if so, I wasn't ready for bold sexual displays. My face was svelte and I hadn't been washing. I had even had the same underwear for three days. I sat on my bunk and everyone was friendly, too friendly that the social anxiety entered; the eye contact started to dissipate.

There was a large, muscular man from Texas who asked where I was from. I said, 'London.' Never the countryside. Always London.

'Wow, you are from here, dude? Why are you in here?' As he said it, it was as if six months flashed before me, showing me step by step of how I ended up here. And I made my answer.

'I'm renting my flat out, on Airbnb, you know?' And they

nodded with conjunct recognition. The Spanish guy in the corner and the Australian girl and the others all now understood. And I hoped and prayed as my hands shook that they didn't ask too many questions. I smiled, the deranged smile from cheek to cheek.

I managed to brush my teeth but could not release my sweat-ridden clothes. This was because I hadn't been paying attention to a golden rule: feet dry. I had feet so moist that that the liquid within the socks squelched and spread as I walked. I knew that, if the socks were released, the smell would permeate and destroy the room. And so, I stayed in my clothes and shoes and lay motionless on the small bunk-bed. Putting the duvet over me as the Australian girl got up again and fiddled around with headphones. Her tight shorts and neat physique paraded around the perimeter.

Then, I saw that somebody arrived late into the room. At the other side where the Texan man was bunking. It was a woman, older than the Australian but just as sexy and… she stripped. Not a mild strip, she stripped so she was only wearing a thong and her breasts were fully exposed. I had seen some things, but this… she seemed to direct her attention to the Texan who was looking at me looking. I thought to myself, 'What would Ritchie say?'

The boys would try to make a move as their macho self-talk would make me believe. And, for some reason, some known only to the Gods, I got up. Fully clothed and thought that perhaps, if she was horny and I walked past, she would want me instead of the Texan. I started to walk but she recoiled and retreated back to her clothes and the handsome and broad Texan looked petrified. I was not sure if he was petrified about her, me, or the entire situation but he was. And I had fucked up immensely, forgetting that I wasn't in a state for this in the first place.

I went to the bathroom to piss, to look as though I meant to do that all along and I returned to bed in retreat. In the morning I thought to myself that I was not sure if I could do that again. Although I had much more sleep than the tent, the intensity of people and the price-per-night presented their own issues. It would be a day by day, and it all depended on the night in question – would it be a friends? Or would it be a corridor on Oakley Street.

Chapter 31

Investment – Part 2

*'What's the difference between a Ferrari and depression? I
don't have the Ferrari.'*
– unknown

I couldn't believe it. Somehow, amongst it all, I had sealed a
second meeting with the investor. The first meet was a long ball
opportunity. Now, it was becoming increasingly likely,
increasingly important, increasingly necessary for me to attempt
to close this out-of-the-blue transaction. I bought a new, more
detailed presentation to him. Ten thousand for thirty percent…
which was a steal. An almost desperate and mathematically
flawed attempt to climb from the bowels of destitution. You see,
it could have been so much more. Looking at the trajectory and
potential of the business, it should have been so much more.

'Okay, so that celebrity you worked with, yeah? I like this
yeah? That's cool.'

I was lucky that he had a penchant for celebrity.

I had the feeling he was interested in being 'cool', of being
liked in certain circles known for glamour and social prestige.
Ten grand was worth the risk for him, and this was a cool
opportunity. Just like last time, there were girls sipping
champagne. Very tight dresses and plumped lips and giggling.
Probably about how poor I looked and Jez noticed the giggling

and stated, 'John, we do need to get you a new suit, yeah?'

And he laughed with the girls and I laughed because if only they knew that I may well be sleeping in a ditch tonight. And I laughed that they were such superficial twits that avoided the necessity of adversity. They were likely penniless themselves and hung on the back of Jez and his unlimited champagne, his hotel-esque apartment opposite Harrods, and his hip-hop tunes.

Was he helping these people?

I handed over my final presentation and he had an expeditive look as he told me that he would look at it in more detail. He said that H had verified me as a good person. H, she had verified me, and this was not to be underestimated. Then again, we had made a deal that I would give her ten percent of the investment.

Jez, as always, was ready to party and my mind only went to one person. I'm not sure why, but I wanted Solus to see this – to see the champagne and the Knightsbridge chic, the brutalist tables and the carefree energy. She was hanging with Tonny – Tonny who had been repudiating the scene for a short while, now I knew she consummately ingested these toxins other than coke, toxins unacceptable in the real world. In any world. It didn't mean that I didn't like her, on some level, based on memories from our illustrative but irregular past. They both agreed to come, and I briefed them so that they did not ruin my investment.

Solus arrived in a sleek black dress but Tonny was in Shoreditch nineties jeans, held together with a contrived piece of string. She had Dr Martens boots and an oversized T-shirt. When I saw them both, I knew where they had been. I could not see Tonny's pupils – they had had contracted so small. All you could see was a sea of blue and turquoise. I wondered if she could even see through the violent glaze but she seemed fine. More than fine. As if she was attentive to each movement, as if any reaction had a heightened effect on her strained psyche. Solus dropped her head in shame as she saw me glaring at Tonny with suspicion. Jez greeted them with a smile. 'Hello, girls, let's get some champagne in, yeah?' And Jez's assistant, the skinny unassuming fellow with a waistcoat, topped up the drinks to the brim. Solus made herself at home, flirting with Jez and all I could think to myself was: 'Please, I beg you... telepathically... not your tits, please do not release your breasts.'

Suddenly, Jez put down his drink on the brutalist table and made an announcement to the room. 'So, listen, yeah – I have a club I'm part owner of in town yeah and we are going to go there tonight for dinner and drinks, John, you can come too!'

I thought to myself that it would be a given that I would come but noticed that his beeline was towards the girls; any talk of business was forbidden, and Solus cheered and clapped at the idea of the restaurant.

'Can we do drugs in here?' One thing about Jez: he didn't tolerate drugs in front of him. Solus was ordered to the loo to do a line and Tonny did not follow her – this was unusual. Tonny wasn't communicating and her blue eyes were wide and lambent. She sipped a glass of champagne and sat upright while Jez tried to talk to her. She would smile and nod, violently and quickly. I went over to her and she didn't acknowledge, she sat upright and didn't look in my direction.

'Tonny... Tonny...' and she ignored me. I pulled her oversized T-Shirt and she turned briskly towards me.

'JOHN, CAN YOU STOP TOUCHING ME, YOU'RE REALLY PRANGING ME OUT!' The way she said it, filled equally with venom and panic.

The other girls that were there in their tight garments and slick hair decided to leave and kissed Jez on each cheek before exiting. Jez was indifferent as there were new folks for him to entertain. I wondered if he ever thought about marriage? Does all the drinking, partying and succubae become laborious? Jez beckoned the underweight servant. He whispered to him but I could hear it. 'Go get the Ferrari,' and he went to get keys and left outside. 'Okay, girls, yeah we are about to drive. John, you can get in yeah too.' And we did. A blue Ferrari with white interiors and I went in the front with Jez's driver, not the underweight servant but a Hench and tall guy with a ponytail and an Eastern European accent. He reminded me of a story that H had told me, how Jez's 'sexy' driver once drove her home to her lover's house in Harrods village. She sneaked him in and fucked him in the cinema room – I wonder if Jez knew of this... or H's lover.

The driver revved the Ferrari engine and Jez smiled with the champagne glass in his hand as we drove with haste down the narrow road. Past Harrods and towards the West End at increasing speed. And as the breeze hit my face, I heard Solus giggling and even Tonny let out a smile. I thought to myself – this is great. The adrenaline kicked in, shadowing the vast horse-power and, for that second I forgot my issues and gave into the rococo and glamour. Jez and his care-free life and I felt rebellious, for that second. For that very second – it was all fair .

Then, Jez became bored and fidgety. Even though we were five minutes from the Piccadilly stretch, even though he had two girls semi-draped around him. 'We need some more girls, yeah,' and he spotted two model-like figures on the left – at least five foot nine or ten with elegant dresses. 'John, John, get out of the Ferrari and get those girls yeah, go talk to them and – you know you are a good-looking guy, yeah, bring them to the club. You know where it is, yeah, off Berkeley street?'

And the girls gave me a lost but indifferent look. I hesitated for a second, but thought this may impress Jez and help with investment. So, I got out of the car and heard it briskly drive away without a care in the world. As careless as when I was in it not so long ago.

The girls' eyes on the left followed the hum of the Ferrari, but they had seen me get out of it. As I approached, purely because of this reason, they were interested in what I had to say. 'I erm, am supposed to pick you up and erm, take you to the club with them?'.

They said, 'Is that right?' I knew their resistance could be easily overwhelmed but instead, and I was not sure why, I started to walk backwards. Backwards and away from them.

'I'm sorry, I'm sorry,' and they were unperturbed and entertained by my strangeness as I got back to the Brompton Road and started to run. Past Harrods and all the rich middle-easterners with their Gucci loafers and Lamborghinis; and I ran across the road towards Walton street. Towards Scatty Alice's. For now, things had changed once more – from the glamour of the penthouse to the muddy and cold depths of the bocage. The gap between rich and poor beautifully realised with my run in the dark. It would take an elite to get me out of this. One of the partying and frolicking five percent, the ones carrying but crippling the western world.

I swore that I would never tent it again, but it was too late to book a hostel. I was hoping and thinking that I would stay at Solus's or even Tonny's but this was now unlikely. I took my tent and felt fine. The earth and the squalor was where I belonged, back in the cold, on the wet-kissed grass with the weekend coming. I would have to get up early tomorrow. Too many people. Perhaps I shouldn't have left the girls with a stranger but I knew they would be fine, and they had my number. Tonny messaged me at two a.m., 'Are you still up?'

As a matter of fact I was – I would constantly wake to my shivering body. I texted Jez, I said that I couldn't get the girls to come, so I thought I would go home. Importantly – he understood.

Chapter 32

Endgame

'People who are homeless are not social inadequate. They are people without homes.'
– Sheila McKechnie

It was the joyful weekend. Although I had been caught sleeping in the office, I would hang there in the day to keep out of trouble. To eat and nap and stay away from the elements. I went for a stretch on the Cornhill and noticed an older guy, one of Amy Tez's friends, he was a member of what seemed to be every club in London. He was a strange man, always looked down to the floor and sometimes it took him five minutes to respond to a comment you made. Having said this, he did respond to questions:

Me: What you doing around here?

Peter: I just went to the gym...members club. What you doing around here?

Me: Oh, just some weekend work.

Peter: You see that building over there?

Peter pointed towards the large building of what used to be the Midland bank. A vast, towering piece of baroque architecture.

Peter: That is going to be the biggest members club you have ever seen. I am already a member there. Swimming pool on top, 1920s courtyard...'

I didn't want to hear of progress, or glamour, or people being happy until I secured this investment. And so, I found a way to leave him as soon as possible, walking with my back towards the open air as I mumbled my tepid goodbye. I sat at my desk in the office, microwaved some vegan lasagna and worked on my laptop. It was still strange being there on your own, alone, with the Dickensian and Roman ghosts, haunted the ageing hallways and dark corners. I again decide to sit at another desk as to not face the dark hall on the right that lead to the kitchen. I looked at the sales of the fashion range, two more sales… we really were doing it weren't we? But not enough – some cash stored including business and personal but I desperately wanted to order just to get out of this world and its pressures.

My sister called, 'John, John, where are you? I'm in Chelsea. Can I stay over tonight?' I needed to think of something quickly.

'Oh hun, so good to hear from you, I'm not in at the moment.'

With that, she paused but continued: 'Okay, but can I stay there tonight?'

This was not good, I had to come up with something and quickly. 'Oh, babe, I would love to you to stay I really would, but they are renovating the flat at the moment – I'm actually staying in the office.' I tried to laugh it off in order to escape her deafening silence. I could hear the limited cogs in her brain working, and I remembered how she liked to stir the family pot.

She thoughtfully stated, 'I'll call you back.' I knew what that meant. What that meant was that she was going to call my Mother and my Mother was soon to call me. And so, I tried to do some work as I waited and, soon enough, my Mother was on the phone.

'John, John, can you hear me?' Unfortunately, I could. 'John, what is happening with your flat? Do you actually have one?'

I patronized, 'Of course I do, Mother, they are just renovating at the moment, I will be back in there next week.'

She thoughtfully paused, just like my sister.

They knew me better than I thought. They knew I would be the kind of person to fuck up and lie about having a flat but they were not sure. 'I hear you are staying in the office, why don't you come to the Country for a bit, John?' And as she said it, it started to seem like a beautiful idea. A beautiful and warm idea. A week or two among the semi-neat hedgerows and flat fields, to straighten my head and ingest pure air. To enjoy pure sleep on a bed and walk in space. Not to be consumed by the gridded buildings and carbon monoxide and narcissists. I could even wheedle off cocaine.

There were three issues with the idea: firstly, I was freelance and did not have holiday. I would not be able to take time off when I was so desperate to save. The second, the temptation to see Tammy would be hard to get over. And the third was Mother's second call: 'John, John, I have just thought, there is no internet down here – you wouldn't be able to do work or anything.' And it was an omen for me, to make sure I did my own things in my own way – I was relieved in that very moment. And sometimes I felt it in the tent, a visceral freedom of living life yourself at all costs. Even when you are freezing or cannot afford to eat, it was still only you and the besieging world. Besides, my parents had done their part.

My sister and mother said that they were going to come down next week, to check on my flat as soon as they had finished refurbishing and I had to, 'Make sure I got a rent reduction.' And so, I needed to plan how I would play this – time was running out and it was certainly getting colder.

I managed to stay on a couch on Saturday, some random party towards Brixton. Sunday, I decided to book a hostel in the square Mile, far from the hedonism of the Holland Park. But first, I would hang in Chelsea on the Kings Road and hit the cinema. "Trolls" was showing – another children's film that I had to stealthily enter. Through the dark theatre full of toddlers and parents and there I was, sitting at the back with a rucksack, trying not to draw attention.

I got a call halfway through the film and it was a call that would change my life – it was Jez: 'Listen, yeah, don't ever bring that Solus over near me, okay?' I thought I was in trouble but I didn't ask what Solus had done, I didn't even want to know. Then, Jez changed his vibration. 'Now, listen, I have seen your presentation yeah and I like it very much – you are a smart guy yeah so I am going to invest. Make sure you give H a reward yeah?'

I responded as reservedly as I could, 'Thank you so much, Jez, you will not regret this.'

He turned away from the phone to state to some party guests to keep the noise down. 'Make sure you make my returns, yeah?' And I would, I would have to make money year after year. The projections predicted his return on investment in year one, and double year two. But it is also one hurdle at a time and my current objective was to get away from living with the dark and tumultuous streets.

I returned to "Trolls" and the children and it was as if I had been transported back to their age. An age of bewilderment and innocence and the wonders of the world are only beginning. And in the dark, I felt amazing. The Trolls broke into song and I would have joined if I was familiar with the lyrics.

Although I was in the dark, I could still feel that it was getting dark outside; I realised that I hadn't asked when I should expect the ten grand and, in turn, when I could start.

I left my spot in the cinema and tried to call Jez for clarity. My phone had died and as I frantically fumbled in my rucksack, I could not find my charger. Not only that, I needed the hostel check-in time. I looked across the road and saw some fourteen-year-old Sloane's, they were chatting and giggling on the small green, cross legged, smoking a cigarette. I carefully approached. The careful approach was essential, to avoid the perception that I was a creepy man with sinister intentions.

'Ladies, ladies, hi. I was wondering if any of you have an iPhone charger that I could borrow for five minutes – I will pay you five pounds?'

They giggled but seemed unthreatened. It was then I realised I was approaching them with worn clothes and an unshaven face – a self-fulfilling prophecy, whilst being the tramp, I had become the tramp. Although, inside I didn't feel like a homeless person. But what does that mean? Because physically and literally that was exactly what I was. Just because I had some opportunities, just because I had a job. Just because I used to live in a flat – it didn't mean that I was not homeless. I was not a superior because of my background or past which, I now know, is as finite as money or life. Just maybe it made me think differently. That, deep down, I maybe knew this was temporary. But I knew how tough it was, how tough it had been – I knew that many were thrust into the situation that had no redeeming light at the end of a cold dark tunnel.

The girls seemed to ignore me and started talking to themselves. I upped the offer. 'Okay, ten pounds!' But I realised that this was as expensive as a charger itself. I was keen to talk to Jez for clarity. Some sure timelines to escape the floor sleeping and all the depressing shit that comes with it.

It was Sunday and getting dark and the electrical shops on the Kings Road would certainly be closed. To the ten pounds, one of the girls responded.

'Okay for real, ten pounds?' And the other girls looked at her with the upmost snobbiness, as if to tell her that this was not social etiquette. Not etiquette to exchange trades with an older, dirty and potentially deranged man – and I realised, that in this country, specifically in London, specifically in this decade; the worst thing you could be was poor or destitute. Or at least come across as poor or destitute; you must at least pretend to be something. Post yourself on a holiday on social media or a restaurant, purchase luxury clothing, buy a dog. Just do something.

Little did these girls know that ten measly minutes before, I had the phone call of my life. A phone call that would provide me with relative affluence and success. A defining moment to a humiliating one within ten succinct minutes. I had to walk with this girl who was cautious with our proximity, and I pulled out the ten pounds from the cash point. I gave her the cash and agreed to return the phone charger as soon as I had it charged. Fifteen minutes in a public house.

She paused and looked up at me with her youthful face 'Keep it,' and I tried to interrupt her but she insisted, 'Just keep it, I have another.'

I felt uncomfortable, I wasn't sure if I had misplaced mine or lost it and the rigorous outside activities did not bode well for my battery. And so, I accepted her request. She could buy another with the money I gave her.

I managed to charge my phone in the pub but I did not call Jez back. It was getting late and I decided to enjoy the moment, even if it wasn't clear – the coup d'etat... I would see if it was real tomorrow. Or, if like the rest of this year, it is part of a collective blur. To the fourteen-year-old girl on the Kings road, wherever you are... thank you.

I made my way back to the City on the eleven bus. A reprobate with shaven hair was insulting the entirety of the upper deck so I moved downstairs. I hated downstairs. The views of skylines and the bigger London picture were impeded, and it was cramped with children and buggies. I arrived at the destination, a large door on a small, cobbled street opposite St. Paul's where the streetlights had not graced us with their presence. I went in and noticed it lacked the glamour of Holland Park: lots of peeling walls and dilapidation. The man on the desk asked for identification and showed me to the floor. I went up and there were numerous bunks in rooms and a décor that had not been renovated. The showers looked like jail - but they were showers.

The presentiment was not as perilous as Earl's Court; no sweat-ridden predators who controlled the windows, and there were younger students and teachers prowling the dated hallways. I slid onto my bunk and Ellie the Freeloader texted about a party. I said no. I was better than that now while laying in my hostel, looking at YouTube videos in fashion and sanctimoniously waiting for pot-luck investment.

I would be able to sleep for longer; work was a ten minute walk and I packed light but this was not to be. For there was a man who got up earlier than the City birds. A fidgety, scrawny man who kept fidgeting with all his loud and clingy belongings and then, he kept coughing. A regular and constant cough as if to fuck us off on purpose. There were other men in the dorm but nobody seemed perplexed or angry. Perhaps it was because he wasn't directly under them, but I couldn't take it. His energy and his coughing were intentionally in my space. If this were jail I thought, if this were jail, I would reveal a 'shank' that I had probably hidden in the peeling wall and stab him several fucking times. His blood would splatter over the other sleepers. I mumbled with aggression, but loud enough for him to hear me for now I was prepared for confrontation as I remembered the pseudo-raper in Earls Court. I pronounced the words to him with exactness and rigour: 'SHUT THE FUCK UP!'

Chapter 33

Flat Hunting

'Nothing is certain in London but expense.'
– William Shenstone

I had nervously been waiting for Jez to get back to me. I decided I couldn't ask for the money directly as that would be too much, too eager. It may have revealed that something about me was untoward, and he would subsequently see through my pathetic attempts to cover my destitution. I re-sent the projection sheet to which he responded positively. But I was still flitting from here to there, from hostels and people's floors and I missed Whip Girl's warm flat and carpeted bedroom. I panicked and thought that I would run away to Tammy's house, in the depths of the country, and disclose my undying love in front of her new finance man. I would do it in order to move this side of Christmas and hope she would greet me with open arms.

H would text me occasionally, stating that I owed her money. Money for which I had not received yet. Money that I still may not receive and money that may not exist. And there was the ticking time bomb of the family – they still threatened to come to the imaginary flat when the 'renovations' were over.

I would work in the office in the City and I would freelance in Hackney and try to impress Monica by showing her flats online. Now, she avoided the room at all costs, although she was supposed to be working on the same projects as me – I thought she was personally avoiding me, that was until they organised a Christmas party. She messaged me (she had my number for work reasons) and asked me to come to this party. As much as I found her beautiful, as much as I would like to see her out of the work setting. I never attend work parties. The mixture of alcohol with people that will tell you what to do the next day lies uneasy with me. A mix that shouldn't be, like the multi-coloured unnatural strains that occupy London puddles. These strips of wet when walking from the bocage. The rainbow-like colours made from when the car oil hits the water. The elements resist each other, showing that the concept is impractical.

Tammy used to say to me, 'All this social anxiety shit, whatever you have is fake, because all you do is socialise with people.' Yes, we have to have human contact, and I profusely socialise and party but only with people who are so self-indulged they do not see between the lines. That's why all my friends are crazy, why they all have stories. They don't cross-analyse me to my face. We just sit on our phones and snort lines and exchange the necessary energies with the least effort. When it isn't that way: family events, work parties, sober events – that is where the issue lies.

Monica asked me to come. 'Just come for a bit.' I was enticed. I said I wasn't sure about the party, but I could meet her just before to say hi. She said, 'Come to the party and I will meet you first.'

I paused and considered but even for her, her long brown hair and large eager eyes, I couldn't. Even for her beauty. I said I would try but I could not guarantee, I knew I had missed my only chance.

H called again, 'Where's my money, bitch?'

One night, I decided to stay at Simon B's house. He was my neighbour in Edith Grove who had shacked up with Bex, Bex the uncommon, Bex the man impaler, immediately after she tried to get me beaten to a pulp by her dealer. She tried to blame me for her own drug debt, but this is a different story for a different time – I was glad to hear she had recently moved to Bristol.

Simon B's flat, which he occupied by himself, was a lifesaver that night. Warm and carpeted and, as I looked outside and at the window condensation, I could not help to wonder about the tramp on the Fulham Road. Simon B was not to be confused with Si, Ritchie's flatmate, although, they were soon to have a girl in common. Simon B obtained his flat from insurance after a serious car crash. The rest of the passengers had died including the driver. 'J, I'm thirty-seven but do you know why I act and look so young? It's because I am still stuck in that event through trauma, many years ago, my brain hasn't processed to change. And that passes to my physicality.'

This assessment had potential, but what was everyone else's excuse? He grinned and explained as we sat down with a beer and with perfect timing, Solus called. She had been exiled from her house and needed somewhere to stay.

'John! I have coke, John!' and we let her enter Simon B's without resistance. Solus and Si flirted at pace and, as we all sat there, the phone rang late into the evening. It was Jez yet again. 'Okay, so listen, yeah, I have got the projections all good. Please take a look at the contract that we have signed over, and we will have the money to you by end of the week.'

'Thank you, Jez, many thanks. I'll hit the ground running.'

I needed that call. The Gods of this metropolis knew I did and I promised myself to look for flats immediately – immediately after this party that is.

301

I walked back to the sitting room from where I could hear giggles and I entered, dauntless and self-assured, as Simon B's head was moving from side to side between the naked breasts of Solus. They had met thirty minutes ago. I should have known it would be this way. Solus, tilting her head up in laughter and ecstasy as she entertained his nuzzling. I saw the drugs on the table and the previous year felt distant to me. As if my conscience was saying, what you have been doing is counter - productive, it was perverse and this should be a new beginning. As if to say - this is beneath you.

But these were the people that had been with me since the beginning, these were the people who had stopped me freezing to death. They were there, of sorts, when nothing else was. Without a second thought, I went to the table next to where Simon B was nuzzling Solus's breasts; I snorted a large white stripe. I tried to join in as much as possible, listening to Simon Bs weird rave ditty's and dancing at proximity, but soon the deep fatigue came and I slept in his spare room. All I could hear is them, almost all night, and they were definitely fucking; laughter followed by regular spouts of silence. Laughter and somebody sneaking periodically to the bathroom. I didn't feel I owed Ritchie.

The next day I woke up, left Simon B's flat without saying goodbye and went to look for flats. The one in Earl's Court, the one I should have attained that perilous week, it was available. Well, not exactly that one, the one upstairs from it but I arranged a viewing nonetheless. Until then, I had to wait for the money. Instead of moving from Hostel to hostel, I decided to chance Airbnb, yet again, and I rented a bedroom in a multi-bedroom flat on Brick Lane. It was close proximity to the City job and Hackney. At only twenty a night I could have it for two weeks.

Now, I didn't have to worry so much about savings. The savings that categorically failed for various reasons. Many of them my own issues though I couldn't imagine many saving in that situation – it was best to live moment by moment, eat on the move and spend to forget.

I was a distance away from the destructive social circles, the other side of London. I mean, I would not want to live East but it was creative. A hub in the shadow of the great financial institutions. Their buildings towered above us; we were constantly in their shade.

My friend, Kat, drinks but no drugs, had moved from Fulham, right on the Bishopsgate stretch and into East London obscurity. This was perfect. No snort and she could keep me company if needed – we would frequent the Jack the Ripper pub for a few and I would walk her home in the quiet night. One night after drinks at the Ten Bells, we walked through Spitalfields and stood in awe at the Coca-Cola truck, a beacon of our childhood. I would walk back through the graffitied streets of Brick Lane to my small bedroom. With my energy, I filled it with gratitude.

I went to see the flat in Earls court, and I put the offer in in lieu of receiving the money but then, you should have heard what they wanted from me.

'Okay, John, so we need: proof of salary, at least two and a half times the rent, we need a reference from your bank or six months' worth of bank statements – your choice. We need a guarantor, a credit check, a holding fee down which is non-refundable. A character reference. A letter from your employer who we will also call.'

This privatised City, this economy measured on rising house prices – I thought of the bald tramp by Marks and Spencer, I thought of the transvestite tramp in the City. I thought of the The

Strand. It was a renter's market and although there were improvements for buyers, everyone was renting. That was if they could. The unemployed, the vagrant, part-timers and freelancers would struggle to make any screen checks. I was some of those things. To rent was now a privilege, even a sign of status that you managed to 'make it'. A truly warped way of 'making it as you gain nothing in the long term. This generation, Generation Rent.

And so, I had to pull a few strings. First of all, I had to tell my parents that the flat I was living in was untenable and that I had to move. I then asked father to be the guarantor. My mother called me and said, 'Listen, something isn't quite right., but I would like you to keep safe, please keep safe, John. Your father is willing to be your guarantor.'

The money came in as Jez said it would and I couldn't believe it. I didn't feel excitement or happiness. More a feeling of being in the present. In present rather than fixating on past mistakes or the anxiety of the future. Time seemed slower and my brain seemed nimble. But I was tired... so very tired.

I could not get a flat without paperwork and move-in dates were done to their timeline. Among many strings, one to pull was my salary. Combined, it was not two and a half times the amount of the flat but I could still afford it, especially with the business coming in. If you earned over two and a half than the amount of this flat, with a non-finance full-time job, you were the minority... and this flat was a discounted one bed twelve hundred pounds. Why not a flat-share again? I struggled and as per the plan before, living on my own would inspire me to make more money. Besides, a flat-share is almost as expensive, especially when you have to eat out and stay out to avoid them.

I already had an idea to Airbnb out the flat. The tenants were sparse and nobody would notice for two days at a time. I was slowly approaching thirty. Psychologically, it was time for my own space. At the end of the day, wage growth is nowhere near the pace of rent growth and this was not going to change anytime soon – you have to find angles.

And thus with the angles, I had to bend the law to get the flat. The Estate agent told me that there was once a guy who had a hundred grand in his bank. Could pay six months upfront but still failed the checks. He was probably a money launderer but still: crazy times.

I asked the finance lady in the City who had been kind when I was extradited from the office. I asked her to create a generic letter, stating I earned a combined total of thirty-six thousand pounds a year. It was sort-of-true with the business sales. I showed her my bank balance with the investment, and the business sales to show her she wasn't fabricating. This and the letter was kept very vague. She did it for me... to her, thank you.

To whom it may concern,

This is to confirm that John Dohmen earns a total of 36,000 pounds per annum.

It did not state where I got this from, it just stated it. I owed her a lot for this, a true gem, without it I would not have got the flat. For they did call to check, and, as I could no way let them see bank statements, I had to get a letter of reference from the bank.

The bank was delayed in getting back to me, the same bank who let me get scammed. They came again to ruin my life from a distance. I called them numerous times from the office and I was delayed and delayed again until finally my call was answered.

'This is really important. Can you please get back to the estate agents!' The man paused, somewhere in the middle of Birmingham or the Midlands and you could hear other phone people in the background. He paused, as if my tone wasn't acceptable, but he had to be nice.

Nonchalantly, he said, 'Okay we will fast track it.'

The estate agent called me shortly after. 'They said no, John? The bank did not recommend we take you on for the costings.' I was in disbelief; these cunts, these banking cunts had screwed me over once more. I explained to him that it was not my fault and that I earned enough. He said this:

'Listen, we have your Dad as a guarantor, if you can show me any recent in-goings via bank statements, as well as three months in advance we will let it go through.'

The wonderful bank who made sure I was not able to move in the summer, was making sure I couldn't make up for it. Treading on the neck of a man that they wounded.

And so, I went to the bank and charmed the lady to give me an income-only statement. Only for the last month which would include the ten grand and I thought to myself: imagine if I didn't have the investment? Imagine if I didn't have my father? I thought of the bald man by the Marks and Spencer's, I thought of the transvestite in the City, and I thought of the Strand. I thought of the thousands, and the hundreds of thousands that are unofficial.

This story is dedicated to them.

Finally, it went through and I had to spend a significant amount of the investment. I would have to be frugal and cost-wise, but that is another story for another time. I had to pay Tammy some of the investment as well as pay-per-bag. I felt bad for Tammy because the business was worth more, but these were

306

desperate times; austerity Britain and my situation – it had to be done with blistering pace.

I left my place on Brick Lane for the final time as I was moving into Earl's Court the day after next. As I looked outside, my bedroom had a high view and above all the purpose-built graffiti I could see a great omen. It was a vodka brand that were advertising by covering half a building with a temporary billboard. 'Viking' it said in large letters, as clear as day it said, 'Viking'. A fitting sign for the end of Ironside.

Chapter 34

Final Night

'A friend to all, is not a friend to anyone.'
– Mike Skinner 2013

I went to see Solus and I said hi to the grandma, I thanked her with the upmost expedition: thank you for all you have done for me.

I gave her a Christmas card and she kissed me on the cheek. Then, I called Nayarra amongst others to thank them. I took Solus to H Club and H decided to join. I had to pay her and she wanted to do it in-person. This was code for cash as she did not have a bank account. I obtained the money from the bank with a passport just like my scammers should have had to do. But they didn't. The three of us, frolicking in the club and, of course, I had to get the drinks. I asked H and Solus if they had heard from Ritchie. H proudly expressed that they had not heard from Ritchie since Solus and H had a threesome with Si, his flat mate – and Solus looked down in shame.

A surprise guest was to join, it was Whip Girl. She had decided to forget the past but, to be honest, Solus and she had been hanging at Si Bs house without myself and my apprehensive ways. Solus teased, 'John and Whip Girl had a thing,' and H seemed to resent this. Not because she loved me in any way – it was a matter of territory.

'Wait, what is this bitch's actual name?' H said. Me and Solus looked at each other, we knew it was a choice of two… but we said we did not know.

The cold outside was brutal. You would smoke and breathe out the vapour, or not smoke and breathe out the vapour as your body started to shiver. Solus and I said to ourselves, 'WINTER IS HERE!'

Solus went downstairs to get Whip and H grabbed me, pushed me outside and started to kiss me. I could see a camera in the corner and she had never been like this before. 'Who is this Whip Girl, hey?' She put her hands down my trousers and said to me, 'Fuck me, fuck me right now.' But the extreme cold and the prompt pressure…. we had fucked once before, many years ago and I was scared to refuse her. This was no excuse, of course I wanted to. I could not say that I wasn't attracted to her, because I was. This time, the camera and the cold made me unable to operate.

She tried to blow me in the arctic conditions until she gave up. And so, we promptly went inside where Whip and Solus were already waiting. H did not mention anything.

We drank and snorted and we all needed somewhere to stay for one, last, homeless night. I thought I would sleep at Solus's or maybe Whip's but the dynamic did not seem to allow. I could not contemplate trying the cold in any way and I agreed to get one, final Airbnb. Airbnb was where it started of sorts and Airbnb would be where it finished. There was one available. It was near the grass square in the bad lands of Shepherds bush. As we were leaving, the bouncer had a word with me.

'Listen, I am not saying anything's going to happen but you need to keep your guests in check.'

I asked him, 'Why, what happened?'

He said that, 'the little one' i.e. Solus, had shouted at guests and had tried to piss in the plant pot, they had it on CCTV. I was relieved that he didn't see me and H. That would ruin my membership and my only status. These friends could destroy everything if I let them. For all my friends are heathens.

We entered a cab to Shepherds Bush and H was condescending to Whip, rolling her eyes whenever she spoke and tapping her foot in anger and anxiety. Whip started to lash back and me and Solus, with our split loyalties, tried to diffuse the situation. 'All right, everyone calm down!' That was until H decided to light a cigarette in the taxi. 'H, put it out please!' She was in the wildest of moods, even for her. I had never seen her like this before. A franticness that was not thought out. Not as calculated. It was pure compulsion.

Inevitably, we had to leave the cab and Whip threatened to go home while trying to get a taxi on her phone. H started again with the prompt sexual needs. 'Kiss me right now, John, kiss me right fucking now!' I will scream if you don't.' And I thought to myself I could quickly kiss and appease her while Whip Girl's back was turned, then I could go and deal with Whip. But she grabbed me and held me as we were kissing as Whip inevitably turned to see.

'John, are you joking? Are you fucking joking?' I told Whip to come in a cab with me and that I was sorry. I told her throughout this incredible, frightening, destitute but somehow exhilarating and reflective time, she had been a gem.

Solus and H got a cab and so did we and we met at the adjoining road by the large roundabout at Shepherds Bush. I had the man who was letting his flat on the phone, he was frantic and kept repeating, 'You aren't going to damage my flat, are you?'

It was a large council block, behind the old mall and it was not advertised like this but, of course, with Airbnb I had no expectations. We went up to what was the highest floor, so high you could see the top of the Westfield Centre and its strange red lighting. The man was present and tidying and said again, 'You aren't going to party, are you?' to the point where he was a nuisance. I was with three girls and we clearly had been drinking, of course we were going to party.

We were relieved when he left and we released the gear which we snorted on his recently cleaned oven. 'No, no! Get a plate,' said Whip, Whip was always the clean one. The one who could measure and ascertain limits. I did a line with H and, for some reason, I felt as anarchic as she did. It went through my veins and affected me. I felt her irreverence while her tight jeans and plump breasts were at close proximity. She rubbed the tight jeans on my thighs and I was at the point of capitulation. She went to kiss me again and me, high on stimulants, didn't give a fuck about Whip Girl, well, for that very second, only for that very moment. We smooched heavily until Whip Girl and Solus entered. Whip girl froze. 'John, again? Are you fucking joking?' and my life flashed before me with an upmost realisation. This was the problem all along: the short term – the buzz and excitement over something meaningful. I felt I didn't owe Whip after her flirting with Ritchie and she hadn't been talking to me but, yet again, my etiquette was depleted.

And to that? Solus karate kicked me in the rib. 'Do you think you are some kind of stud? Some kind of Casanova!' and I said something careless and selfish.

'It's not like we were going out, I haven't seen her in a while!' And to that? Whip girl left.

I wasn't as upset as I should have been. Perhaps it was because I thought I still had H. But H, now that Whip had gone, ignored me for the rest of the night. And this was what she wanted all along: to be in control, in sexual control. For her territory to not be threatened and for her ego to remain intact. No relationships survived near H.

I was duped and sat alone, bored and twitchy. H commenting on how nice Solus's arse looked. I thought it was banter until I went in their room to snort a line. They slammed the door, barricading me out. 'Can I have some snort?' I meekly asked and they eventually let me in. Solus was unclothed and H was in a bra and it was then I knew that these two were shagging on the regular. Ritchie's main girl... was fucking his sister.

I took the snort, went in the other room and listened to some Radiohead. Then Florence - Falling. I heard them fucking for a further two hours before they left to another party. The sex seemed violent as furniture seemed to shift and clang while they eloped. They didn't even say goodbye. This was supposed to be my night, to celebrate me not being homeless. To celebrate my Coup d'etat but instead I lay there, depressed and confused like so many other times. These people – they would destroy everything I have if I let them. But there is the other side of the grey: H had help me obtain investment, Solus let me stay at hers in some of the most vulnerable nights.

I didn't hear back from Whip for quite some time but I heard a story on the grapevine: two months later she was sojourning with Solus. Solus decided to have stentorian sex in Whip's bedroom with a random guy from a Greater London bar. Whip girl was kicked out of her premises, back to the flatness of the provinces. The flat mates had finally had enough of the random guests and unnecessary scenes. For this, I felt bad. She had taken us in out of her own will. On the coldest nights she may have saved my life only for her to lose her London foothold with such denigration.

The first thing I knew I would have to do. Me, with this new life was to give up the drugs and the people that enable them, Solus and the others, and stay clean or as clean as possible. I had paid H her cut and now I owed them nothing. They must be a memory of what seemed a different era as I try to eek out profit from the business. I must keep the investor satisfied. I must keep everything satisfied. Solus only came to the flat once, she leaned out of the window and paused in her own thoughts:

'Good spot,' she said. After that night, I never saw her again but to Solus: thank you for the times you were nice.

I moved in fully the next day. I didn't have much stuff but I collected what I had from Scatty's who came out to meet me.

'How are you doing?' she asked. 'This bloody weather, I need to pick up my winter coat but I have left it at the dry cleaners and I just haven't had the bloody time to...'

'I'm good, many thanks,' I said to her, interrupting her fast flow. 'Final day now all this stuff will be gone'

'What are you going to do with yourself now, John?' and I told her.

'I am going to live in Earl's Court, do a business and write a novel.' She gave me a puzzling look, as if to say she may miss the phantom-like company. As if she was worried about the danger of my future plans. We hugged each other goodbye in an eerie silence and parted with mutual understanding. 'Scatty Alice, you are a gem.' I took a detour to see the bald man outside Marks and Spencer's, he was luckily there. I said hi to him and I gave him my ninety pounds sleeping bag, far superior to his and recently washed. 'For colder nights,' I said to him. He looked confused but moved, smiled which made his eyes narrow into their sockets and slowly revealed a thumbs up. Then, I walked briskly to the brand new Earl's Court flat - the place was dark. It was small but sleek and the kitchen joined with the sitting room. There was a separate bedroom and a separate bathroom. It was luxury. No fleas, no rapists and no ghosts...well, to my knowledge.

A man had dropped off a sofa for me which I purchased online and I left it outside while I re-calibrated. I went downstairs and a group of youngsters were sitting on it. A music band, I hadn't seen one of those in a while. I hadn't seen many guitar-swinging youngsters since the vacuous culling of live venues. I told them it was my sofa but they didn't believe me. They remained staunchly quiet and did not move. Their arms folded in resistance. I was far too tired to squabble with three youngsters, so, I offered one of them a fiver to move it up to me flat with me, up the long and winding stairs. He acquiesced my request and saw my dark and minimal flat as he pivoted in the sofa.

'Cool flat, man,' he said. He was northern, a little like the Beatles or something, and his comment and his youthful perspective moved me. Almost to the point of tears, he alone had validated my existence. I promised to see his band at the Troubadour some day and, as he left, I went to go to the shop.

I closed my front door and realised I had left my keys inside. And I laughed erratically as I now had to sleep in the hallway, homeless again for one last night. In a hallway with temporary lights until I obtained the spare keys from the Estate Agent's the following day.